Hunting with the Tigers

HUNTING WITH THE TIGERS

How to Achieve Commercial Success in The Asian-Pacific Rim

An essential primer on doing business in: Hong Kong Indonesia South Korea Malaysia The Philippines Singapore Taiwan Thailand and Vietnam

Claudia Cragg

MERCURY

First published in 1992
by Mercury Books
Gold Arrow Publications Limited
862 Garratt Lane, London SW17 0NB

Set in Palatino by TecSet Limited, Wallington, Surrey
Printed and bound in Great Britain by
Bookcraft (Bath) Limited, Midsomer Norton, Avon

British Library Cataloguing in Publication Data is available
ISBN 1-85251-156-7 (hardcover)
1-85252-152-X (paperback)

To Anthony L. T. Cragg,
without whom this book would not have been possible.

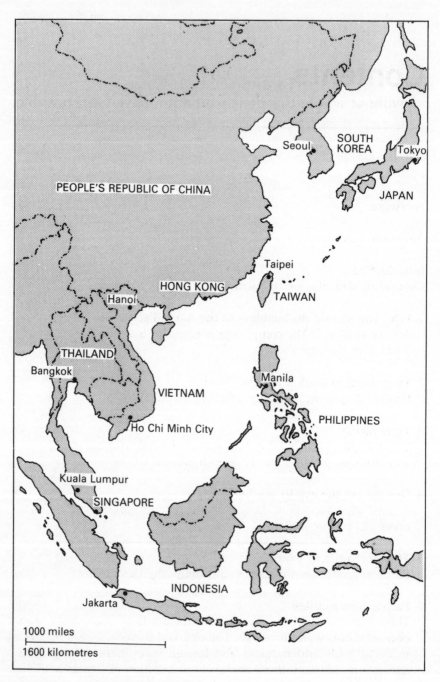

PEOPLE'S REPUBLIC OF CHINA

SOUTH
KOREA

Seoul

Tokyo

JAPAN

Taipei

HONG KONG

TAIWAN

Hanoi

THAILAND

Bangkok

VIETNAM

Manila

PHILIPPINES

Ho Chi Minh City

Kuala Lumpur

SINGAPORE

INDONESIA

Jakarta

1000 miles

1600 kilometres

The Asian-Pacific Rim

Contents

Additionally, for each country except Vietnam, an all-important Confidence Survey, conducted by *Asian Business Magazine*, of businessmen in the market.

7 **The Asian-Pacific 'Little Black Book'**   255
The real people of influence in the Asian-Pacific Rim, these businessmen should be on your contact network. A gameplan to bring you into their sphere.

8 **Have you got what it takes?**   264
A self-test questionnaire designed to assess the suitability of expanding your particular business/service into the region.

Foreword

If a Derbyshire brick manufacturer can sell his product to Japan and The Body Shop can do so well with a range of toiletries in plain packaging, surely you can sell your product to the emerging Asian-Pacific Rim economies? That is the lesson of this book – and it is an important lesson.

First, the Asian-Pacific Rim has been the most economically vibrant and fastest growing region in the world over the past decade, a growth advantage over Europe and America which, if anything, is set to increase. If you are not a part of this region, you will be missing out on crucial volume.

Second, many of your most vigorous competitors are, or will be, in the Asian-Pacific Rim; hitting them in their home market is an important defence, while the increasing quality consciousness of this market will provide a crucial competitive discipline. In short, if your products and marketing are good enough to sell in this region and to Japan, you will be able to sell anywhere.

Of course, there are problems: the Asian-Pacific Rim economies are distant both geographically and culturally; they are also difficult because they are so competitive – and so close to the Japanese powerhouse; and there are still problems with trade barriers.

Yet these difficulties are too often exaggerated. After all, the well-known brick manufacturer whose products have done so well in Japan is almost completely excluded from the Irish public sector market because of unofficial 'Buy Irish' policies, while sales to Germany are hampered by existing tied brick distribution arrangements. A Midlands manufacturer of high-quality chocolates found his products selling well in Japan and the Pacific Rim, but was all but prevented from marketing in the United States because of non-tariff barriers posing as 'health regulations'.

So markets which are near at hand or culturally linked are not always as open as some people think; by the same token, the difficulties of the Asian-Pacific Rim markets are habitually overstated. Obstacles, of course, do exist, which is why this excellent book by Claudia Cragg is such an invaluable and thorough guide through the labyrinth. Arm yourself with it and sell. For those who take the easy option of sticking with traditional markets will find themselves increasingly left behind as we move into the late 1990s and the next century.

Phillip Oppenheim
House of Commons
July 1992

Acknowledgements

In the course of research for this book, the following companies were contacted at the highest level. Many people very generously gave their support for the project and let us into some of the best-kept 'Tigers' secrets of commercial success in the Asian-Pacific Rim.

Allied Colloids PLC
Allied Dunbar Assurance PLC
Amersham International plc
Amstrad
Apple Computers (UK) Ltd
Astley International
Baring Brothers & Co Ltd
Baxter Healthcare Ltd
Blackwood Hodge PLC
Body Shop International
British Aerospace PLC
British American Tobacco PLC
British Chambers of Commerce
British Consultants Bureau
British Petroleum Co PLC
British Telecommunications PLC
Cadbury Schweppes PLC
James Capel & Co
Caradon PLC
Chartered West LB Ltd
Charterhouse Bank Ltd
C & J Clark Ltd
Clerical Medical & General Life
   Assurance Society
Coats Viyella PLC
Compair
Compaq
Courtaulds PLC

Continental Can
Coopers & Lybrand
Dale Electric International PLC
Delta
Digital
Dixons Ltd
Du Pont (UK) Ltd
Dun & Bradstreet
Eagle Star Insurance
Esso Petroleum Co Ltd
Federal Express
Ferodo Ltd
Fitch & Co
Foseco PLC
General Electric Co PLC
Glaxo Holdings PLC
Glynwed International PLC
Guinness PLC
Hallmark Cards
Hanson PLC
Harrods Ltd
Hewlett-Packard Ltd
Hongkong & Shanghai Banking
   Corporation
Horsell Graphic Industries
Hyatt International
IBM United Kingdom Ltd
Imperial Chemical Industries PLC

Inchcape PLC
Johnson Wax Ltd
Killick Martin & Co. Ltd
Kodak Ltd
Landis & Gyr Ltd
Leica Cambridge Ltd
LinPac Billoway
Logica Ltd
Lloyds Bank PLC
Mars UK Ltd
Matheson & Co Ltd
Meridian
Metal Box PLC
Midland Montagu Trade Finance
Mobil North Sea Ltd
Norsk Hydro UK Ltd
Pepsi-Cola International
PL Thermal Sciences

Polaroid
RTZ Corporation PLC
Rank Xerox (UK) Ltd
Reader's Digest Association Ltd
Reuters Ltd
Revlon International Corporation
Robertson Research PLC
Rolls-Royce PLC
Rowntree Mackintosh PLC
Saatchi & Saatchi
Tate & Lyle PLC
Thomson Holidays Ltd
3i PLC
Trafalgar House PLC
Unilever PLC
United Distillers
Virgin PLC

Special Acknowledgements

Patrick Walsh
British Overseas Trade Board – Lord Reay
British Tourist Authority – Mel Montgomery
Commercial Attachés – for all Pacific Rim countries
Confederation of Trade & Industry – Andrew Lawson
Department of Trade & Industry – Ann Sweet
Export Credits Guarantee Department
Foreign & Commonwealth Office
Hong Kong Government Office – Ian Howard
Imperial Chemical Industries PLC – Michael T Simmons
International Monetary Fund – K. Young
Insead
London School of Economics & Political Science – Library
Marks & Spencer plc
Marshall Library – Donald Ross
University of Sheffield & Korea Trade Services – Judith Cherry
Virgin PLC

The author is indebted to Katie Cross and Diane Hart for the many
hundreds of hours of research and co-ordination that they put into this
complex project and to Roger Jordan for checking and correcting the
material so thoroughly. We would also like to thank Angus Baxter of
Smith New Court, Far East Ltd. for his kind permission for access to
supporting statistics for background information.

We are particularly grateful also to Jack Maisano, publisher and editor-in-chief of the Hong Kong-published *Asian Business* magazine, for his very generous permission to reprint the material in Chapter 4, *Debunking the export myths* by Leon Richardson, and also for the Confidence Index for each country which is reprinted at the end of each of the profiles.

Introduction

On trading with the Asian-Pacific Rim

'I do not believe that trade with eastern Europe – or any other bloc or economic region for that matter – could have achieved the same ends for this company in terms of a contribution to our commercial success' – John Binney, *Allied Colloids PLC*.

'A breath of fresh air blew through the company as a direct result of our trading in the Asian-Pacific Rim. It is now the biggest overseas market for us and growing. In the beginning, we had to 'take on' new attitudes, or fail. We had to listen, not just hear. We had to reply, not just respond and we had to sharpen up our whole attitude to quality in every sense of the word. But successful trading with the Asian-Pacific can only come about for those who have an entirely open mind, and are positively both receptive and adaptable' – John K Corner, *Astley International*.

'The Body Shop now has franchise stores operating in Hong Kong, Singapore, Taiwan and Malaysia and is exploring Thailand, the Philippines and Indonesia. There are a great many issues to be addressed. Korea is also being closely studied to see whether the market can sustain a viable operation.

Our basic philosophy in international trade is that we do not want to exploit, nor to be considered to be exploiting, the local people in any country, whether in the Asian-Pacific Rim or anywhere else. It is always a prerequisite of our business operations that we somehow put back more than we take out. We are also deeply involved in projects in distressed areas through our 'Trade Not Aid' programme, creating work for local people by making the best use of local industries' – Robert Gluckmann, *The Body Shop*.

'The aviation sector in the Pacific Rim as a whole is likely to grow to three times its present size by the turn of the century. Given this and the

1

fact that the area will account for a quarter of all world air travel by the year 2010, it is a particularly valuable market for British Aerospace Commercial Aircraft, the world's largest manufacturer of regional aircraft. We have already had considerable success in placing our products in the Asian-Pacific region of the Rim, in Taiwan, Korea, Thailand and Indonesia, not to mention a strategic breakthrough into the Japanese market. It also could well be that Asia-Pacific will offer the combination of skilled workforce, physical infrastructure, finance and willingness to collaborate that will underpin the manufacture of the next generation of airliners' — Sidney Gillibrand, *British Aerospace PLC*.

'British Consultants Bureau member firms have worked successfully in most countries in the Asian-Pacific Rim and have set up joint operations with local professionals. Many have offices in the region, particularly in Hong Kong, Singapore, and Malaysia, and more recently in Thailand. These countries now form a key part of the world-wide operations of British consultants' – Tony Boam, *British Consultants Bureau*.

'Part of BP's world-wide strategy is to focus future development on nations in the Asian-Pacific Rim. The growing importance of this region to BP was underscored when it set up a new regional headquarters in Singapore in 1990. Hugh Norton, a BP managing director, was relocated to the new office as chairman' — *BP Asia Pacific & Middle East*.

'The attitude of British business as a whole to the region is getting better but there is a lot of room for improvement. Distance seems to be the problem. Company executives who have never been there are very negative and many seem to have decided to stay ignorant. On the other hand, those actually doing business there were very enthusiastic indeed.

In terms of investment, the British presence is very much in the service sector which is not a bad thing. British companies are very good at service.

There is always a niche somewhere, for example for products the Japanese can't be bothered to make, in particular those items which will fit into pieces of Japanese equipment, providing of course that they are properly made. A large number of British businessmen have successfully explored this kind of potential.

The basic CBI policy towards the region is that we would like to increase the British presence, one way or the other. We do our best to tell people what a great place the Asian-Pacific Rim is. At the end of the day, it is the company that makes the choice. You lead the horse to water but he decides whether to drink' — Andrew S. Lawson, *Confederation of British Industry*.

'Asian-Pacific Rim markets are less mature than those of Europe so there is a 'second bite' opportunity to make strategic corporate decisions which were missed at the same stage of development in Europe. The 'if only we'd done so and so 15 years ago' syndrome and 'missed opportunities' the first time around can be recycled in the Asian-Pacific as they go through similar development to Europe.

You cannot expect to penetrate these high-rise markets exclusively from an exporting factory in the UK. In market-places which are developing, both horizontally and vertically, you have to establish a local presence whether that is in sales, liaison, technical or a service office, or by manufacturing part or the whole of the product locally. The idea that the UK is the world's workshop is no longer valid. Asian markets want local service and support, within their own time zone and ethos.

In commercial success, remember that the Asian-Pacific Rim is not a short-cut to instant profits. The markets are world-wise and know how to buy well. Guile has to be matched with guile. In terms of fast-track recovery from the present recession, the Asian-Pacific Rim represents the best options because demand has been barely affected by the recession and there is an ingenuity which is survival- and progress-based – Iain L. Dale, *Dale Electric International PLC* and chairman, *South East Asian Trade Advisory Group (SEATAG)* – DTI.

'For several years it was not easy within our industry to export into the Asian-Pacific Rim area direct from Europe because of the low prices offered out there by small but numerous companies already established throughout the region. Now however we maintain a reasonable export business to the region of materials of a higher quality than those locally available, for example highly sophisticated materials to serve the vehicle manufacturers in Japan, Korea, Europe and the USA.

A product exported from Europe or from the US must be of quality high enough to overcome what, with tariffs, must be its uncompetitiveness. Our success has come about with the help of our local partners and, more particularly in Korea, by allowing the products to speak for themselves. It soon became apparent to the premium market that a high quality product at a higher price was not only safer but also gave longer service and therefore saved cost' – Ron Cooke, *Ferodo Ltd*.

'Success in the Pacific Rim is based on knowledge, trust and an approach which recognises and adapts to the commercial and cultural sensitivities of the East.

Guinness has a long tradition of successful trading in the Asian-Pacific Rim countries. In that sense, the market is not 'completely foreign' to us. Clearly, ownership of quality brands is important in determining the level of success in this region. Given that, the continuing success of Guinness depends upon maintaining the trust which has been built up, continuity of contect and careful attention to detail' – Brain F. Baldock, chairman *Guinness Brewing* World-wide and deputy chairman *Guinness PLC*.

'In a review of ICI strategy for the 1990s and into the next century, we believe that about 43 per cent of future growth in the chemical industry

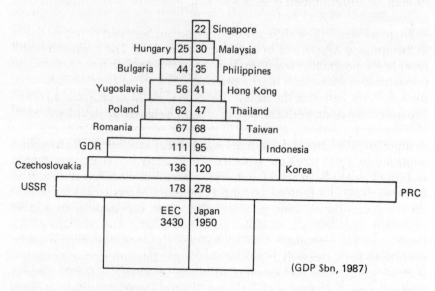

Figure 1 Asia and eastern Europe
(*Source*: DTI)

will be in the Asian-Pacific Rim to the year 2000. Most of the growth rates in the territory make even our sometimes sky-high inflation rates look modest and countries in the region are disappointed if growth falls below seven per cent. There is clearly a great deal of opportunity.

It is not inconceivable that ICI would have someone from the Asian-Pacific Rim as an executive director or even as chairman. We've already had Soichi Saba (ex-president and chief executive officer of Toshiba Corp) as a non-executive director on the ICI board and there is a huge pool of talent out there. In my view, the average Chinese is extremely capable. Every company should have its purchasing department staffed by Chinese. They are the most superb buyers of goods and brilliant negotiators, usually getting everything at the best price. What we have done is to shift the management and leadership of the territory to the 'coalface', so it is now led from Singapore in the same time zone, not from here' – Michael T. Simmons, *ICI*.

'The factors contributing to Marks & Spencer's success in the Asian-Pacific Rim have been, first of all, that we had a history in the market-place. Secondly, our stores were seen to offer standards of presentation, cleanliness and service which are still unmatched and that was appreciated. We have several hundred Chinese employees in the region now and our working conditions have caused the word to spread, just as it did in this country. It took a hundred years here, though. Your reputation goes before you and word of mouth is the best ambassador.

There are really few differences in principle between doing business in Europe and America or in the Asian-Pacific Rim. The approach is still completely pragmatic: learn the lessons of the market-place, assess the opportunities and weigh up the priorities. We are in the Pacific Rim for the long term and over the next 20 years it is bound to be a major area of expansion for us on both the supply and the selling side. Our food range is successful out there, at about 20 per cent of our total range and is a definite growth market. Last time I was there, I saw someone struggling manfully trying to work out what a Cornish pasty is. We arrange a lot of tasting of products in stores and explanatory leaflets. That is all part of learning to be international' – John Poppleton, *Marks & Spencer plc.*

'In the Asian-Pacific Rim, success in business can depend to a great extent on one's ability to establish good connections and relations with a large network of people. Once established, these relationships must be nurtured, both through business meetings and informal gatherings, such as golf games and evening drinking sessions' — Judith Cherry, formerly senior analyst with *Salomon Brothers* (now consultant at *Korea Business Services*, and lecturer in language, history and politics, *Sheffield University*).

'Rolls-Royce PLC greatly values both its existing and potential new customers in the Asian-Pacific Rim countries. At any one time we will be running a number of major sales campaigns in this region. It has never been "a completely foreign market" for us, although we have of course increased our business in individual countries over the years and gained new customers. On the civil aviation side, Hong-Kong based Cathay Pacific Airways is a good example of the former, while Garuda and Thai airlines are illustrative of the latter. We have gained extensive new orders in the power generation field from Singapore and Malaysia in particular, with bigger orders usually following the confidence gained by customers on smaller projects' — *Rolls-Royce PLC.*

'The most important aspect of business in the Asian-Pacific Rim is learning to deal with the people and their very different cultures. In the broadest possible terms, the Koreans (like the Japanese) are Confucian and value their corporate or family relationships above all else. The Chinese, however, value their more individual human contact network. Who introduces you to the person you hope to do business with is of the utmost importance' — Richard Cross, *Rudolf Wolff & Co Ltd.*

'What are the necessary personal qualities for success in the Asian-Pacific Rim? Only that anybody who is set in their ways and has only preconceived ideas will never adjust to working life there. Those who do well are good at their jobs as well as highly professional and are likeable. If you don't have a nice personality back home you certainly won't find

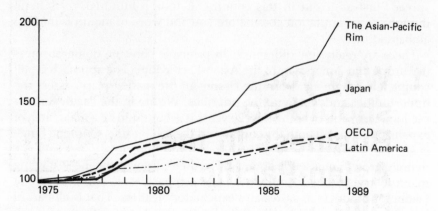

Graph 1 GDP growth
(*Source*: DTI)

life any different out there' — Jane Kingsley, *Russell Reynolds Associates Inc.*

'Richard Branson has been careful to spend a lot of time in the Asian-Pacific Rim because of the long-term importance of the region to our corporate growth. Our first moves in, through Japan in our case, came about through spontaneous thought. They were not strategised by management consultants – we never do that. Common sense dictated to us that the Virgin brand name was very strong out there and so could be maximised in those markets for both the retail operations and the airline. The goal for the airline is to fly to the 12 most important world capitals out of London and in this region. We are aiming at Seoul in 1993, Singapore in 1994 and Hong Kong not long after' — William Whitehorn, *Virgin PLC.*

1 Why you should do Business in the Asian-Pacific Rim

When Captain James Cook discovered the Hawaiian islands during his third voyage in January 1778, not even the most prescient thinkers of his day could have foretold that the surrounding far-flung nations would someday become the world's most dynamic region, 'The Pacific Rim'.

As we move towards the twenty-first century, however, it is becoming increasingly clear that the world has turned. The industrialised nations are being thrown up against the hard reality of an economic volte-face. The major cities bounding the Pacific area, Los Angeles, Sydney and Tokyo have made a bid to replace the old established cities of New York, Paris and London. Despite world stockmarket upheavals and even recession, their success looks ultimately inevitable if not increasingly imminent.

The modern school of 'geopolitics' has always emphasised that in theory the heartland of the world shifts in successive economic cycles. Large-scale trade started in the Mediterranean before shifting to the Atlantic. The 'Age of the Pacific' is clearly at hand. Since the turmoil of the Second World War, the Pacific's share of world trade has increased until now in the 1990s, the volume of trade in and across the Pacific Ocean has finally surpassed that of the Atlantic. The rapidly maturing economies of the Pacific nations provide constant new opportunities for trade and investment.

Historical changes, such as the end of the Cold War, inevitably cause structural shifts in the world's economy. Close to home, all businessmen throughout Europe and North America are well aware that the eastern European countries are shifting to try and become market economies. Western Europe is now trying to consolidate the European Community

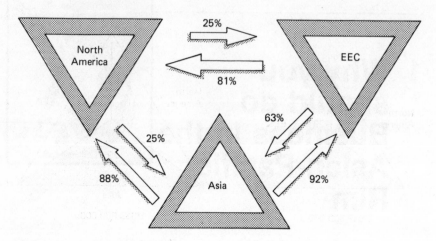

Figure 2 Trade patterns
(*Source*: DTI)

and North American nations are signing new economic agreements. The question now is, will the Asian-Pacific Rim, the most active economic area in the world today, form an economic bloc and will its might continue to grow?

John Naisbitt, the distinguished social observer, trend forecaster and co-author of *Mega-Trends 2000*, is now only one of many respected gurus to confirm the new orientation in world trade. He believes that 'The shift to the Pacific Rim is economically driven and at a pace that is without precedent'. *The Economist*, summing up the sentiments of many, has published a number of articles with the same theme that, as part of the entire Pacific Rim, 'Asia looks like the best thing to happen to the world since America'.

It was President Ronald Reagan who set the tone for the United States' business reorientation towards the Pacific back in June 1984 when he declared, 'This century has brought the Pacific nations many hardships and many difficulties and differences remain. But what I found everywhere [on a recent tour] was energy, optimism and excitement. More and more there is a sense of common destiny and possibility for all the peoples of this great region. The vast Pacific has become smaller, but the future of those who live around it is larger than ever before'. He went on later that same year to state that 'The Pacific is where the future of the world lies'.

Of course, the United States is already a key player in this emerging region, if only because of its lingering historical influence and because it undoubtedly sees it as a gigantic market for the region's exports and commercial activities. Its influence, however, is on the wane though in

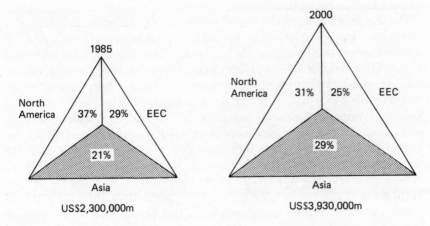

Figure 3 World manufacturing
(*Source*: DTI)

direct proportion to the decline in its aid. They know full well that remedial action must be taken because the growth in consumer spending alone in the nine countries featured in this book is enough to cause the average US manufacturer to holler for joy.

There are five states on the west coast of the country which all stand to gain significantly if the Pacific Rim does go on to fulfil its promise: Washington, Oregon, California, Nevada and Colorado are already the recipients of investment and tourist interest from the region. In this part of the US at least, ideas and culture, and a large volume of tourism exchange is showing a profound influence in the ways of doing business in terms of markets approached and even in culture and the foods people eat. Japan has already paved the way by stealing the thunder in a large number of major US and indeed European cultural events in the last five years or so and where she leads the others in the Asian-Pacific will surely follow.

The first signs that a move was afoot in the USA came perhaps as long ago as 40 years when the Pacific Area Travel Association was set up to promote both tourism and cultural exchange, as well as to report trends and ideas from throughout the Pacific Basin. While US travel to the Pacific has increased about nine per cent over the last five years, travel from nine Pacific nations to the US has increased by 15 per cent. This is aided and abetted of course by the large numbers of people whose families originally stem from countries in the region, who are now transplanted to the USA and making very full use of their connections with those back home to create new business. Who would ever have believed that a hamburger-eating nation could grow to love raw fish with such enthusiasm? There is now a sushi bar or Thai eatery on almost every Main Street in the US.

On the other side of the ideological coin, in the once 'Evil Empire', Gorbachev too was swayed by the distinct possibilities offered and took a keen interest in the region. He has spoken of the 'renaissance of world history' that has been taking place there and encouraged his citizens and ministries alike to form cohesive policies to maximise the possibilities for new business that will increasingly present itself. The Pacific Rim also suddenly became the 'sexy topic' for MBAs and CEOs alike and US companies for the most part have been solidly working to open up the region to their commercial influence and grab some of the gain for themselves. To what extent, though, is this a classic example of American marketing hype? Are we to believe that, in some far distant land, there really are better commercial opportunities than we can find much closer to home, for example in the revitalising economies of eastern Europe?

Tigers, what tigers?

In the simplest possible terms, it is the Pacific Rim including China that will hold two-thirds of the world's population in the third millennium, while Europe will contain only six per cent. That in itself is uninteresting. You could possibly discuss the potential of, say, the Indian sub-continent in the same way. However, in the case of the Pacific Rim this involves a $3 trillion-a-year market growing at the rate of $3 billion dollars a week. This growth is the key, so much so that any further yardstick which is then applied, whether geographic, demographic or economic, only serves to underscore the characterisation of the Pacific Rim as a powerful global presence. The sum of the gross national products of Japan, China and the 'tigers' (Hong Kong, Korea, Singapore and Taiwan) alone will, by the year 2000, be equal to that of the United States, and that is even before you factor in the gross national products (GNPs) of the emerging tigers such as Malaysia, Thailand, Indonesia, the Philippines and Vietnam. Major economists now predict, with good evidence, that the Asian GNP will overtake North America's by the year 2011 and Europe's by 2015. We have less than 20 years to get ready for the onslaught.

It is a serious and all-too-common mistake to believe that somehow the area's growth has come about solely because of the involvement of both the United States and Japan, or that continued dependency on these two is the *sine qua non* of its progress on to maturity. These two countries were undoubtedly of paramount importance for the initial spurt, that is unquestionable. The yen was strong, the dollar was weak, the US, western Europe and Japan were enjoying stable economic growth, and in 1990 oil prices dropped to half their 1986 level. The conditions were all there. The progress that has since been made, ensures that the region's future strength is virtually assured.

Even though economic growth has been slowing over the last year and has therefore had a knock-on affect on the Rim as a whole (no one in the world has been immune), South Korea, Malaysia and Thailand have managed a growth in their gross domestic products (GDPs) of about 8 per cent despite the Gulf conflict, while Taiwan and even Indonesia grew at a rate of more than 6 per cent. Consider then that, by comparison, economic supergiant Japan only managed about 3.5 per cent growth, while the figures for the UK and the USA do not bear discussion. Something other than mere trading interaction with established countries is clearly fuelling the countries onward and upward to greater realms of growth.

These 'tigers', that we now have to learn to hunt 'with', rather than regard merely as our legitimate commercial quarry, have significant characteristics in common. Sadly, none of these are qualities that we can or would even wish to emulate so that we might perhaps put our own house in order. All those countries involved are extremely adept at importing manufacturing and other techniques and in implementing them with maximum cost-cutting in the process. They have a dynamic and growing consumer market and a growing middle class, and they increasingly have greater disposable income. They are no longer just the vendors that we once egocentrically thought they were (and some wished they might stay), but are fast becoming independent marketplaces in their own right. Our management consciousness seems to be clearly lagging behind history in this, so much so that many companies cling stubbornly to the idea of these places only as producers of items for Western entrepreneurs to sell. These cataract-ridden executives are missing the new opportunities to sell into countries where consumer demand can become so hungry that it almost threatens to run riot.

If these 'tigers' can flourish in such financially unsound times, at the same time grappling with their own widening current account deficits, rising inflation and infrastructure bottlenecks, they could well be unstoppable given a better world economic picture. Maybe we shall never have such good times again in order to test the theory. However, even with only a modest US recovery over the next year or two, a regional rebound of at least more than commensurate strength will follow. The focus for business in the twenty-first century, whether we like it or not, will undoubtedly shift dramatically, and this can only be accelerated by modern technology (satellite links, the ubiquitous use of modems and electronic mail) and supersonic, less expensive air travel daily bringing the possibilities so much closer to home.

What all managers must now ask themselves, therefore, is not are they bold enough to brave the emerging markets, but how they can dare not to. If just the minimum ingredients do come into play, can anyone afford to risk missing what could be a phenomenal opportunity? At the end of the day, if for whatever reason the region does not come together as a whole up to the present high expectations for the Association of South East Asian Nations (ASEAN) – on a par with, say, the EEC – can those in charge really deny the existence of the very real opportunities that are undoubtedly presenting themselves right now. As they say, the future is already here.

The nature of the beasts

This book intentionally avoids covering the entire Pacific Basin. Japan and China are well-covered by numerous tomes on the shelves of every business library, and no one, I hope, needs lessons or encouragement at this late stage in how to do business with Australia, New Zealand, or the US. It is on dealing specifically with the other, often ignored, nations of the Asian-Pacific Rim that guidance, solid information and some measure of hand-holding is required. It is here, in the very core of the Rim as a whole, that the world's most dynamic area of future trade and economic expansion can be found and it is here where the best opportunities for new business can be scented out.

The focus is on nine key countries, 'the four tigers' (South Korea, Taiwan, Hong Kong and Singapore), together with the 'tiger cubs', the new growth economies of ASEAN, Thailand, Malaysia, Indonesia and the Philippines, and the emerging market that is Vietnam. The latter's inclusion is justified by the growing interest the country has been receiving from businessmen travelling and investing in the region and it looks as though it has all the ingredients to one day become a powerful feline in its own right. It is these nine countries that together with Greater China and the king of the Pacific jungle, Japan, will eventually dominate the entire Pacific Rim. (Note: Brunei has not been included, and neither has Macau because of the still low volume of business and opportunities.)

This area can be viewed as a miniature of the world itself characterised by the coexistence of a wide variety of cultures and religions, by different stages of economic and political development and by different levels of endowment in natural resources and population. The area in question holds a large portion of the world's remaining untapped human and natural resources and, in equal measure, the prospects, hopes and (to some extent) track record for economic development and progress.

It is while these tigers are still 'developmental states', so-called because they are not yet 'newly industrialised countries' (NICs) that they provide the best conditions. A point worth making is that while the tigers are still in economic pubescence, the survival of their individual political regimes takes absolute precedence over every other domestic concern as a matter of expediency. Concerns with nation building and the growth of liberal democracy move down the list of priorities so that economic growth can be allowed to provide the solid and indeed only foundation of political legitimacy. If the growth falters, then so does the regime. If the growth is sufficiently great to mollify the people with the compensations of greater capacity for consumer spending, the country continues to grow, all along allowing for further consolidation and therefore more solid foundations for further growth in the future. It is when a tiger is fully grown that it then starts to face, and hopefully learns to handle, more complex political problems and resolutions.

The basic ingredients that are vital to the successful execution of the young tiger's game-plan are strong government, flourishing collaboration between the state and private enterprise, an open-armed welcome for foreign investment, a willingness on the part of the majority of people to put off reaping substantial personal reward for the long-term good of their country (through the acceptance of low wages in the interim) and the superpower security umbrella which will play a role for another two decades or so.

As you read through the profiles of all nine countries discussed in this book, you will clearly see that even those who have not yet been identified as NICs have already gone a long way towards at least establishing the framework for their future role as part of the ambush (the collective noun for tigers). Whether they now succeed in achieving the dizzy heights of such a formal economic classification depends as much on international trade and investment as it does on the particular strengths and weaknesses in their own systems. Each chapter will start you off on the road to complete awareness of all that is going on in these markets, such as the conditions of trade and industry, the manufacturing and general support infrastructure, the people, their politics and economics. Above all there is one vital ingredient with which no businessman could fail to arm himself, solid information. The 'primer' chapters will at least equip you with essential details of the countries concerned and are the ideal basis for you then to go on and absorb as much detailed knowledge as you can in the specific market or markets of your choice. Most of all the material is served up as food for thought and will hopefully whet the appetites of those you of who have not yet given the region much attention.

The leaders of the pack

It is agreed that the tigers in themselves might just be individual examples of economic maturation, as spontaneous and coincidental as a number of heavy clouds bursting forth with rain. If that is the case, then it is all the more remarkable that they are now, disparate as they are, trying to find a way to work together as a pack for the mutual benefit and protection of all. The vulnerabilities of life as a lone economic animal could easily, the idealists amongst them say, be countermanded by life as an economic pack. Just look at Maastricht!

The Association of South East Asian Nations (ASEAN) was formed in 1967 by Indonesia, Malaysia, the Philippines, Singapore and Thailand and was the first attempt to improve links between countries in this region. At the moment there are various moves for a wider pan-Pacific association drawing in other countries. The rapid development of the 1970s and early 1980s created a clear need for stronger trade links and greater co-operation between ASEAN nations in order to consolidate economic gains into some sort of political clout. The region as a whole, with the benefit of its double-digit growth economies, soon became a major force to be reckoned with. It also began to provide the best opportunities for both businessmen and investors looking for new expanding markets which are as yet largely unrealised.

It is more or less certain that politics in each of the countries can be expected to become more pluralistic, but not in the democratic mode of the West. Indeed, it can even be argued that political competition is not a process that is well understood in these countries, either in theory or in practice. It is more often than not regarded as a state of mind that can only lead to violence, not the accommodation of differing points of view. Satisfying these competing democratic groups will become more and more difficult as new voices find a means of expression. The result may be that some countries become preoccupied with their internal problems and therefore less inclined toward regional collaboration of either an economic or political nature. On present form, however, the clamouring for union of some kind between the region's nations shows no sign of abating. Should a union ever become enough of a reality for them even partially to pull together, their combined might could prove overwhelming.

Getting into the lair

Even if the 'Pacific Rim' concept ultimately turns out to be nothing more than hype put out by a few influential management gurus and business thinkers, few businessmen can afford to ignore the fact that in an economically hard-pressed world, it is these new economies in Asia that provide the best hope for sustained business growth for both European and North American companies. As the Royal Institute of International Affairs summed it up, with masterful understatement, 'Even though the

Pacific Century itself may never materialise, the region will surely take a more prominent place in the world of the twenty-first century'.[1]

In Europe we have been more sleepy-headed in tackling the region than our American cousins. We have the ultimate excuse of course that (unlike the Americans who are neighbours and indeed, on their west coast, an important part of that region), the Pacific is a very, very long way away. This is the lame excuse most often cited when companies were questioned as to their involvement in the Asian-Pacific Rim. The other is that, to their minds, eastern Europe is a lot closer to home and therefore less trouble to deal with.

There are surprisingly few common threads among the countries on the Pacific Rim. The people involved speak between them more than 1,000 languages and are exceedingly diverse ethnically, politically, socially, religiously, and geographically. How then, with domestic markets shrinking, can businesses capitalise on the potential profits in this new trading arena which will soon offer a market of some 80 million new consumers hungry for our goods and services?

During the course of this book, we set out to establish (informally and with no attempt at real statistical significance) to what extent hundreds of British companies, as well as major multinational corporations, seriously consider the Asian-Pacific Rim as part of their corporate plans for future growth and development. From those with an established interest, we sought practical advice. Those who declared no interest at all in the region or in its possibilities were asked to elaborate on their reasons for inactivity. The results, while eye-opening and useful, were fairly shocking but a selection of the very best and most useful of them are reproduced here in this book for your edification. These are the 'secrets' of achieving commercial success in the Asian-Pacific Rim that are so very hard to elicit during the course of normal business.

The conclusion has to be drawn that the real level of interest across the board, despite the very best efforts of the Department of Trade and Industry (DTI) and other promotional stalwarts, is still minimal. There is a clear reason for this. Eastern Europe, we were often told, is a great deal closer and a lot less trouble to deal with. That misconception was instantly corrected by Michael T Simmons, manager, Asia Pacific Liaison, at ICI group headquarters, a man of profound capability and practical wisdom on the question of cross-cultural commercial literacy, whose insight is relayed to you in a later chapter. Given the fact that ICI is already well established in North America and in Europe (in common with a great many other successful companies), the Asian-Pacific Rim is the natural choice for expansion. He believes that present indications are

---

[1] *The Royal Institute of International Affairs in Pacific Asia in the 1990s,* by Masahide Shibusawa, Zakaria Haji Ahmad and Brian Bridges, 1992.

that as much as 43 per cent of future growth in the chemical industry will be in the Asian-Pacific Rim to the year 2000. No one could ignore such shining prospects. Eastern Europe may have potential but it does not have what the Asian-Pacific abounds in, he says, entrepreneurs and a cast-iron work ethic everywhere you look.

Intrepid business pioneers from the industrialised world, from companies such as British Petroleum, Marks & Spencer, Body Shop, ICI (already mentioned) and Virgin, and a great many others who have generously contributed to this book, have been increasingly lured to seek out these lucrative new arenas by a sense of challenge and adventure and by receding domestic markets. Far from being hurled against jagged and unseen commercial rocks, they have usually had their brave and often expensive economic forays well rewarded. Tales are filtering back of the profits to be made in Asian stockmarkets and of machinery and equipment orders to be won in the newly industrialising countries. These are the people who are hunting with the tigers. Others must now join the throng or take the risk that, one day, they might just be eaten.

2 To market, to market . . . *Quo Vadis?*

The decision you make when choosing your target market is a fundamental corporate investment decision and must be treated as such. A foray into uncharted waters can be very expensive and time-consuming in terms of company resources if it proves to be fruitless. With the changes that have taken place in eastern Europe, as well as the likelihood, eventually, of a bottoming out of the general recession in the US and UK, many companies consider themselves opportunity-rich at the moment. Companies, of course, have to be very selective and many, therefore, are unnecessarily dismissing the valuable and long-term opportunities in the Asian-Pacific because of this need for selection. This is a mistake. No damage at all can come from a thorough and detailed exploration of the possibilities for you and your company in an area that without doubt holds some of the world's best commercial promise.

The Asian-Pacific Rim may be loosely classified as a regional market with national characteristics. This is essentially because the countries concerned are at different stages along the same developmental path. In very broad terms, it can be said that they are all looking to improve their infrastructure which means that there will be sectoral opportunities in roads, transport, communications, power, water. All are looking to increase their export industry capabilities and so need all the goods and services which make up a dynamic industrial base: processing, production and finishing machinery, as well as major infrastructural construction such as docks and airports.

A great deal of this growth has already taken place and there are relatively new pockets of very high wealth and capital in a number of cities. Major cities in Thailand are already showing the characteristics of a newly industrialised economy. Malaysia is quite clearly going the same way and Singapore is already there. There are growing consumer markets in these areas, particularly for high quality western goods. The growth also requires a solid base of development of welfare policies, so serious opportunities in health care, education and training will also become more apparent. A concern for the environment is perceptible, barely, although it is not yet highly developed. It is unlikely, though, that south-east Asia will become as big a market as, say, Japan or Taiwan, or Korea for high technology environmental protection equipment because the level of public awareness of environmental issues does not seem to be properly developed.

ASEAN members are considering setting up a free trade area by the year 2000. Even if a cohesive region were to exist, in some form or other, it is questionable whether the appointment of one agent to cover the region would ever be ideal. A good parallel is to imagine just how succesful it really would be to appoint an agent in France to cover the Benelux countries. There is, however, a Chinese or 'Greater China' factor at play in these markets. Since most small companies could not afford a local man in each market for assessment purposes, a Chinese-run trading company, say out of Hong Kong or Singapore, may provide an alternative.

There is the example, however, of one very large company which formed a joint venture run by an expatriate who took two to three years setting up in the market getting ready to sell its products. When he went to see what he had hoped might be their most lucrative client, their attitude surprised him. Why, they wondered, should their company do business with him in particular? The expatriate went through all the usual reasons of value for money, the highest quality and so on, only to be rejoindered with the remark that he was not the client's friend. In other words, no relationship, no business. That aspect of Asian-Pacific business alone absolutely requires you to have a community presence there.

Many products must be adapted for sale in Asian-Pacific markets, often because of the climate. One of the key selling points that needs to be looked at, apart from the cost of market entry is the education and training component. Training must be considered as part and parcel of you and your company becoming a respected member of the community. Countries in the region want to enhance the technical base they already have and the skills of their work-force in order to develop products for their markets. They are not always merely seeking to acquire foreign goods. A high degree of willingness to train can therefore be of the utmost importance in achieving successful business results. This may cause a problem for UK companies which are concerned that their investment might ultimately be lost, as it has sometimes been here in the UK in some industries. Generally speaking though, there is a high degree of worker loyalty in south-east Asia.

There are some geographical pockets where skilled labour shortages are causing a wage price spiral. This applies to Bangkok, for example, and to parts of Malaysia, as well to a certain extent to Singapore and Jakarta. The same skilled employees tend to do the rounds of three or four companies over a period of time, only to come back to their original employer at twice the salary. On the whole, though, you can expect good loyalty from a pretty able work-force. Apart from Singapore, most of these countries would like to attract labour-intensive manufacture, involving processing or adding value to their natural resource base, ie fishing.

The 20 key market selection criteria

The initial interest in the market should be followed up by a thorough investigation of (a) the market potential, (b) the competition and (c) the political environment. Using this book as a starting point for general background information, you should collect as much current information as possible on the country. Banks with strong financial links to the region, eg, the Hongkong & Shanghai, as well as multinational banks, usually have a wealth of information that can be made available to prospective clients. The embassies of the countries concerned should be contacted for general business information. This is also a very good way of getting the 'feel' of the country with which you are planning to do business, as well as an indication of how you will cope with their relative degrees of bureaucracy. Bear in mind, though, that the staff you will come across here are expatriate and therefore more acclimatised to your ways. Explore the possibilities of further information resources from specialised libraries and associations, resident representatives of international agencies, lawyers, business consultants and by contacting other people in your broad field with known experience in the region.

There is a whole host of very detailed considerations that must first of all be very thoroughly explored and then applied to your specific circumstances. This is primarily so that a unanimous financial commitment at the highest level in your company can be made to develop the chosen market. Market intelligence and research is best undertaken by any one of the specialised firms working in the region. After the final assessment of the potential of the market, and before commitment can be made, familiarisation visits must be made to sound out the possibiities with known contacts. This must not be, as it often seems to be in so many cases, the first step. Going on a 'look-see' to a market that you just happen to be passing through on the plane, will not provide a solid foundation for future business success.

The twenty basic factors that must be considered in selecting the market or markets to target for your business are, in no particular order, as follows:

1. Is there an *identified need* for your product or service in the country or countries of your choice and the infrastructure to sustain that need?

2. Is there a *large availability of potential customers* for you and your company?

3. What is the *competition* and does it enjoy significant advantages over you that might make your business unviable?

4. Is there a *wide availability of market information* on your product or services for that country from specialised professional sources?

5. What about the *advertising, public relations, and general promotion* of awareness of your business in that country?

6. What is *the maturity and level of the product* and/or service in the market

7. Is there an *industry using your products* whose demands you could meet?

8. What is the availability of potential *outlets, agents and distributors*?

9. What are the *long-term prospects*?

10. What are the options in the market in terms of *exporting, licensing* or using *a local subsidiary*?

11. What is the *availability of financing* in the market?

12. What are the *costs of market entry* (set-up, as well as re-engineering, repackaging and translating) and what of the distribution channels?

13. *How easy* is it in that market *to ensure payment*?

14. How will the *legal and accounting framework* in that country, i.e. the general operating environment, impact on your company's usual business practices?

15. How passive or regulatory is the *government's attitude* to foreign businesses (foreign equity and ownership) and what of *tariffs and quotas* for your product?

16. What are the possibilities of *incentives*?

17. How sound is the country's *political stability*?

18. What of the *costs of facilities and* the cost and availability of necessary skilled and unskilled *workers*?

19. How difficult are both *cultural inter-action* and the spoken *language(s)* in terms of doing business?

20. To what extent will *your company's goals* and interests be met by being located in this market or markets?

Follow my leader

In very general terms, the majority of companies which are currently active in the Asian-Pacific Rim seem to find that Hong Kong is the market that most satisfies these criteria for their products and/or services. Close rivals are Singapore and then Malaysia who both seem to be catching up with Hong Kong in the run up to the Chinese takeover of the territory in 1997. It is of course not surprising that these destinations are so appealing, since these old 'pith helmet' countries have in place the vestiges of a profoundly British way of doing business, albeit highly localised in practice. English is also widely spoken in daily business life and the legal and accounting systems are familiar. A smaller business, with limited funds may well want to look closely at Singapore which is a warehouse for the rest of the region and is, in its own right, a small but wealthy market. Singapore is also a fund of information for the whole region in that, using it as a base, you can unearth a lot of pertinent and valuable sectoral information as well as potential business contacts.

The Philippines has good trade links both ways with the UK but the country has a lot of domestic problems. The outward mission scheme that the DTI runs is done on an annual basis, with sponsors and trade associations invited to bid for support. The companies who are already trading in the Philippines are doing quite well, particularly in the form of joint ventures. The country is unlikely to prove to be an interesting export market for some considerable time, but there is still further potential for joint ventures as well as investment opportunities.

The other markets – South Korea, Taiwan, Thailand and Indonesia – follow on close behind because the continuing growth in their GDPs and in their consumer markets is making them far too attractive to ignore. Vietnam, while interesting for those in the financial, construction and energy sectors, is on the whole still too new and uncertain a business destination for most inexperienced companies. The very weak infrastructure and persisting problems with trade with the US (the total veto that was a legacy of the Vietnam war is still in place) do not yet make the market sufficiently attractive to warrant the necessary risk, effort and expense. Most companies nevertheless believe that when the US does 'normalise' its trade relations with Vietnam (as it is expected to in the near future), the country will probably witness the most rapid development of entrepreneurial energy that the region has seen to date.

Already a large number of Hong Kong companies have their eyes on Vietnam as an alternative bolt-hole if Hong Kong should come to grief. You must look at the markets and recognise them for what they are. There is a lot of development still to come, and many still have a very poor infrastructure. The bureaucracies of Indo-China are also yet to be tested in terms of developmental growth. Vietnam is some 30 years behind Indonesia on its road to becoming a market economy and there are vast sums of money that need to be spent on investment in infrastructure. The countries may well be wealthy in natural resources, and have an abundance of cheap and highly trainable labour but industrialisation is nevertheless still a considerable way off.

Where to get help

It is the body of British businessmen that make up the British Overseas Trade Board (BOTB) who collectively advise the government through the DTI on the promotion of exports by sitting on various area advisory groups. Within the Asian-Pacific Rim, as defined in terms of this book, there are four groups with which should concern yourself. These are the Anglo-Taiwanese Trade Committee; the Korea Trade Advisory Group; the Sino-British Trade Group (for Hong Kong and the Greater China economic region), and the Southeast Asia Trade Advisory Group (SEATAG) which looks after the six ASEAN markets, three Indo-China markets and Myanmar (formerly Burma). (See Appendix, for details of addresses.)

Outside western Europe, North America and Japan, other so-called 'top priority markets' have been identified and in the Rim. These are Korea, Hong Kong, Taiwan, Thailand, Malaysia, Indonesia and Singapore. These markets are thoroughly monitored in terms of prospects, potential and opportunities for serious business. The DTI's upstream work creates awareness of the markets and, to a certain extent, covers aspects of how to do business there. Excellent information is available on people already conducting business successfully in the region in the magazine *Overseas Trade Magazine*, and in the regular SEATAG bulletins. Seminars are frequently held on the region generally as well as on individual market or country's prospects. Some look at particular sectors (eg the situation and prospects for IT, power generation, or packaging in south-east Asia). For these, hard copy material is available and there are usually a number of expert speakers brought over to the UK from the market concerned. For a recent roadshow on Indonesia, two speakers experienced in the market briefed the audience.

In addition, the DTI also holds seminars on particular aspects of business life in south-east Asia with an emphasis on cultural awareness. These explore potential problems for the first-time visitor to an Asian-Pacific market, illustrating business 'dos and don'ts'. A recent topic was the 'dos and don'ts of exhibiting products' in the region. Another has been on that thorny subject, 'appointing an agent'. In these, it is the cultural element and how it practically applies to the business environment that is emphasised.

It does look as though some UK companies are put off entering markets, not only by a lack of awareness but also because they may consider the business environment too alien to their own. It is true that on the whole, we are not used to the ways of doing business in the area. What many chief executives and managements fail to realise, though, is the high degree of communality in business practice in the different countries in the area, even though approaches may vary slightly along the way. The DTI seminars also look at the tactical aspects of doing business, for example, joint ventures, mergers and acquisitions.

It is important too that the attention is caught of the corporate decision-makers and/or company business strategists so that they are armed with information that will appeal to sales staff, market planners and the sales directors whose task it is to identify future markets for corporate expansion and for greater resource allocation. The DTI gently but persistently tries to goad sales staff into taking south-east Asia seriously, while also pulling in decision-makers to brief them fully.

Once a company has taken the initial decision to go ahead, and interest in expansion to the area has been declared, the DTI may then help in the acquisition of both general and specific market information through the Overseas Trade Services Bureau (see Appendix) or from outward missions, exhibitions and inward or outward technical seminars, for which the DTI is sometimes able to provide grants to sponsors. Most of these activities are sponsored by local chambers of commerce or trade associations. Regional briefings are usually held six months ahead of a trade mission's visiting a chosen market in order to recruit and encourage potential participants. For the outward trade missions themselves, the DTI provides as much assistance and advice to individual companies as they need in the hope that the businessman stepping off a plane in a new market for the first time will be well-prepared and thoroughly appraised of the precise business reasons for his visit.

All kinds of UK companies, both large and small, request DTI assistance in countries like Indonesia and Thailand where there is no strong history of trade links with Britain. Some are seeking opinions on who should be contacted to provide more information or to find reputable agents, distributors or partners. To a certain extent, the DTI does present its opinions as being those of experts, even though as civil servants their experience is not gained through practical business dealings.

The conscious level of awareness amongst UK companies on the potential earnings from the Asian Pacific has certainly increased during the last four to five years. The government would like to believe that most of the UK exporting population is trying to get to grips with Asian-Pacific in one way or another. Those who tend to be successful realise that the region as an entity offers different markets for different companies and products, and so take the approach of tackling one pre-selected country as a jumping-off point.

The ten cardinal commercial 'sins' of the Asian-Pacific

1. Inadequate preparation.
2. Inadequate strategic planning.

3. Inadequate resource commitment.
4. Too short-term an approach.
5. A lack of understanding that the markets operate in a different way.
6. Failure to recognise the importance of relationships (not so different from the UK).
7. Failure to establish a sound local base.
8. Too heavy a reliance on the efficiency of agents, who normally peddle a large quantity of similar products/services.
9. Infrequent visits to the market by face-giving VIPs from home base.
10. Commercial arrogance.

It cannot be emphasised enough that companies must not only put down local roots but also take steps on the road to becoming a respected member of the local business community in order to be considered a serious player. When companies neglect this side of operations, their Asian-Pacific business can only ever remain marginal even if they may have had larger expansion plans in mind.

Do not attempt to cover every and any export possibility. Selective decisions must be made and sometimes mistakes in selecting a market will be made. With increasing interregional trade in the Asian-Pacific area, and increasing investment in Korea, Taiwan, Hong Kong, Singapore and other south-east Asian markets, an embryonic regional market could be said to be emerging.

This could mean that current business operations in Singapore at the moment could well lead to future business in Taiwan. The relationships you now establish in Thailand or Malaysia, for example, might well lead to business in Vietnam. That is the nature of the Asian-Pacific entrepreneurial mindset. This 'third country business' approach also applies to your present dealings with the Japanese. If you sell yourself and your product in Japan, you can also – through the same connections – sell the same to other parts of the world. This is also true of Korea and is becoming increasingly true of Taiwan. A seminar on making the most of Japanese trading relationships in south-east Asia is currently in the pipeline.

The Japanese presence in the region is often seen as an obstacle to British trade. Remarks are made about the Japanese domination of the markets. The final realisation by peaceful means of her 'Greater East Asia Co-Prosperity Sphere' ambitions is perceived as making entry for others more difficult. This dominance by foreign multinationals, however, may also provide a valuable window of opportunity if you already have a history of dealing with these trading concerns.

Plenty of advice is also available on 'different business practices', a matter that may cause some concern when dealing with countries such as the Philippines and Indonesia. Corruption is seen by some UK companies as characteristic of the region and can be very offputting.

The more experienced observer will be aware sooner or later that it need not be as problematical as it seems, if handled correctly. While 'baksheesh' of any kind should never be indulged in or encouraged, the 'old hand' will normally come to judge its practice somewhat leniently as an 'alternative form of social welfare'. In a social context, the intelligent businessman will begin to appreciate the factors involved and manage the situation more effectively. Where major sums of money are involved though, there are ways and means of influencing the final outcome in hot competition for business that are substantially no different from those practised anywhere else in the world, ie straight-forward lobbying.

The truth is that business life in the Asian-Pacific is not all that different. The bottom line is and always will be money. The most sound advice that can be given to anyone embarking on a venture out there is not to do a deal unless both sides are winning something. Cashflow is of the greatest importance and is a tenet in the Asian-Pacific that you will be understood and respected for.

Practised business practitioners in, say, western Europe or North America should not experience too many difficulties. The businesses and peoples of the Asian-Pacific Rim are looking to deal with Britain and like the country and her people. The British, it can be said, start with a number of real advantages in that the UK is one of the leaders of European trade investment in the region and the English language is also the natural tongue for business. Above all, good governmental relationships have been forged with countries in the region. The conditions are such that businesses should make an attempt to go forth and multiply but should not expect immediate cash returns. They should also not be surprised if market conditions, and the *modus operandi* if they are, are not exactly the same as in the UK.

3 Tiger tactics

If ever there was a true Pacific Rim pioneer it is that canny East-Ender, Alan Sugar. It would not be true to say that Amstrad, one of the most successful consumer electronics concerns in Europe, owes its success entirely to the Asian-Pacific region. That success is Sugar's alone. However, it is generally agreed, I believe, that without the nimble fingers, productivity, and intelligence of the component-manufacturing abilities that are so widely available throughout Asia, Amstrad would never have achieved such heights of corporate success.

It is indeed strange that Sugar and his company, who started out with the 'British made' tag, were then severely rounded upon when they did what their well-honed business instincts naturally told them to do. The company was forced to turn to the Asian-Pacific as a source so that it could keep products competitive for consumers in the domestic markets, at the lower end of the electronics market.

With hindsight, it is clear that Alan Sugar's only 'sin' was a real prescience that allowed him to see that world manufacturing and trading patterns were changing and that corporate survival, in so many cases, must mean finding the least inexpensive sourcing for parts.

It was Amstrad's operations base in Hong Kong that allowed the sourcing of cheaper production in the whole of the region, but especially in Taiwan, South Korea , Hong Kong and later on Malaysia. The cost involved was not perhaps as reckless as the continuing product development that occurred which was crucial. This came about because of his local Chinese engineers' gifted ability to continually pick competitive products apart and build them, better and cheaper.

Not only was Sugar right to set and develop the trend (dozens went out to try and emulate his success, therefore decreasing his own competitive margins), but he was rattling around in small back offices in downtown Seoul and Taipei in the mid-1980s when most chief executives had not even given the region a thought. As it now turns out, Sugar was doing exactly what the Japanese, who are always one step ahead of the game in the Asian-Pacific Rim, can now be seen to have been doing all along and at exactly the same time: moving their main production sources to markets where they could take advantage of cheaper labour and production costs. (Remember the Greater East Asia Co - Prosperity Sphere?)

It was the sharp decline in the yen exchange rate in Japan back in the early 1980s that made it impossible for their firms to maintain competitive prices in their export markets in Europe and the USA, so they were forced to manufacture offshore. It was this Japanese investment, first in Korea and Taiwan, and later in Singapore, Hong Kong, Malaysia, Thailand and Indonesia that caused the catalyst to react into the rapid development of the markets. Even now, these lessons are not being learned in Europe and the USA. There are still opportunities for foreign firms to establish operations as down-stream suppliers to these industries, ie threads, buttons, dyes to garment industries, varnishes, lacquers, preservatives to furniture industry, components to auto-industries and they should be vigorously pursued.

Alan Sugar, in fact, could be said to have opened the floodgates for others from the West and to have helped to open our eyes in a profound way. What he did, though, was what Jardine Matheson, Butterfield Swire and dozens of other 'hongs' in the region had done for nearly a century before him. It is the present generation which has been so slow on the uptake. A certain amount of 'education' of the local people in the area was needed, admittedly, on how to handle and work with 'gweilos' (foreign devils), till then usually thought of as green-eyed monsters, and what better man to do it than Alan Sugar. A harder lesson in commercial tolerance and exploration would be hard to find. For our part, we also needed to be brainwashed into an understanding that commercially we are not always right (contrary to our deepest instincts) and that it is perhaps us who are 'foreign'.

In order to get a handle on how these perceptions and prejudices on both sides affect business strategy in the 1990s, a number of key commercial players in the region have ingeniously come up with some important thoughts. These are not so much 'rules' as 'philosophies' (as in so many other ways in the East), but they are best thoroughly digested, preferably with an ice-cold glass of rice wine on a hot, sunny day by a Malaysian stretch of sandy beach. When the pleasant glow evaporates, wake up immediately and incorporate these ideas into your Asian-Pacific Rim business strategy.

Find your 'Schwarzkopf'

There will be two outstanding contributing factors to your success in the market, according to Richard Humphreys, president of Saatchi &

Saatchi Advertising World-wide. The first is that you must have a solid base of international activity which will generate the necessary cash flow to run the business. You must also have the credentials to attract both staff and new clients. Above all, you must have the right chief executives running the local operation. These are what he says are best described as 'marine entrepreneurs'. The person selected for the job must be an astute businessman, finance manager, public relations expert, personnel manager, finance manager, strategist, and new business tactician – with the heart, courage and leadership of General Norman Schwarzkopf.

Bend like a willow

Successful trading in the Asian-Pacific Rim can only come about for those who have an entirely open mind, and are positively both receptive and adaptable. This success in the Asian-Pacific Rim is based on knowledge and on trust, as well as an approach which recognises and adapts to the eastern commercial and cultural sensitivities.

You must learn to be flexible. The Pacific Rim has a strong regional cultural overlay to its Japanese-inspired business orthodoxy. In the Pacific Rim, there are socialist, capitalist, Buddhist, Islamic, Confucian, and Christian-based influences at play. If a salesman is to create the rapport and synergy which is so essential to sustained business, he has to recognise particular cultural traits and adjust his positioning accordingly. This is what academics call 'cross-cultural literacy'. Even in individual countries, the tribal differences which affect relationships and reactions to trading approaches are challenging. In Indonesia, for example, you may be dealing with Dayaks, Batiks, or Javanese, all of whom have different behaviour modes. In short, the diversity of the Pacific Rim, in a relatively compact area, will hopefully teach you to be culturally aware and more precisely reactive.

Unanimity of intent

Do not consider export to Asian-Pacific unless all senior colleagues in the business are fully committed. This means an absolute understanding at the beginning that these markets are long-term and will never realise a desire for short term gain. On the first few visits *always* leave time at the end of the trip for impromptu second and even third meetings. The buyer is almost always unwittingly looking for commitment and will immediately spot the parachutist who arrives with an empty order book believing it will be filled in two days and then he will be off again.

No instant profits

Remember that the Asian-Pacific Rim is not a short cut to instant profits. The markets are worldly-wise and know how to buy well. Guile has to be matched with guile. In terms of fast-track recovery from the present recession, the Asian-Pacific Rim represents the best possible options because demand has been barely affected by the recession and there is an ingenuity which is survival- and progress-based.

Not one Siamese twin

A number of major corporations confirmed in response to our questions that they are indeed looking these days at ways of increasing their business in the region, specifically with the six member nations of ASEAN and with the tigers of South Korea, Hong Kong, Singapore and Taiwan. Thrown in for good measure very often are the developing markets of Indo-China, such as Vietnam. In tackling these markets it is essential that each is looked at and dealt with separately. The countries that make up the Pacific Rim are all different. Each has its own business traditions and practices and unique national characteristics. In some there is a high degree of government regulation and involvement, and this needs to be taken into account when contemplating business in these markets. Other governments may insist on an element of offset in any business deal. There are also likely to be varying rules governing the use of intermediaries or advisers and there are frequent changes in laws and applications throughout the region reflecting its state of permanent growth.

Getting a toe-hold

The comparative ease of setting up businesses in some of the Asian-Pacific Rim markets (eg Hong Kong, Malaysia, Singapore) has enabled a number of companies to get a toe-hold in the regional markets to a greater extent than they otherwise could. This has in most cases given the companies concerned a much greater market share than would be possible if exporting from the UK. In those markets with less liberal investment laws, the same level of penetration might otherwise be impossible.

If only . . .

Many decision-makers pointed out that, because the Asian-Pacific Rim markets are less mature than those of Europe and North America, there is frequently a 'second bite' opportunity to make strategic corporate decisions which were missed at the same stage of development in Europe. The 'if only we'd done so and so 15 years ago' syndrome can really come into its own to a company's advantage. Missed opportunities first time around are recycled in the Asian-Pacific as the countries go through similar developmental stages as the West has in the past.

Macro-prompts

Pay careful attention to macro-economic developments in the region. For example, 'windfall' benefits from fluctuations in oil prices might well prompt you to consider a diversion of resources in anticipation of a new need. This can often lead to export business in a new market in the first instance and then to the establishment of a local presence to further penetrate the market.

Find that niche

Do not attempt to break into a market with your products on a like-by-like basis. You will be defeated by intense local competition and undercutting. A joint venture to develop a niche through a combination of both partners' expertise has a very much higher chance of success.

The perfect product?

Allow your products to speak for themselves. If they are of the highest quality in their field (and they should be to warrant the investment of your time, money and resources) it will soon became apparent to the premium market that the high quality product at the higher price is safer, gives longer service and therefore saves cost. In any case, a product exported from Europe or the USA simply has to be high enough quality to overcome the inherent lack of competitiveness because of tariffs.

Make your mark

Build a brand and maintain control of it from the beginning. Acquisitions often provide short-term savings but entail long-term costs both direct and indirect.

Protect your rights

Anywhere in the region make sure your trademark and all other intellectual property rights are fully protected. It is essential to have the best possible professional advice on this from lawyers well-versed in your chosen market. A high quality product or very sound service idea will necessarily attract pirating and in the less industrially advanced countries there is little recourse possible. Full details of the protection of intellectual and other property rights are available from the Department of Trade and Industry country desks (Overseas Trade Division, 1 Victoria Street, London SW1H 0ET tel 071-215 5253/5489) or from the commercial section of the relevant embassy.

In their own time

You can't expect to penetrate these high-rise markets exclusively from an exporting factory in the UK. In market-places which are developing both horizontally and vertically, you have to establish a local presence whether by setting up a sales, liaison, technical or service office or by manufacturing part or whole of the product locally. The idea that the UK is the world's workshop is no longer valid. Asian markets want local service and support, within their own time zone and ethos.

Time is looked on differently. Westerners are always in a hurry and a year seems a long time. To the Chinese 50 years can be a short time.

Attitude

You must develop new attitudes to doing business. Throw all deeply entrenched preconceptions out of the window or you must fail in your endeavours. Flexibility and adaptability are crucial. You must listen and understand exactly what is required of, or being said to you. Passive hearing, or failure to pay attention to cultural nuance (when 'yes' really means 'no') can only cause problems. You must sharpen up your whole attitude to 'quality' in every sense of the word, and follow through each thought with a deed that is as perfectly executed as it could possibly be. Quality means 'doing your very best' in Asia. Half-baked service and products are thrown straight out of the proverbial window..

Not today, thank you

Never cold call the market. It indicates lack of commitment as well as muddled thinking. The person who makes the introduction on your behalf to a person with whom you wish to do business is absolutely vital. The Chinese phrase is 'valuable person' and no one is more highly prized in Asian society. It is an extension of the Western idea 'Show me your friends and I will tell you what and who you are'. If you are introduced by a low-life, it follows that you must mix in those commercial circles and must therefore be an unworthy person to do business with. You cannot spend too much time getting this aspect right. Of invaluable help in this is the British embassy in your market of choice, as well as the CBI and DTI (see Appendix) back home who will all be very well aware of suitable 'valuable people' and arrange for you to be introduced. Develop products to suit the Asian-Pacific Rim market needs. Always keep your options open and if and when necessary move your production around the region. Indulge in a bit of 'cherry picking', not for the sake of it, but to find the best opportunities, capabilities and prices.

My friend, the fax

As a general statement, it is true to say that anyone serious about exporting needs to have personal contact with their prospective customers. This is particularly true when dealing with the Pacific Rim countries. Anyone expecting to conduct business solely through an intermediary agent, or via facsimile or telephone is unlikely to succeed.

Love my company, love my family

A complete understanding of the Chinese extended family network is all important. The corporate entity and the family have no demarcation lines. When you are buying into a company, you will find nine times out of ten that you are also buying into a family. Eighty per cent of the economy is controlled by 20 per cent of the nation's families.

Once personal links have been established, and cultivated on a *regular* basis, business negotiations can proceed. A sound knowledge of the market and a degree of patience are two invaluable commodities required for winning business in the Asian-Pacific. When a good business relationship exists, with trust on both sides, there is then a real prospect of tapping into a series of markets that show some of the most exciting growth rates anywhere in the world.

Where possible links orchestrated on your behalf between the business world and the academic world are highly desirable, if not essential. In this way you can tap into regional behaviour patterns with, hopefully, broad minded individuals who can win friends for you so that you can influence people.

The protocol of 'face'

Always have plenty of business cards printed on the reverse in the language of the country to be visited. This is simply and effectively arranged at the business centres of all the best business and five-star hotels. The price is high but the 'face' you are accorded by the proper cards is invaluable.

Your card in Asia is an extension of yourself, not an *aide mémoire* for future business use as it is in the West. Always remember to hand them over to all those present at the very beginning of a meeting with prospective clients/customers. It is according to your company and rank in that company that those in the Asian-Pacific may then decide how to deal with you in terms of the status you are accorded.

This might seem unforgiveably rigid, it is also inflexible and, from the Asian point of view, ensures that no one is caused a loss of that most highly prized commodity 'face'. Do make sure that your card and particularly title is not mis-translated. When this has happened, as of course it sometimes does, it can be the cause of a great deal of hilarity and mirth on the part of the people you are doing business with and a great big red face for you.

The ties that bind

Find the right sort of partner for you. This could, in your case, prove to be a small entrepreneurial and hungry organisation and not necessarily a giant of a corporate beast. The appeal for the Asian-Pacific company in doing business with you lies in the possibility that with your support they may blossom and grow.

In the broadest possible terms, the Koreans (like the Japanese) are Confucian and value their corporate or family relationships above all else. The Chinese, however, value their more individual human contact network.

You must establish good connections and relations with a large network of people and once established, these relationships must be nurtured. This can be done both through business meetings and informal gatherings, such as golf games and those legendary evening drinking sessions. It should be remembered, for example, that in Korea and other countries here the signing of a contract is commonly seen as the official start of a new relationship that will develop over the years to come. It is not meant to signify, as it usually does for us, the successful conclusion of negotiations, which frees both parties to turn their attention to other matters.

Fair dues

In a number of these markets, you will find that prospective partners will need help with financial, production and labour management. In return, you will undoubtedly be greatly impressed and rewarded by an exchange of technical innovation.

You should realise that your partner in some of these countries may not easily understand the concept of sharing decision-making and reporting results. The cost of putting in your own financial or technical people is likely to be prohibitive to the local company if charged in full.

Energetic, but contained, enthusiasm

The real key to your success will be the enthusiasm of your sales people and the healthy working rapport they will establish with your Asian partners. You must find local partners who will enjoy working with you and vice versa. Make sure right from the start that the quality of your local representation is equal to that of your home-based personnel

First time lucky?

Never anticipate or expect an order on the first visit or even perhaps the second and third. These visits are expressly for getting to know one another with a view to establishing a sound base for future business. Business is a 'relationship', not a casual commercial encounter.

Diction, comprehension, misunderstandings

One Monday morning in South Korea, a chief executive was having a cooked breakfast of scrambled eggs. He asked the waiter if he might have some 'pepper', to which the waiter replied that he was very sorry but they didn't have any on Mondays. At which point the executive looked befuddled. No newspapers are published in South Korea on Mondays!

The sun rises further

Remember that if you are successful in the Asian-Pacific Rim you will often find yourself dealing, if successful, with major Japanese trading companies or stores since they are a vital route to new business in the region. Bear this story in mind. After one chief executive officer (CEO) had sold his first trial order to a Japanese retailer operating throughout the Rim, they then recognised a particular design that they wanted the CEO to develop to increase the range.

After careful thought and discussion, the CEO said 'no', but explained that this was only because they did not have the specialist manufacturing capacity to take on more work of that nature. He was very scared that the company had blown their only real chance at that time of a major regional coup. Almost immediately, however, the store responded by not only re-ordering the current lines but increased the value to far greater than the initial order. This is what we in the West invariably call 'inscrutability' even though it makes perfect business sense. Then a year later, the CEO remembered the enquiry and was able to develop capacity in the specialised area. They informed the clients by telex and by return received a request for samples and prices. These were supplied, negotiations were completed and a surprisingly substantial initial order was placed for the newly developed range for which exclusivity was agreed.

Looking back ten years later, this single experience built business that in six years placed this client as the company's largest single export customer, and after eight years and to date, the client is still the largest single customer for the company in the world. In 1990 their business alone exceeded the total of all the company's business into the US.

The overall Japanese 'quality culture' (the dominant management influence in the region) and techniques with regard to inventory management, 'just in time' and quality control have provided a role model for a number of Western companies working in the region to follow. They have found that a growing customer base in the Pacific Rim has helped to establish the international credibility of their products. This is because, they say, it is widely known that Pacific Rim countries are very demanding in their product evaluations and therefore success in itself speaks very highly.

As the Asian-Pacific is Japan's captive territory (with 24 per cent of the total trade), many of the Asian-Pacific's values are Japanese-based although this may be in a diluted or slightly variegated form. All those 'good business' disciplines we originally learnt from doing successful business in Japan are now doubly important in the Asian-Pacific Rim. Chief of these are the needs for perseverance and commitment, for establishing mutual loyalty, and complying with stereotypes. One key success factor is the consistent and expeditious provision of responses to every enquiry from the customer. In the US the customer is king: in the Asian-Pacific the customer must be treated as though he were a god. There is a very high expectation of quality service from potential suppliers and it must be provided.

Back to school

Remember the value of the implementation of training local staff back home. In a market where you already have some success with products that have been well supported, you should be getting new orders. Bigger orders can usually be expected after establishing confidence in your partner through preliminary dealings. In this case, initiate a programme of training of the Asian-Pacific staff at your Western headquarters. You will find that with every new trainee you will be adding a newer stronger bond to the relationship with your overseas partner. Between you, you are extending and embracing each other into a genuinely international business family.

Syllogism

Remember that your values are not necessarily shared. As an Indonesian businessman told one CEO, 'You must remember here that whilst Britain rules the waves, Indonesia waives the rules'.

Don't you dare . . .

Some CEOs say there are no real taboos. They maintain that if you are pleasant and understanding with your contacts and they, in turn, respect you there will be few problems. Under such conditions of mutual respect, any glaring *faux pas* will be excused. The worst behaviour anywhere in the Rim is being loud and extrovert. Lay low and behave in a slow, polite, measured way.

Everyone has seen at some point or other the archetypal stetson-wearing Texan in the foyer of the major hotel who, when not understood by an interpreter, shouted louder. When still not understood, he shouted louder still. Such impatience in communication anywhere in the world is unforgiveable. Otherwise most Asian-Pacific cultures are increasingly tolerant of innocent Western cultural mistakes so, short of straightforward crass behaviour, you are unlikely to give irretrievable offence. Having said that, sensitivity to local customs and protocols will significantly improve your chances of developing the crucial personal element to business relationships.

Buddhist people in particular, and there are a great many in the region, are forgiving. Because of this, out and out taboos are rare in several markets but Moslem Indonesia is particularly sensitive. At cocktail parties in Jakarta, for example, do not stand hugging an alcoholic drink as you talk. If you do take a drink, place it on a side-table and sip at it only at appropriate times. If you are offered a drink at an office meeting, which in Indonesia will of course be non-alcoholic, do not take a sip until the host has drunk first.

The main point about these so-called taboos is that if there is the slightest chance they may irretrievably damage your prospects by your failure to observe them, then you must make sure that you behave absolutely correctly at all times. Even if the chances of such damage are very rare, it is still a question as to whether you can enhance your performance through the development of empathetic behaviour thereby creating fruitful opportunities.

One particular mistake to be avoided is trying to conduct business from the home base. Visits are essential. As with anywhere else in the world, letting potential customers down is unforgiveable as is continually changing your team. That ubiquitous Western 'arrogance' that was so prevalent back in the so-called 'good old days' is instant commercial death.

It is important to study the local culture and customs, just as you would if you were going to do significant business in France or Germany but many managers feel this is now becoming much less important as the foreign visiting population increases. Respect for culture and tradition is a two-way flow; you also have culture and ethics. It is the business on offer that is the most important factor.

Do as you would be done by

A seemingly crazy example cited by one manager, but so often reported as seen and heard by others.

Businessman: I am here to sort out this wretched mess and I must leave here tomorrow evening by plane at 5pm. Believe me, I intend to get it straightened out before then.

Local Contact: We very much regret, sir, but no meeting is possible until 4.45pm tomorrow.

Result: Nothing gained – this is not a taboo. It is just bad business. Anywhere.

Food for thought

One CEO in the early 1980s arrived in Taipei from Hong Kong with a bad cold, having brought some honey-based medication *en route* out of mainland China. This was in his suitcase in the original wrapping. In those days, there was no tolerance of mainland China in Taiwan and as always at that time his suitcase was opened and searched. The customs officer spotted the medicine at once and berated the owner that such packaging with Chinese characters could not be allowed into Taiwan.

He removed the phials from the pack and tore up the packaging. The CEO remonstrated angrily with him and told him that the kind of examination given to business visitors in Taiwan could be found in no other country on earth. In high dudgeon, he closed his suitcase and went out to meet his agent. The agent spotted him and took him and the suitcases outside to wait for him and the car. After 2–3 minutes, there was a tug at the CEO's elbow and he looked around to find the customs officer with his duty free bag containing an expensive bottle of Cognac and the 200 cigarettes he had bought in Hong Kong to give to his agent. During the contretemps with the customs officer, he had left them behind. He certainly felt humble.

4 Debunking the export myths

Ten commercial secrets of export success in the Asian-Pacific Rim

Leon Richardson, a lifetime Fellow of the Sloan School of Management, MIT, has been running a highly successful business operation in the Asian-Pacific Rim for a number of years. There is very little about doing business in the region that he does not know and here he offers some short, sharp advice that debunks a great many of the myths that are likely to be raised within your own company or operation when you moot the idea of exporting to the countries involved.

Exporting requires heavy investment and a large staff

Successful export businesses have been started with one sales person visiting all the target export markets and establishing local organisations to do the importing, warehousing, distribution and selling. With modern communications and jet aircraft, overseas markets are easily accessible and can be approached without excessive investment.

To compete, you have to manufacture in the export market

For a hundred years, Coca-Cola has been exporting its secret formula syrup made in a factory in the US. It gets local companies in each export market to bottle and distribute the product. Coca-Cola's main profit is in exporting the syrup. Local bottlers can buy other ingredients such as water locally, thereby saving freight costs. The local bottler acts as Coca-Cola's banker, as its local management, manufacturer, warehouser, distributor and seller. Coca-Cola's local investment is marginal.

39

Hunting with the Tigers

To export you must sell your product cheaply

Of all the myths, this is perhaps the most dangerous yet the most widely believed. It is spread by bureaucrats, economists and accountants – none of whom has ever exported anything. Specifically, these people believe that if a country's currency is devalued, its exports will become cheaper and sales will rise. In the real world, the opposite is more often true. With some categories of exports, certainly, a competitive price may be essential but in addition, the goods that sell best in foreign markets are those that buyers believe will give them premium benefits and satisfaction when compared to cheaper local brands.

Anyone embarking on an export endeavour would be wise to specialise in a range of up-market, higher quality products and this is true for any type of product apart from raw materials. Premium quality requires premium price, but an exporter can make a profitable trade-off between premium pricing and premium quality. To tell a buyer that you can supply a product with a better cluster of benefits for the same price as a lower quality cluster is to insult his intelligence. Everyone knows that you only get what you pay for. Any time that a manufacturer improves his product, he must ask a higher price for it. Usually, low-cost products are already available in an export market, so another
low-price product is not required and will probably not succeed. What may not be available, however, is a premium quality product. Products that offer more benefits to the customer are always welcome. A premium price does not impair export. On the contrary. It helps sales, provided that the promise of superior benefits (the product plus special features, such as appearance or extra service) is fulfilled.

Export opportunity, system, and structure are determined by the characteristics of the product

The product is a mere incidental. Indeed, the greatest single mistake is to make export decisions focused heavily on the product. The only attention that should be allotted to the product is to determine:

- What type of customers will buy this category of product?
- Who makes the decision to buy?
- What does the buyer want? With what benefits must the product be packaged in order to fulfil this requirement?
- When is the buying decision made?

In short, the would-be exporter must find out what is needed to satisfy the final customer and then work his way back from there. Exporting is not about things. It is entirely about people, and people do not buy a product. They buy a promise of benefits and satisfaction.

Eliminating middlemen reduces export costs and increases profits

Middlemen are often the best profit makers because they can perform certain services more efficiently than you can. A local middleman, whatever label you put on him – distributor, retailer, wholesaler, agent or partner – knows the local culture, has local banking arrangements, and provides invaluable contacts. He can also handle such functions as transfer of title, customs clearance and warehousing. But the most important thing the middleman does is sell the product. In selling, the person making the offer is often more important than the offer itself. We all buy from people we know and like, and in any market that is unlikely to be the exporter.

The primary function of the foreign wholesaler or distributor is to provide a warehouse for storing goods

This common myth is wrong on at least two counts. First, the primary purpose of foreign middlemen is to deal with people, not to be warehousemen. Second, this belief assumes that storage is a key factor in success, but no product makes money when it sits in a warehouse.

Administered exporting channels are more efficient than non-administered channels

An 'administered export channel' is one that is controlled and administered by a single organisation, whether through franchise, ownership or force. The exporter can force products that customers do not want through a distribution system. He can force commitment by all parties to planning, scheduling, advertising and promotion. If the customer does not want the product, however, he simply will not buy it. Very often it is more successful for the exporter to share the administration with local wholesalers, distributors, or retailers. The exporter must be demanding on some basic standards, such as honesty, ethical behaviour and operating systems, but local matters can be delegated to local institutions within the distribution channel.

A good method of doing export business is to get on tender mailing-lists with foreign government and other agencies

A tender is a suicide pact which guarantees the thinnest profit margin for the exporter and the lowest quality of product and service for the buyer. Usually the tender issuer will list specifications in the belief that all products that vendors quote on a tender are equal, so long as they meet the specifications. In the real world this is not the case. A reputable exporter will supply products that exceed specifications to provide extra quality in order to build long-term repeat customers and brand loyalty. A wise exporter will not participate in a tender unless it specifies his brand, and further stipulates 'genuine exporters' product only: no substitutes acceptable'.

Trade missions are an excellent way for exporters to develop overseas markets

The value of trade missions depends on the exporter's objectives. If his aim is to make contacts at a political or chamber of commerce level so that someone can follow up later and conclude the transaction, then trade missions can be very worthwhile. It is rare, however, for participants in missions to come back with firm business, such as purchase contracts or letters of credit.

It takes many years to make a profit from exports

Why? Why not plan your export business so that you will be in profit from day one? Locate local companies that already have a business providing good cash flow, but which are not already doing business that would compete with your own. A key argument in persuading the company to be a partner would be that the partnership would cost very little, since it would use the distributor's existing assets to generate additional profits and growth.The perfect partner will have a specific number of assets including (1) a warehouse in which to store the goods and from which to service clients; (2) adequate funds or adequate banking facilities to finance an initial order, pay sales agents and finance local clients who tend to require 30-day payment terms; (3) basic essentials, such as an office and telephone, a clerk to type invoices, a means of delivering to customers, and the various other faciities for modern marketing, such as sources for legal, accounting and other professional services.

5 The mechanics of export

The clinching of a successful sales deal is the beginning of an intricate process that can be very confusing for the exporting novice. Freight forwarding, insurance and customs clearance have to be arranged and so your main concerns suddenly shift from a dogged determination to score sales hits in a country to the problems of getting the goods in. You also have to make sure you get paid for them and on your terms. Customs the world over delight in bureaucratic melodrama that can hold up both the flow of goods and of payment. The procedures can be learnt and when applied meticulously pose few real problems in practice. The exporter who is one step ahead of the game takes expert advice before going into the market so that he is absolutely sure that all the hidden costs are factored into the total price before he begins negotiation with a client in a foreign market-place.

The British Exporters Association (16 Dartmouth Street, London SW1H 9BL; tel 071-222 5419) can make everything a great deal simpler by giving you a specialised list of the names and addresses of those in the Asian-Pacific Rim who will buy goods outright from manufacturers and arrange to have the goods delivered to their home market at their own expense. If you wish, you could instead pay a set fee and deal through a confirming house whose function it is to place orders with entities such as department stores and who will then manage the bureaucracy and transportation for you to your chosen market. Remember though that under this scenario the control that you will have over your chosen market and the marketing of your goods will be virtually nil even though the process is made very much simpler for your company. Freight forwarders and shipping companies will get your goods to their destination and handle all the issues regarding transport, documentation, customs clearance and insurance.

However, the six essential factors for consideration for those who do elect to become involved in the whole process of exporting goods to countries in the Asian-Pacific Rim are:

1. The terms of the price of goods, 'delivered', 'ex-works' and in which currency?
2. The handling of delivery and documentation.
3. The cost of insurance against buyer default and credit risks.
4. Safeguards against fluctuations in currency.
5. The need for, and terms of, pre-shipment finance.
6. The terms of payment and affects on cash-flow.

One godsend on the paperwork side is the Simpler Trade Procedures Board (SITPRO) (Venture House, 29 Glasshouse Street, London W1R 5RG; tel 071-287 5751, fax 071-287 5751), who will guide you through the documentation maze by supplying a list of experts in the field who can take over the task on your behalf. There are now a number of tried-and-true methods of document preparation available and you will be advised on the suitability of each for your own particular export needs. Not all documentation is remitted in hard-copy form nowadays, however, and SITPRO has become the world leader in Electronic Data Interchange (EDI) whereby trade documents are remitted round the world in a paperless form, like electronic mail. The benefits of this are the speed, the lower cost involved in preparation, and greater security for purposes of just-in-time inventory control. This can be managed direct from your office with a PC fitted with a computer modem through which you may then access the computer-link or value added network.

When you negotiate the sales price of your goods, you must build in a 'cost escalation clause' that will cover you in the event of currency fluctuations and inflationary costs during manufacture and the export process. This then allows you to adjust the price of the goods to a pre-defined level when invoicing the goods for shipment.

The decision as to whether you quote prices in sterling or in the local currency of the buyer may well require expert advice. If you decide to accept a non-sterling price, you are then exposed to the risks of currency fluctuations. This potential problem can be dealt with through your bank who can arrange, if they consider it expedient, a forward contract. This means that the foreign currency that is due to you will be converted into sterling and then exchanged at the rate of exchange fixed at the time of the acceptance and signing of the contract.

How to get paid

Getting the necessary funding to cover the appropiate length of credit, sometimes as long as two or three months, can be a major financial headache. Money is needed to cover the manufacture and packaging of the goods, the transportation costs by air or sea, and the period of credit that you choose to extend to your buyer. Banks are required to be very sympathetic to exporters and so the promise of good new business overseas should incline your usual bankers to extend an ever-helpful hand. He will want very thorough substantiation, however, of the degree of risk involved and you should be prepared to take him into your fullest confidence about the contract and the buyer.

You may then arrange for the buyer of your goods to open a documentary credit in your favour which will allow you to get paid upon presentation of the right documents. Alternatively, the buyer may want a bill of exchange allowing him to pay after an agreed period, or he may want to pay upon receipt of the goods. The methods are open to negotiation.

The Export Credits Guarantee Department (ECGD) — PO Box 272, 50 Ludgate Hill, London EC4M 7AY; tel 071-382 7000 — can make all the difference between success and disaster in an export enterprise by helping you to ensure against the risk of not being paid for your exported goods. The exporter faces not only credit risks and the possibility that the buyer default on payment, but also exchange controls and demurrage charges which may be imposed causing serious problems. The ECGD will also arrange for factoring (the system whereby 80 per cent of the total monies due are paid at an early date after the shipment) and for guarantees to banks for the export of capital goods so that finance can be arranged at a good rate. For further information about the requirements for export licences for your goods, you should contact the enquiry unit at the Export Control Organisation (Room 711 Kingsgate House, 66-74 Victoria Street, London SW1E 6SW; tel 071-215 8070).

Glossary of export terms

Acceptance: The bill of exchange is the means by which the buying party accepts the responsibility for payment for the goods.

Airway bill: This is the receipt for the goods (and therefore the document of title), as well as a contract between the airfreight forwarder and the airline company that will carry and deliver the goods to the destination, according to the precise requirements of the order.

Bill of exchange: This is a demand for payment by a specified date of monies owed which goes together with the bill of lading/airway bill and other documents to a bank overseas. When the buyer signs this document, he is undertaking to meet the demand for payment either on demand or by a specified date, either 30, 60, or 90 days ahead.

Bill of lading: This is the receipt for the goods (and therefore the document of title), as well as a contract between the exporter/shipper and the shipping company that will carry and deliver the goods to the destination according to the precise requirements of the order.

Documentary letter of credit: These are bank instructions issued on a buyer's request that ensure you get paid upon presentation of the correct documentation. You should have this double-checked by your bank in this country to ensure that eveything is in order and that the document is 'irrevocable'. This means basically that it cannot be altered in any way without the agreement of all the parties concerned.

F.A.S. (Free alongside ship): This means that the price agreed includes for the goods to be packed and ready for shipment and delivered at the exporter's own expense to the quayside where the ship will be loaded. The cost of getting the goods on to the ship for sailing therefore is not included and will be charged as an extra.

F.O.B. (Free on board): The price at which the goods will be delivered on board the vessel at the exporter's expense. Most foreign buyers, however, are interested neither in FAS nor FOB prices and want to know the delivered cost to them of the goods in their own country.

C and F (Cost and freight): This price if for the cost of the goods being delivered to a named destination port excluding the costs of insurance.

C.I.F. (Cost, insurance and freight): As above but including the insurance charges.

Force majeure: This clause allows for unpredictable incidents such as dock strikes or the impounding of goods so that the rights and duties of the parties are clearly defined when something goes awry. This is of course something that should only be handled with legal advice.

International customs tariff numbers: Goods in transit are identified by these numbers on the relevant documents which are issued by the customs authorities. Advice on this can be obtained from your local office of HM Customs & Excise.

Performance bond: This is a means of drawing up a contract so that it is awarded subject to the provision, on behalf of the contractor, of a performance bond whereby a percentage of the contract price is guaranteed by a bank or other financial institution.

Further information

Very useful in learning more about the whole export process are:

Croner's Reference Book for Exporters: A loose-leaf volume which is kept up to date with amendments, costs £87.25 for the first year, and then £54.00 each year thereafter.

ECGD Information Pack: Full details on the various types of insurance policy offered by the ECGD which is freely available from all ECGD offices.

Export Digest: Also from Croner (above), a monthly magazine covering every aspect of exporting.

Export Today: The journal of the Institute of Export (64 Clifton Street, London EC2A 4HB; tel 071-247 9812) published bi-monthly.

Hints to Exporters: A series of British Overseas Trade Board booklets giving essential information on more than 100 countries which have been produced for exporters intending to visit these markets. From BOTB offices, at £5.00 each.

Sources of Finance for the Smaller Company: Available from the Institute of Directors.

The four major British retail banks, Barclays, Lloyds, Midland and National Westminster produce useful publications for the exporter, covering such subjects as documentary letters of credit, exporting for the smaller business and services for exporters.

Pacific Rim profiles

HONG KONG
(British Crown Colony)

Nominal GDP: US$70bn/HK$546.1bn
GDP real growth: 2.4 per cent
Exports: US$82.0bn (+ 12.2 per cent)
Imports: US$82.7bn (+ 14.1 per cent)
Net foreign debt: n/a
Trade surplus: US$0.7bn
Population: 5,709,000
Work-force: 2,750,000
Unemployment: 1.6 per cent
Average factory wage: US$680/month
Inflation (annual CPI): 9.8 per cent
Savings rate: 34 per cent
Overseas visitor numbers: 5.5m (1989)
Head of State: Queen Elizabeth II
Head of Government: Governor Sir David Wilson
Ruling party: n/a
Other political parties: n/a
Capital city: Victoria (GMT+8 hours)

(Figures for year ending 1990, except where stated)

Membership of international organisations: Asian Development Bank, ESCAP and The Commonwealth (Associate Member), GATT, IMO, Interpol, Multifibre Agreement, UN, UNCTAD, WMO.

Brief history

The late foreign correspondent and author, Australian Richard Hughes dubbed Hong Kong 'A borrowed place on borrowed time'. For many years the phrase seemed to be an almost inconsequential and well-worn cliche as people rushed around Hong Kong, too busy with their own success to care very much about the future. Now, however, as 30th June 1997 looms – the date of the handover of the rule of Hong Kong by the

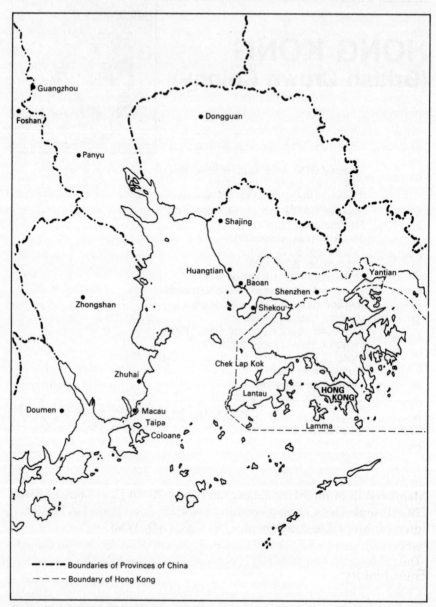

Guangzhou

Foshan

Panyu

Dongguan

Shajing

Huangtian

Baoan

Shenzhen

Yantian

Shekou

Zhongshan

Chek Lap Kok

Zhuhai

Lantau

HONG KONG

Doumen

Macau

Taipa

Coloane

Lamma

— · — · — Boundaries of Provinces of China
— — — — Boundary of Hong Kong

Hong Kong and the Pearl River Delta

Hong Kong (British Crown Colony)

British Government to the authorities of mainland China – it has never seemed so apposite.

The greatest fear, one that strikes right through the heart of the colony's dyed-in-the-wool businessmen both Chinese and foreign, is that Hong Kong will simply cease to function in the way that it has so successfully till now. The undeniable efficiency and verve of the place is rather idiosyncratic, to say the least, but it works and all Hong Kong people constantly strive through self-improvement towards commercial perfection. Hong Kong, along with Korea, Singapore and Taiwan is now solidly established as one of Asia's tigers, or if you like a 'little dragon'. The city, once just another aggressive manufacturer and exporter has now successfully metamorphosised into a highly interesting market in its own right.

The territory, which has lived on its business instincts and sheer hard grind for over 150 years, is soon to be handed over to China. The people and the stockmarket are not happy about it, despite some well-publicised bullish protestations to the contrary. Xinhua, the official Chinese news agency does a great deal of public relations work in a concerted effort to show the local populace that all will be alright on the night. As yet, however, there are no watertight guarantees for civil, personal and commercial liberties after the takeover, nor can there be. The rule of law, as we in the West understand it, will no longer apply. Most of the six million plus people in Hong Kong are there because they, or their parents, fled the Communist rule in the People's Republic of China (PRC) at some point during the last 40 years. Under an efficient, *laissez-faire* British colonial administration, the island Palmerston described as a 'barren rock with nary a soul upon it', is now a powerhouse of trade and industry. Its tiny population, with an estimated work-force of nearly 2.75m, does more trade than the whole of China's 1.1bn population put together.

Since the Tiananmen Square massacre in 1989, however, few people in Hong Kong have been inclined to take the PRC's word that a 'high degree of autonomy' will be allowed. Similar promises were given over Tibet and Hong Kong people are all too well aware what has become of that country. Hong Kong Chinese are now emigrating at a rate of 1,200 a week and seem to be taking their money with them, mainly to Canada. The brain-drain (some 62,000 people left Hong Kong in 1990) is pushing up prices, depressing growth, and undermining Hong Kong's value to China, ironically its best guarantee of being left alone after 1997. The UK parliament passed the Hong Kong Passport Bill, giving passports to 50,000 Hong Kong professionals and their families, although with very stringent – some would say unfair – requirements, take-up was slow. Those who could meet the requirements had long ago made provisions for alternative boltholes. These days too, armed robbery, fraud and 'Triad' gang warfare are all on the increase, as are the numbers of boat people still flooding in from Vietnam, despite the fast changing situation in that country.

Relations between Britain, China and Hong Kong are still at a low ebb despite the resolution of some of the problems regarding the construction and financing of the new airport, and tension is likely to increase as 1997 approaches. Hong Kong will still be far better off economically than the rest of China, no matter what the outcome on the local political scene, but its days of being the pacesetter in the Asian-Pacific Rim are probably over.

The Japanese, though, could change this ending into a fairy tale, for them anyway. At the moment there are 40,000 Japanese in Hong Kong and there are more Japanese banks in Hong Kong, accounting for 60 per cent of the banking sector, than in the whole of the City of London itself. They clearly believe that it is a good place to set up shop regardless so that they will be able to take immediate advantage of developments if the Chinese economy should continue to open up.

Apart from one or two provisos, it must definitely be said that Hong Kong's economic situation looks healthy enough, especially given the anticipated recovery in the US economy to which Hong Kong is still heavily exposed. The one major trip wire still hanging loose is the continuing problem over intellectual properties in the mainland and therefore the potential loss for China of its trade status as a 'most favoured nation' which would impact very heavily on Hong Kong. This has been extended for a while and remains conditional on the release of pro-democracy demonstrators in China and Tibet, as well as on a ban on missile sales to Syria and Iran.

It is not completely unlikely that the United States' Congress, if pushed, will possibly at some time impose Special 301 trade sanctions on a number of mainland exports which would correspondingly increase tariffs by as much as 100 per cent. This could cause Hong Kong to lose as much as 44 per cent of her re-exports to China which come from the US, a total loss of as much as seven per cent in her overall trade and as many as 43,000 jobs.

Hopes for the future must now lie in the possibility, however slight that when the Chinese leader Deng Xiaoping eventually dies, he will be replaced by a more youthful visionary rather than by a hardline old-style Communist guard. The same has happened all over eastern Europe and the USSR, so the local residents are hoping against hope that it can happen in this former colonial outpost too. In this case, the Special Economic Zone that is Shenzhen, on the borders of Hong Kong, would merge effortlessly into Hong Kong and possibly blend in by special arrangement with Macau as well, no doubt creating the focal point of one of the most dynamic territories on earth.

The country's strengths

• A regional centre for all kinds of business, including manufacturing, finance, shipping, and a major entrepôt for putatively the largest market in the world, the People's Republic of China.
• Together with Macau and Guangzhou, Hong Kong could, with a very large measure of political stability in the mainland, develop into the mainstay of the Pearl River delta area and then on, to be the linchpin of a 'Greater China'.
• The best environment for international and domestic business in the region with no restrictions at all (certainly not until 1997) on direct foreign investment and no quotas for numbers of local staff to be hired.
• No non-tariff import barriers and few duties.
• Sheer dynamism of the local people, synergised with legions of the two per cent of the population who are expatriate and well-versed local managers.
• Non-interventionist government and very limited bureaucracy.

The country's weaknesses

• Political uncertainty about the future stability of the territory when it reverts to mainland Chinese rule in 1997.
• A continuing brain-drain and skilled labour shortage.
• High local housing costs.
• Inflation – the food, housing and services sectors are all under upward pressure.
• The possibility that China could lose its MFN (most favoured nation) status and cause some of the larger companies to shift elsewhere in the Asian-Pacific Rim.

Goals

• To tackle the 1997 political transfer with the maximum of ease and the minimum of economic disruption.
• To stabilise the brain-drain from the local work-force.
• To contain local inflation and ever-rising housing costs.

Politics

Politically, more sober-minded observers must still have some serious concerns. The People's Republic of China undoubtedly offers huge advantages, both real and potential, for Hong Kong as it is both a large neighbouring market and a source of much needed labour and space. The development of the special economic zones close to Hong Kong has been remarkable and it is the access to this resource that has saved Hong Kong when its own cost competitiveness has been seriously diminished. Despite all potential for commercial reciprocity, however, the two countries – if Hong Kong may still be called a country – remain political rivals. In any serious battle of will, few can now doubt which party has the most to lose.

After the failure of the so-called 'model' Communist regime in the USSR, the geriatric and reactionary Chinese leadership now stands alone against the widespread movement for democratic reform. Conventional wisdom, at least when publically voiced, tends towards one of two contradictory trains of thought. One is Beijing's line, as put forward originally by Deng Xiaoping, that 'two systems, one country' will apply from 1997 and that Hong Kong will be left to get on its own merry money-making way while the mainland will persist with the Socialist ideals it believes to be necessary for a country as diverse and populous as China. The other is that the PRC will inevitably be forced to change and will go the way of the USSR and eastern Europe, and that, more importantly, this transition will be smooth, peaceful and seamless.

The problem lies in the fact that neither of these options looks entirely realistic. However considerable Hong Kong's financial and commercial value to the mainland, the fact remains that it represents a hotbed of precisely those forces the Beijing regime is most determined to resist. Despite the PRC's economic liberalisations, there is little real evidence at all of its willingness to extend these reforms into the political arena. Those who argue that the attitude of the Beijing hierarchy has changed were also arguing, prior to the Tiananmen massacre, along the same stubbornly and unfoundedly optimistic lines. There is little sign that they are any more correct now than they were then.

During the Hong Kong elections of 1991, a prominent local reformer was elected with a convincing victory and Hong Kong citizens have now visibly demonstrated their desire for greater democracy. One could be forgiven for imagining that the 'two systems, one country' philosophy might allow a decent measure of democracy. In the event, the vote for Martin Lee was greeted by a senior Chinese official dealing with Hong Kong, Lu Ping, with a mixture of derision and contempt. Speaking at a conference on the future of Hong Kong held in London, he said the victory by the United Democrats of Hong Kong 'cannot represent the orientation of political reform in Hong Kong'. A lot lies behind those typically bureaucratic words. Martin Lee has already been branded 'a subversive' by Beijing, it would seem, and it is clear that in PRC officialdom's eyes, there are plenty more where he came from in Hong Kong. Not that many are prepared either to emulate Baroness Lydia Dunn's stance of appeasement and conciliation towards China.

Even though the people of Hong Kong had merely exercised the sort of freedom which they had been promised for life post-1997, that expression of free choice proved clearly unacceptable to the Chinese leadership. The more the leadership feels threatened and isolated against what they choose to interpret as the hostile forces of capitalism, liberalism and democracy, the more they will regard Hong Kong as a breeding ground of political dissent. In the past five years, Hong Kong people have quite naturally got more and more feisty and independent of mind and it is disturbing to try to envision how the monolithic mainland establishment might try to deal with them in a few years' time.

After the takeover in 1997, the Chinese army will be physically stationed in Hong Kong. Until then, we can only guess how tactfully and delicately any hint of a freedom movement will be dealt with or even suppressed. One ugly incident and the fragile confidence so vital to Hong Kong's economy and stockmarket will be easily upset.

Even now prior to the handover of course, China exercises considerable influence, not to say control, over Hong Kong's affairs. The prime example of this in 1991 was the political controversy over the Hong Kong Government's proposal to build a new airport. Agreement was finally reached for an airport core programme (ACP) which is estimated to cost HK$98.6bn (US$12.6bn) in terms of 1991 prices. This was achieved only after very considerable modification in the light of PRC objections. Despite the pressing need for a new airport, China was clearly determined that as much money would be left in what it sees as Hong Kong's coffers when it takes over the political and financial reins. Under the agreement, although the Hong Kong Government's share of the cost may be as much as HK$68bn, it still has to hand over at least HK$25bn in fiscal reserves in 1997 to the authorities of the Hong Kong Special Administrative Regional as Hong Kong will then become known.

Domestic economy, current economic policy and forecasts

Generally speaking, Hong Kong is classified as an 'Emerging Financial Market'. Even though it has adoped a *laissez-faire* attitude in most aspects of financial management, it nevertheless has tightly controlled interest rates and does not allow foreign banks to have more than one branch in the territory.

The biggest spoke in Hong Kong's economic wheel, however, continues to be inflation. The food, services and housing sectors of the consumer price index (CPI) are all being pushed up. Having hit 13.9 per cent during 1991, inflation did show a modest decline attributable mainly to a cut in certain tax charges but the rate of increase in CPI is still a worrying 12 per cent. There cannot be said to be any great scope for cooling off in the next couple of years. Double digit inflation looks set to continue for the time-being due largely to the tightness of the labour situation pushing up salaries (exacerbated by continuing emigration).

Meanwhile, so long as the HK$/US$ peg remains in place, the Hong Kong Government is naturally unable to temper inflation through its monetary policy of anti-inflation measures. Indeed, with the recent reduction in prime to 9 per cent, it looks as they they have given up the attempt. Not only is inflation unlikely to fall much in the foreseeable future, but there is a strong case that by 1995, it could reach 15 per cent as a result of the increased pressure of the massive new airport project.

Banking and finance, equity market outlook, stockmarkets

The best-known banks are Hongkong & Shanghai Banking Corporation, Standard Chartered Bank Ltd, Nanyang Commercial Bank Ltd, Bank of East Asia Ltd, and Shanghai Commercial Bank Ltd.

It is in her banking structure and the multiplicity of her sound financial institutions that Hong Kong finds her greatest strength. It is under their auspices, and particularly perhaps under the watchful eye of the most famous of the 150 or so licensed banks, the Hongkong & Shanghai, that the infrastructure of the city state has evolved. The grand old lady with branches on virtually every street corner, now houses its headquarters in Central in the most stylish of buildings built by English architect Norman Foster.

Like its age-old counterpart, the Standard Chartered Bank, both have a very large number of offices around the region and extensively into the Middle East and other areas, making them the most sensible choice for those attempting any kind of global commercial operation. Most of the staff is now localised with only a very few expatriates still left in the upper echelons.

There is no central government bank, a counterpart to the Bank of England, since all financial affairs fall to the brief of the Government Secretary with the Financial Secretary in supreme command. The ultimate responsibility for banking operations rests with the Commissioner for Banking who also has a watching brief over the many deposit-taking companies. Efforts are being made to make banking regulations as watertight as possible so that as much of the banking structure as possible will remained unchanged in the years after 1997.

The Hong Kong Stock Exchange which lists some 250 companies is housed in the Central district of Hong Kong in Exchange Square. Hong Kong's stock index is known as the Hang Seng Index. The exchange now houses as one body what comprised, until 1986, four different entities, the Far East, the Kam Ngan and the Hong Kong and Kowloon exchanges. The intelligent building is equipped with the very latest in electronic trading facilities and stock activity display. All activity is regulated by the Hong Kong Commissioner of Securities (38th Fl, Tower Two, Exchange Square; tel 842-7666, fax 810-5385) while the exchange library for research is at the Far East Exchange Building (8 Wyndham Street, Central; tel 852 526-6833). Exchange Square also houses many of the leading stockbrokers and related services operating in Hong Kong. Hong Kong is also the region's headquarters for fund managers specialising in the region's stockmarkets and nearly 30 billion US dollars' worth of major overseas institutional investors' and pension funds' money is said to be managed in the territory. The situation is constantly changing, however, as the threat of increasing instability causes financial companies to relocate to Tokyo for their regional headquarters and as the brain-drain steals away more and more of the managers to settle elsewhere.

After a long period of underperformance, Hong Kong was one of the world's best performing markets in 1991, partially as a result of the HK$–US$ peg. The general economic picture in Hong Kong is currently brighter than it has been for a while. After the relative (for Hong Kong) stagnation of 1989 and 1990, when GDP grew less than 2.5 per cent, the economy is expected to expand to as much as 5.5 per cent in 1992.

In the all-important property sector, activity has picked up considerably in the low- to mid-range residential property market. A couple of new developments sold within hours and apartments of less than 1,000 square feet are clearly in demand and prices have firmed significantly. There are however still serious questions about the Hong Kong property market in general. The vision of prospective buyers queuing since dawn is all too reminiscent of the speculative boom of the early 1980s and there is considerable debate as to how much of the purchasing is actually being done by those who want to live in the apartments rather than by speculators.

Ten years ago, taxi drivers and secretaries commonly owned one or two flats for 'investment purposes' as well as the property they lived in. This time, however, there were reliable reports that even the infamous 'triads', with names like the 'Green Dragon' and 'Black Tiger' gangs, have been involved, muscling others out of the way in order to be the first in line. There is also little real evidence of a similar buying appetite at the top end of the residential property market and the office market remains under the dark cloud of over-supply which is likely to get worse over the next year, keeping rents soft. As for the hotel industry to which many property companies are exposed, while tourist arrivals have picked up since the Gulf conflict, Hong Kong is still afflicted by an over-capacity of quality hotel rooms. Occupancies are still unsatisfactory and discounting of room rates is still apparent.

The market rose strongly for most of 1991 but the Hang Seng Index did encounter resistance at around the 4,000 level and then drifted sideways for some time on low trading volumes. The reduced enthusiasm for Hong Kong stocks was attributable to a number of factors, not the least of which was the faltering in the economic recovery of Hong Kong's biggest market, the United States. Also contributing was the switching by investors out of Hong Kong stocks, which have done well for them, and into other markets, predominantly Japan, which are still at depressed levels and gaining attention. The new laws tightening up disclosure of interest rules for company directors, combined with a general move towards stricter monitoring and regulation of the stock-market after past excesses and abuses, also took their toll.

Above all, perhaps, the deterioration in supply and demand was caused by a flood of new placements, listings and rights issues. Some of these were of dubious quality which in a few cases left the underwriters with considerable amounts of stock which were left over-hanging the market. The deluge of new paper dulled the investors' appetites particularly in the retail sector and also caused a situation where the market required net funding for the year ending 1991 of somewhere between one and seven billion dollars.

In the short term, the market should go higher, driven by strong corporate earnings from a relatively low PER base. The individual attractions of certain counters in the banking and property sectors are strong while companies with sound overseas or Greater China (ie Chinese Asian-Pacific regional connections, as well as into the mainland and the Pearl River delta) or airport connections will probably continue to do well. Right up to 1997, Hong Kong is likely to remain a market where money can sometimes be made more quickly and excitingly than in most other places. What is appealing to the punter, however, is not always of great interest to the long-term investor. The likelihood of reward will remain high but the specific risk attached to that reward has not diminished to any meaningful degree.

Cotton, sugar, soya beans, and gold are traded on the Hong Kong Futures Exchange, while gold is also traded at the Chinese Gold and Silver Exchange and on the Loco-London Gold Market. The currency for gold trading in Hong Kong is the 'tael', about 1.2 troy ounces of gold at 99.9 per cent fineness.

Trade and industry

Of all the countries in the Pacific Rim, Hong Kong is without a doubt the most open for business to foreigners. The government has the most benign of attitudes towards inward investment, positively going out of its way, through instruments such as the Hong Kong Trade Development Council (HKTDC), which has a network of some 30 or so offices spread around the globe, to stimulate interest from the outside world.

Foreign exchange between Hong Kong and other countries is entirely unfettered, guaranteeing the minimum of problems with the movement of capital needed to support or develop your business. Perhaps nowhere else will you find the principles of free trade so thoroughly enacted.

In Hong Kong, business and pleasure are inextricably mixed to the extent that the people, whether 'gweilo' (expatriate or 'foreign devil') or local Chinese, seem to bend over backwards to accommodate you if they believe (as they usually do) that their help to you may result in new enterprise for them. No tricks or inscrutability are involved here – simply a desire to keep the commercial cogs turning at all costs. In an area of the world where mind-numbing bureaucracy can so often be the order of the day, Hong Kong comes as a surprisingly refreshing change.

Red tape of any kind is kept to an absolute minimum and all procedures, whether for establishing multinational corporations or registering new sole trader businesses, are streamlined. Further comprehensive information on the legal formation of a new business enterprise may be obtained from the Registrar of Companies (Companies Registry, 13/14th Fl, Queensway Government Offices, 66 Queensway; tel 852 862-2600; fax 528-5423, tlx 75911) There is no minimum sum required for capital investment unless the operation involved is a full service bank, an insurance or a trust company.

Most major accountancy firms are well represented in Hong Kong and you may want to start by asking your present business accountants to recommend you specifically to one of their associates in the territory, so that the whole process of company formation and procedures may be correctly and effortlessly managed on your own behalf. You can expect to pay something in the order of HK$10,000 (about £1,000) to have the all the necessary work done to create a limited company for you.

If you do choose to take the do-it-yourself route, which is perfectly possible and in Hong Kong's case not inadvisable for start-up, the registration of a new company in Hong Kong incurs a fee of HK$730 (payable annually), and an extra HK$105 for each additional company name. Registration is managed through the Business Registration Office (Inland Revenue Dept, Windsor House, 311 Gloucester Road; tel 852 894-5098/5001).

Staff ratios of local to overseas staff are not stipulated in any way and 100 per cent of the company's shareholding may be held offshore out of Hong Kong, so clearly partial ownership by local interests is not required either. To obtain a copy of the very straightforward local employment regulations, you should contact the Labour Department (16th Fl, Harbour Building, 38 Pier Road, Central; tel 852 528-2213, fax 544-3271).

Whatever type of business you wish to set up in Hong Kong, or whether you are simply involved in straightforward import and export, a vital ingredient in your success is the 'One-Stop Shop' on Kowloon side (14th floor, Ocean Centre, 5 Canton Road, Kowloon; tel 852 737-2434, fax 730-4633, tlx 50151). As gimmicky as it may sound, it is in this office that you will find the very best market intelligence available on Hong Kong and at virtually no cost. You should always do preliminary market research yourself on your service or industry before hiring professional consultants (see Chapter 2, for further help on conducting market research) to narrow down and intensely investigate your specific area.

Not only are the staff here exceedingly well-informed and courteous, but they are directly linked in to the government's executive offices and can theoretically call upon the ultimate authority on your subject with the maximum of ease. Their brains are there for your picking and you do not have to fly to Hong Kong to make use of it. The service is also available from the Hong Kong Government Industrial Promotion offices in Brussels, London, New York, San Francisco and Tokyo.

The Trade Services Department, a subsidiary division of the HKTDC, offers access to its regularly updated database with its store of details on 40,000 local manufacturers, importers and exporters, plus 130,000 overseas buyers of Hong Kong products. Enquiries are currently running at the level of a quarter of a million a year and the staff are still smiling. (Head office: 0900–1800, Mon–Fri; 0900–1300, Saturday; Ocean Centre, Tsimshatsui, Kowloon, 0845–1715 Mon–Fri, closed 1230–1330 (lunch), and 0845–1230 Sat.)

Those in import/export will also want to appraise themselves of the necessary documentation. Full information on this is obtained from the Trade Department of the Government of Hong Kong (Ground floor, Ocean Centre, 5 Canton Road, Kowloon; tel 852 722-2333, fax 723-6135, tlx 45126), or from your nearest Hong Kong Trade Development Office (see Appendix).

Hong Kong's industry is among the most innovative in the region, has the investment and infrastructure to give it the very best support and is constantly aware of the pressure it needs to maintain to stay at the forefront of the region's exporters. The main sectors are textiles and clothing, tourism, electronics, plastics, toys and watches and clocks. All but ten per cent of Hong Kong's manufactured goods produced out of some 50,000 factories in the territory are exported and all involved, whether entrepreneurs or government aides, are concerned to keep pushing for higher and higher standards.

Overseas interests in Hong Kong are now said to employ more than 12 per cent of the total industrial work-force in nearly 700 foreign-owned or partially foreign-owned enterprises. Surprisingly Britain, which many would expect to occupy premier position in terms of industrial investment, is only at a humble fourth position with just nine per cent, preceded by the US with 34 per cent of the total investment, followed by Japan at 27 per cent and China at about 11 per cent. All indications seem

Hong Kong (British Crown Colony)

to be that, in the run up to 1997, Japan has few qualms about expanding what it sees its very useful industrial base there, so may well in the not too distant future stride on up, relatively unchallenged, to the number one position.

The breakdown of activity within the industrial sector shows the continued dominance of light manufacturing with some 65 per cent of the total industrial work-force and some 80 per cent of the entire Hong Kong working population. People are employed specifically in the broad textile industry (including garment manufacture), consumer electronics, toys, watches, clocks and plastic products, which together constitute 80 per cent of the make-up of Hong Kong's exports. Consumer electronics, as well as video and telecommunications equipment of all kinds, together with ICs, and other components are all produced to the highest quality at competitive prices. Other areas of industry include major shipyards for repair and building, aircraft engineering and all kinds of machine tools. Manufacturing as a whole still accounts for 22 per cent of the GDP.

Companies and businessmen of note

Burwill International
Cathay Pacific Airways Ltd
 (part of the Swire Group)
Cheung Kong (Holdings) Ltd
 (Li Ka Shing)
China Light & Power Co Ltd
 (Kadoorie family)
Dairy Farm International
China International Trust &
 Investment Corp – CITIC
 (mainland China's
 commercial interests in Hong
 Kong)
First Pacific International
Hang Lung Development Co Ltd
Henderson Land Development
Hong Kong Aircraft Engineering
 Co Ltd (HAECO)

Hong Kong Electric Holdings
Hong Kong TVB Broadcasting
Hong Kong Telecom Enterprise
Hutchison Whampoa Group
Jardine Matheson & Co Ltd
Kowloon Motor Bus Company
 (1933) Ltd
Li & Fung Ltd
Mass Transit Railway
 Corporation (MRTC)
New World Development
Oriental Hotel Group
Semi-Tech (electronics)
Shui On (Holdings) Ltd
Sime Darby Hong Kong Ltd
Swire Pacific Ltd
Wharf Holdings
Winsor Industrial Corporation

A thorough study of the history, as well as of both the annual and stockbrokers' reports (where available), of the companies of note will give you a good idea of the commercial 'inner game' psychology of the countries in which you plan to do business.

Agriculture

Agriculture and fisheries only make up some 0.3 per cent of Hong Kong's GDP (1988) and crops include small amounts of rice and vegetables, especially watercress, radishes, kale, lettuce, cabbages, yams and sugarcane. The Hong Kong terrain is largely mountainous and infertile except where meticulously irrigated, so much so that only eight per cent of the total land area is suitable for crop farming. Only around two per cent of the labour force works in primary production. Fishing continues to be an important source of work for nearly 25,000 local people who work the surrounding South China sea to provide nearly 75 per cent of the total fish consumed in the territories. It is from mainland China that Hong Kong obtains most of her foodstuffs and all her water.

Tourism

Affected by the Gulf conflict and continuing uncertainties in their domestic economies caused apparently by the world recession, tourists had been visiting Hong Kong in less substantial numbers during 1990–91. Altogether the industry employs around 620,000 people, 500,000 of those indirectly. Some 12 per cent of the 5.5 million people who do visit Hong Kong each year also go on to tour some part of mainland China. Of the total number of visitors to Hong Kong in 1990, tourists from south-east Asia, Japan, Taiwan and South Korea represented over 60 per cent of the total. The figures were up some 10.7 per cent on the previous year.

Infrastructure

The most expensive project coming online is the PADS, the construction operation for Hong Kong's new airport, referred to earlier. An announcement was made simultaneously in London, Beijing and Hong Kong on 4th July 1991 that the British and Chinese governments had initialled a Memorandum of Understanding on matters concerning the construction of the new airport. The international competition for these infrastructural developments will be fierce.

Also under construction, as if trying to squeeze as many buildings as possible into the territory's confined space, is the tallest building in Asia in Wanchai. (The trouble is that Pyongyang, Taipei and Tokyo are also building 'the world's tallest building', the first two are government financed, the latter two monuments to private enterprise.) Other projects include a 1.4km suspension bridge from Lantau to Tsing Yi island, and the Western Cross Harbour Tunnel from Hong Kong Island to Yau Ma Tei in Kowloon. Gordon Wu of Hopewell Holdings is a very pro-mainland businessman in Hong Kong responsible for the China Hotel in Guangzhou who is now mooting a 23-mile Pearl River bridge and a new toll road from Guangdong province into Hong Kong. The journey by car into Hong Kong from the mainland would take just one hour, something that the very farsighted have started to take advantage of even now, before the property prices zoom up, by moving to live in Guangzhou and commuting into the territory for work on a daily basis. There are reputed to be some 10,000 Hong Kong people already living on the 'wrong' side of the border. However, as one local wag put it recently about the new road, 'Tanks don't pay tolls'.

Worth noting, in practical and specific terms, is the Industrial Estates Corporation (Suite 107, Estate Centre Building, 19 Dai Cheong Street, Taipo Industrial Estate, New Territories; tel 852 653-1183, fax 652-2481). It is this statutory body, established about 1976, that procures the land necessary for Hong Kong's industrial expansion. While Hong Kong on the whole offers no special incentives to encourage business activity in the territory, seeing them as contrary to the free trade policy, there are nevertheless some commercial draws to siting a manufacturing operation in one of these areas. A project likely to be suitable is one that would be considered to contribute in some way to the future of Hong Kong, either by expansion or innovation, probably in the leading edge, high-tech arenas.

A new industrial estate, to add to the two already established in Tai Po and at Yuen Long, is to be developed at Junk Bay at an estimated cost of HK$1bn. Phase one of the project is expected to be completed by 1992. Bringing more power to the territory will be a new power station from China Light & Power which will be operational by 1996 at a cost of HK$60bn.

Communications

One of the biggest pluses in Hong Kong is that local telephone calls, both residential and commercial, are completely free. It is only from public call boxes that a HK$1 fee applies. On a much larger scale, Hong Kong is fast developing its own 'silicon harbour' out in Taipo with manufacturers like Motorola from the US and Binatone from the UK basing more and more of their manufacturing operations there. This coupled with the excellence of its native telecommunications company, Cable & Wireless (HK) Ltd and its global network of satellites, plus the local affiliate Hong Kong Telephone, make for efficiency and the very best service for both business and domestic consumers alike. Cable & Wireless (HK) Ltd and Hong Kong Telephone Co Ltd are both part of the Hong Kong Telecom group which is privately owned and completely unsubsidised. Their franchises are up for renegotiation in 1995 and 2006 respectively.

In terms of both computer applications and normal phone use, the Hong Kong system offers every capability including international packet switching (for accessing databases and communications satellites, etc), and private international leased circuits as well as the now everyday facilities of fax, telex and electronic mail (through Dialcom). In addition there is the dedicated IDAS (International Database Access Service) and Infonet. Also available is document transfer by International High Speed Document transfer and, for travel agents, a multi-access reservation system. Videoconferencing is also easily available.

Another subsidiary, Communication Services Ltd provides telecommunications systems, services and paging products including the Viewdata teletext information service. Cellular and portable phone services are available from UNITACS (Unified Total Access Communications) and from Hutchison Telephone, part of the Hutchison Whampoa Group. Like other Asian-Pacific countries, Hong Kong is well serviced by international courier companies such as DHL, Federal Express, TNT Skypak and UPS.

Transportation

As far as getting around the territory is concerned, the transportation system could not be more efficient. The subway system, the Mass Transit Railway is one of the best in the Asian-Pacific and the bus network, both on Hong Kong island and in Kowloon and the New Territories works well even if it is somewhat overcrowded. Using the trams makes more sense than it might at first seem, cutting as they do through the heart of the traffic.

On a grander and more significant scale, the first runway of the new airport at Chek Lap Kok will open in 1997 at a total cost of some HK$79bn. In the meantime, Hong Kong's Kai Tak airport is one of the most convenient airports in the world, situated as it is just 15 minutes from the Central business district on Hong Kong island. It has been known for visitors to be sitting in their hotel room at the Mandarin Hotel just 40 minutes after landing.

The most famous of the 38 airlines flying in and out of Hong Kong is perhaps the indigenous Cathay Pacific. Cargo facilities are handled by the Hong Kong Air Cargo Terminal which handles some 28 per cent of the territory's total exports. For container services, Kwai Chung on the west side of Hong Kong harbour is one of the busiest in the world, with one of the largest freight stations in the Asian-Pacific Rim. There are plans to build two more terminals to cope with the increased demand in the future.

Conferences, conventions and trade fairs

Hong Kong is now one of the trade fair capitals of the world so to establish which of the many that are held is of particular interest to you, and ultimately to help develop your business contacts and standing in Hong Kong, you should contact your nearest branch of the HKTDC (see Appendix 1, page 267) for a copy of the monthly *Businessmen's Calendar*. The HKTDC, which is not dissimilar in many ways from JETRO (Japan's External Trade Organisation) was set up in 1966 to promote Hong Kong overseas as a trading centre. The chairman and 18 council members are appointed by the Governor of Hong Kong and drawn from every discipline within the community and from government to provide the broadest possible fund of knowledge and expertise.

This comprehensive list includes all fairs and related seminars, not just those organised by the government such as the Hong Kong International Toys & Games Fair organised by the HKTDC. A few of the others worth mentioning here are the International Jewellery Show in March, the Gifts and Houseware Fair in April, the Watch and Clock Fair in September and the International Electronics Fair in October. The HKTDC also takes part in more than 80 trade fairs and commercial groupings in 35 countries around the world every year.

Also of great use is the Tourist Association's publication, *Coming Conferences & Exhibitions in Hong Kong*; (HKTA, 35th fl. Jardine House, Connaught Road, Central, Hong Kong; tel 852 524-4191). The telephone information service can be reached on 722-5555. Offices are also located in Barcelona, Chicago, Frankfurt, London, Los Angeles, New York, Osaka, Paris, Rome, San Francisco, Toronto, Singapore, Sydney, Tokyo and Wellington.

For those wishing to organise conferences helpful advice on venues, hotels, restaurants and transportation, as well as shopping and leisure activities, is available from the Conferences and Incentive Travel Bureau, also part of the HKTA. The main venue for conferences in Hong Kong is the Convention and Exhibition Centre in Wanchai with 18,000 square metres of exhibition space, a 1,800 square metre main conference hall and 24 meeting rooms, as well as an auditorium seating a maximum of 600 people. There are further plans to double the size of this convention centre on reclaimed land on the Wanchai waterfront and a second trade fair centre project is being developed in Kowloon Bay at a cost of $1.2bn. The Hong Kong Trade Mart when finished will comprise 100,000 square metres of exhibition, convention and showroom facilities. The Chyau Fwu group of Taiwan is also planning to develop an exhibition centre on Kowloon side to display Chinese and Taiwanese products at a cost of around HK$3.0bn.

All the major hotels also make excellent venues for small and more personal conferences. When in Hong Kong, you may also find it useful to go to one of the free one-hour cultural shows held each week at the Tsimshatsui New World Centre or at Citiplaza in Taikoo Shing.

Taxation

After the swingeing taxes that most of us are used to paying in Europe and the United States, Hong Kong comes as a most pleasant surprise. It is perhaps more suprising even when you consider the territory's well-developed infrastructure that does not appear to have paid penalties as a result of inadequate government funding.

The joke, or conventional wisdom, is that it is the Royal Hong Kong Jockey Club (RHKJC), Hong Kong's so-called 'welfare state' and the vast income from taxes on horse racing that allow such low personal taxes to be levied. Whether the RHKJC does substantially contribute and with charitable intent to the community or not (it does), the fact is that the commercial success of Hong Kong manages to generate enough revenue to more than adequately meet the fiscal needs of its society. If you are in Hong Kong for less than 60 days in any one year, you are not required to pay any tax at all on whatever income you derive from the territory in that financial year. Hong Kong-based companies are also exempted from paying tax on that part of their corporate income which originated overseas, even though they may bring that capital back into Hong Kong.

The three taxes that are levied are salaries tax (15 per cent), profits tax (16.5 per cent), payable on business income sourced from a trade, profession or business and a property tax (15 per cent) which is payable on unearned income from rents on both commercial and residential buildings. Full information is available from the Hong Kong Inland Revenue (Windsor House, 311 Gloucester Road, Causeway Bay; tel 852 894–5098, fax 576-6359).

Exchange rates and currency positioning relative to US$

The Hong Kong dollar is pegged at $7.807 to one US dollar and will, we are assured by the highest governmental authorities despite speculation to the contrary, continue to be so both now and after 1997 and under the new jurisdiction of the People's Republic of China. The Hong Kong dollar is freely convertible and all currencies from around the world may easily be traded in banks throughout Hong Kong. Denominations of Hong Kong dollar notes are $10, $20, $50, $100, $500 and $1,000.

The people, their languages, education and religion

The population of Hong Kong stands at 5.80 million (1990), and is mostly made up of Cantonese-speaking people whose families originally hail from the Guangdong province in China just north of Hong Kong. Whilst the official languages are Cantonese and English, other dialects often heard in Hong Kong include Hakka, and Fukien. With both political and trading eyes increasingly turning towards mainland China, Mandarin speakers both expatriate and local Chinese are on the increase. There is even a local Chinese international school which offers Mandarin as the main language of instruction for the children.

There is a significant element of people from the Indian sub-continent who are deeply involved in commercial life, and perhaps the most well-known of these is the Harilela family. The impact and influence on local commerce they and others from the Indian sub-continent have had is disproportionate to their actual numbers in the community. Even so their future in Hong Kong has not been properly catered for after 1997.

Apart from these two ethnic groups, there is of course a varied mix of expatriates from Europe, the US and Japan, as well as a substantial number of immigrant workers from the Philippines, mostly employed in domestic labour. With the newer, relaxed immigration rules towards countries in the surrounding Asian-Pacific Rim, Hong Kong is also attracting numbers of other people as skilled or semi-skilled workers to keep up with expanding demand. It is likely that the shortage of labour will result in yet more immigration to Hong Kong from the surrounding region to meet the continuous growth in manufacturing and business which will in turn need an ever-increasing supply of workers.

About 75 per cent of the Hong Kong population is said to be literate. Out of the population of nearly six million, there are just over one million children in primary and secondary school and nearly 33,000 students at the universities.

The inhabitants of Hong Kong are not notably religious, although like other 'dragons' in the Asian-Pacific Rim, they do model their lifestyle and attitudes on the basic tenets of Confucianism. Confucian principles acknowledge the importance of ancestors and entail not a small amount of ritual in daily life. The drawing of good luck fortune straws and the obsession with the 'feng-shui' (wind and water) man for divination, even for commercial purposes such as stockmarket selection, are very well known. The Christian church, in many different denominational guises, has some following in Hong Kong and continues to play an important part in education.

Publications of note

The *South China Morning Post* (News International) and the *Hong Kong Standard* (part of the Sing Tao Group, owned by world publisher Sally Aw-Sian), the *Asian Wall Street Journal* and the *International Herald Tribune* are the four daily English-language newspapers of note. The business pages in both *The Post* and *The Standard* remain the very best source of Hong Kong-specific commercial information on local companies and key local businessman. A thorough digestion of both for a few weeks would provide the best possible insight into the workings of commercial and daily life in Hong Kong.

For more specific and detailed information, the *Far Eastern Economic Review* is a must, as are *Asiaweek* the news magazine and *Asian Business* (Far East Trade Press Ltd). The monthly Hong Kong Trade Development publication *Hong Kong Enterprise* is very useful, as are some of its corollary publications on specific industries. It is also essential to train a member of local staff to keep an eye on local Chinese-language papers for new stories hot off the business press. There is sometimes an inevitable time-lag in these 'leaks' hitting the English-languge press, fed as they so often are to the publications of the lingua franca.

Worthy of particular note in the specialised publications market is *Asian Advertising and Marketing*, since Hong Kong is the local regional headquarters of the English-language advertising industry and many of the top advertising gurus are situated in the Asian-Pacific Rim head-quarters here. All major economic and news publications from around the world and the region are also, of course, widely available, not just in international hotel bookstores, but from many street vendors and at the entrances to the Mass Transit Railway (MTR), Hong Kong's subway, and at the Star Ferry which crosses the harbour from Kowloon to Central and to Wanchai. Regional editions of both *Time* magazine and *Newsweek* are produced out of Hong Kong.

Visa and health requirements

Visitors need a valid passport but no visa is required for business travellers from the USA, EEC countries and most South American countries for stays of up to one month. No special inoculations are required for most visitors to Hong Kong unless you are arriving from a virulently infected area.

Rising hopes in difficult time

While the mood certainly isn't one of unrestrained optimism, Hong Kong's executives are less pessimistic than they were one year ago, when the confidence rating plummeted to 60. This year's score of 65 reflects the feeling that the territory will continue to be a good location for doing business.

Although 48 per cent of respondents say they are less hopeful about Hong Kong's economy than they were six months ago, an overwhelming two-thirds of them feel their firms are doing fairly well or very well, while 43 per cent say that their profits have increased.

With the outlook for world markets still uncertain, the factors that most worry executives are insufficient demand and tight competition.

Hong Kong confidence index: 65

Not surprisingly, most respondents in the survey say a new airport is either essential or would be helpful to Hong Kong's international competitiveness in the 1990s. Some 50 per cent of them also feel that China's public statements on Hong Kong over the past 12 months are damaging to the territory's confidence.

What is surprising is that, despite official forecasts that between 50,000 and 60,000 people will emigrate this year, 65 per cent of respondents expect it will actually be easier to recruit white-collar and professional staff than it has been in the recent past.

Finance houses report a flood of resumés sent in by unemployed stockbrokers in cities like London and New York. Unlike most other Asian cities, Hong Kong's doors are open to expatriate talent.

Asian Business provides readers with a Confidence Index for each country surveyed. To compare the results of confidence surveys conducted around the region, we process the data from each survey and (in conjunction with Frank Small & Associates) arrive at a numerical rating for each country. This index measures the following six criteria used in the survey: local market, export market, turnover, profits, company prospects and economy.

ECONOMIC/POLITICAL

National economy: are you more optimistic about the national economy than you were 6 months ago? Less? About the same?

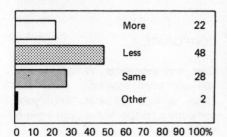

	More	22
	Less	48
	Same	28
	Other	2

0 10 20 30 40 50 60 70 80 90 100%

Local market: During the last 6 months, has your company been operating in an expanding, a static, or a contracting local market?

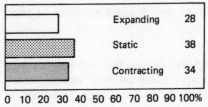

	Expanding	28
	Static	38
	Contracting	34

0 10 20 30 40 50 60 70 80 90 100%

Export market: During the last 6 months, has your company been operating in an expanding, a static, or a contracting local market?

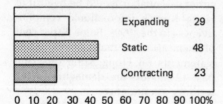

Expanding	29
Static	48
Contracting	23

0 10 20 30 40 50 60 70 80 90 100%

Brain-drain: In the next 12 months, do you expect the recruitment of white-collar and professional staff to become easier or more difficult?

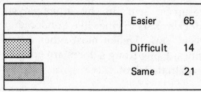

Easier	65
Difficult	14
Same	21

0 10 20 30 40 50 60 70 80 90 100%

New airport: Do you regard the proposed new airport as essential, helpful or irrelevant to Hong Kong's competitiveness as an international business centre?

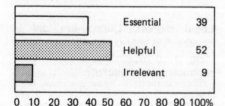

Essential	39
Helpful	52
Irrelevant	9

0 10 20 30 40 50 60 70 80 90 100%

China: Do you feel that recent statements made by PRC officials about Hong Kong have been beneficial or harmful to the territory's economic well-being?

Beneficial	14
Harmful	50
Neither	28
Other	8

0 10 20 30 40 50 60 70 80 90 100%

Economic prospects: On a scale of one, for very poor, to 10, for very good, how would you rate the likely performance of the following economies in the next 12 months?

	Average rating	Proportion who gave a rating
Japan	6.8	94%
Thailand	6.5	90%
Singapore	6.3	91%
Hong Kong	6.2	97%
South Korea	6.2	89%
Malaysia	6.2	88%
Taiwan	5.9	91%
Indonesia	5.9	83%
China	5.6	97%
USA	5.3	98%
New Zealand	4.6	94%
Sri Lanka	4.6	73%
Vietnam	4.6	79%
Australia	4.5	94%
India	4.2	69%
Philippines	4.1	89%

CORPORATE

Company prospects: Would you say you are more optimistic, about the same, or less optimistic about your company's prospects than you were 6 months ago?

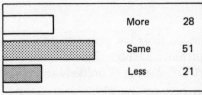

More	28
Same	51
Less	21

0 10 20 30 40 50 60 70 80 90 100%

Company performance: Overall, would you say that your company is doing well, badly, or neither?

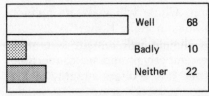

Well	68
Badly	10
Neither	22

0 10 20 30 40 50 60 70 80 90 100%

Gross profits: During the last 6 months, has the trend of your profits been up, down, or the same compared with the same period last year?

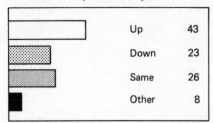

Up	43
Down	23
Same	26
Other	8

0 10 20 30 40 50 60 70 80 90 100%

Turnover: During the last 6 months, have your company's turnover/billings, compared with the same period last year, gone up, stayed the same, or gone down?

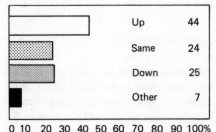

Up	44
Same	24
Down	25
Other	7

0 10 20 30 40 50 60 70 80 90 100%

Staffing levels: Do you expect staffing levels in your company over the next 6 months to rise, fall, or stay the same?

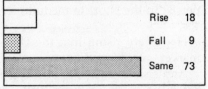

Rise	18
Fall	9
Same	73

0 10 20 30 40 50 60 70 80 90 100%

Concern for company future: Which of the following areas do you expect to be your main business concern during the next 6 months? (Multiple answers possible)

Insufficient demand	22
Tight competition	17
Political instability	16
Labour supply	9
Availability or cost of materials	7
Industrial unrest	4
Cashflow	3
High interest rates	2
Speed of service or deliveries	1
Devaluation	1
Others	16

The survey was compiled by Frank Small & Associates in Hong Kong from telephone interviews with a quota sample of businessmen. Business directories were used to conduct a sampling frame. Eligibility criteria were set for number of employees in the company, and for respondent's seniority, and company quotas were set for different company types. Interviewing took place between 22 January and 11 February 1991. A response rate of 45% among eligible companies was achieved.

Note: 'Other' category in charts includes those who answered 'Don't know' or declined to answer.

Respondents had the following company titles: Manager 42; director 18; general manager 15; vice president 7; assistant manager 4; accountant 4; executive 2; secretary 2; officer 2; company secretary 1; controller 1; owner 1; others 1.

The number of staff employed by the company broke down as follows: under 100 employees, 24 companies; 101-249, 51 companies; 250–499, 11 companies; 500-999, 6 companies; 1,000-2,499, 7 companies. Some 26% of companies were in manufacturing; 25% in banking/insurance/finance; 25% in import/export/trading; and 24% in other sectors.

Investment risk: Hong Kong 64

Hong Kong's investment risk is unchanged from last year. Over the next year economic performance will remain slow. Double-digit inflation will persist in the short to medium term. GDP growth is unlikely to exceed 4%.

Hopes are rising that the US – Hong Kong's major western export market – could pull out of recession by mid-year.

Any risk assessment of Hong Kong must take China into account. Since the events of June 1989, China's leaders have taken a hard-line stance on Hong Kong.

As the handover date draws nearer, China will make its opinions known on an increasing number of issues in Hong Kong.

Nonetheless, the overall business climate will remain favourable. Hong Kong enjoys relatively low taxes, superb air and sea connections, and state-of-the-art telecommunications. It also offers a highly mobile, and well-educated, work force.

Hong Kong scored as follows:

1	Inflation	5
2	Interest rate	6
3	Growth	3
4	Infrastructure	8
5	Labour: strife and shortages	5
6	Bureaucratic impediments	9
7	Government interference in business	9
8	Threat of armed aggression (internal and external)	9
9	Political volatility	4
10	Business confidence	6

Investment risk: **64**
Last year's score: **64**

Reproduced by courtesy of *Asian Business*

REPUBLIC OF INDONESIA

Nominal GDP: US$101.3bn/Rupiah 191,279bn
GDP real growth: 6.7
Exports: US$25.7bn (+ 16.3 per cent)
Imports: US$21.8bn (+ 33.7 per cent)
Net foreign debt: US$52.6bn/51.9 per cent of GDP
Trade surplus: US$3.9 bn
Population: 182.6m
Work-force: 74.5m
Inflation (annual CPI): 9.5 per cent
Savings rate: 31.2 per cent
Overseas visitor numbers: 2,177,566
Chief of State and Head of Government: President Suharto
Ruling party: Golkar (military-bureaucrat-farmers ruling party)
Other political parties: United Development Party (PPP), Indonesian
   Democratic Party (PDI).
Capital city: Jakarta (GMT+7 hours)

(Figures for year ending 1990)

Membership of international organisations: ANRPC, APCC, ASEAN, Asian Development Bank, Association of Tin Producing Countries, CCC, CIPEC, Colombo Plan, EC Trade and Co-operation Agreement, ESCAP, FAO, GATT, IAEA, IBA, IBRD, ICAO, ICO, IDA, IFAD, IFC, IHO, ILO, IMF, IMO, INMARSAT, IPC, IRSG, Islamic Conference Organisation, Islamic Development Bank, ITC, ITU, NAM, OIC, OPEC, UN, UNESCO, UNIDO, UPU, WFTU, WHO, WIPO, WMO, World Bank, WTO.

Brief history

A huge archipelago of 13,667 islands (only 5,000 are inhabited) which sprawl over 1.9 million square kilometres, across the Equator from the longitude of Burma in the west to the Gulf of Carpentaria in the east. The capital of Indonesia, which is one of the largest countries in the

75

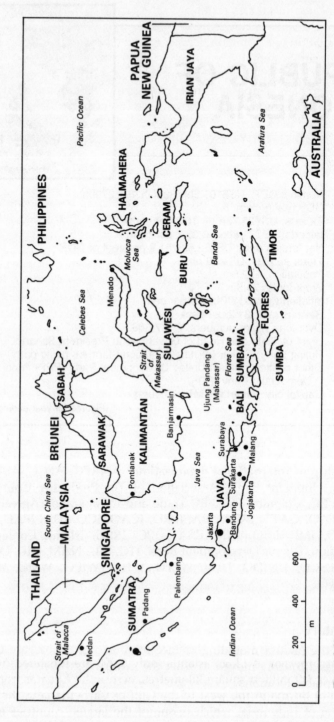

Republic of Indonesia

world, is located in Jakarta on Java on the northern coast. Jakarta was founded in 1527 and is now spread over nearly 580 square kilometres with a population of 6.5 million people, who are predominantly Moslem with Islamic fundamentalist leanings.

Other main cities on Java include Surabaya, Bandung, Semarang and Jogjakarta. On Bali, Denpasar is the capital town, on Sumatra are Medan and Palembang, on Sulawesi is Ujung Pandang, formerly Makassar, and Parepare. Also well-known are some of the settlements on Kalimantan (Borneo) and Irian Jaya (West New Guinea). Altogether, there are said to be at least 31 semi-rural districts with populations over one million, but it is most unlikely during the normal course of business that you will have either the time or the inclination to get to these places.

Hard-bitten businessmen love to tell lurid tales of the difficulties of even attempting any kind of commercial negotiation in these remote spots. Jakarta itself, they are quick to say, is hard enough. So, certainly until you have a firm grasp of Bahasa and of the local mindset (a mastery of winning ways to conquer the inevitable cry for 'baksheesh'), it is probably wiser to give the far-flung spots a big miss.

Be especially careful to give a wide berth to the warring states of East Timor and Irian Jaya where some of the 1.5 million people, who altogether make up the country's 300 different tribes, are engaged in constant internecine warfare with the Indonesian Government over their rights for self-determination. There continues resistance to the 1975 occupation of East Timor and its incorporation as Indonesia's twenty-seventh province, which was carried out with considerable brutality. Both the Revolutionary Front for an Independent East Timor and the Free Papua Movement are still waging their independence battles.

In November 1991 there was what *Time* magazine referred to as a 'graveyard massacre' when government troops gunned down dozens of Timorese civilians with automatic weapons after 1,000 Timorese had marched to a cemetery in memory of a young militant who had been killed. The European Community, along with the US and Japan 'vehemently condemned' the killings. One excuse given was that a soldier had been hacked to death with a machete so the masses were mowed down in too hasty a retaliation, while other commanders admitted it had all been a ghastly mistake. The trouble is, these so-called 'mistakes' have a nasty habit of happening in Indonesia whenever ethnic minorities start to break out of line. Kalimantan and Maluku (the Moluccas; remember the hijackings?), formerly known as the Spice Islands, are also best avoided. The Suharto regime is stubbornly insistent that all Indonesians melt into the Jakarta moulding or face annihilation. Tribes are being uprooted and forcibly moved to what the government considers to be more acceptable locations.

Today Indonesia is the dominant power in the six-nation ASEAN grouping but much of its fortune is vulnerable to the rise and fall of world commodity prices. With a population of nearly 188 million, more than that of the other five members combined, and abundant natural resources of oil, tin, natural gas, nickel, timber, bauxite and copper, it is now seeking a greater role on the world stage. In recent years it has played a leading part in the search for a political settlement in Cambodia. The combination of the work-force of the forecasted population for the year 2000 of some 222.7 million people at a growth rate of two per cent, plentiful resources, and growing infrastructure and technology transfer all make Indonesia a country to watch.

Historically speaking, Indonesia has its roots in Hindu and Buddhist culture in the first century. Islamic culture was subsequently introduced to Sumatra in the fifteenth century from where it then spread throughout the rest of the islands. By the sixteenth century, the Portuguese had come hunting for cloves and other spices and imposed their influence. The Dutch then arrived in the early seventeenth century, during which time the area became known as the Dutch East Indies. Next it was Britain's turn to occupy Indonesia unlawfully during the Napoleonic wars.

Today, the country's internal politics are at best confusing to the outsider. President (General) Suharto who is said to be something of a misanthropist with only a vast liking for his family (especially his sons and daughters to whom he hands out the ill-gotten largesse of 'empire' – tolls from toll roads, for example) has been in power for 25 years. There is no other sign at the moment then that he clearly intends to run for yet another five-year term in the March 1993 'election', in which army representatives have the controlling voice and will therefore vote him back in. They would hardly dare do otherwise.

Though most Indonesians would like to see the back of Suharto and his grasping family, no alternative candidate has yet emerged. No one will ever dare, unless they are hell-bent on self-destruction, real or imagined, to run against Suharto. He always muses vocally to the Press, every time an election comes around, about the wisdom of standing down but it is all so much empty talk. Dictator that he is, he would at least like to be seen pretending to be otherwise. It is always said by those who know Indonesia really well that there is a vast political resentment swelling up below the surface which will sooner or later burst forth into a revolution. What is more likely to happen is, motivated by the increasing wealth of its neighbours in the region, Indonesia will continue to potter along quietly but industriously till before long it is catching up. 'Slowly, slowly, catchee monkey.'

The country's strengths

- Abundant resources.

- Export-led growth: broadened manufacturing sector and non-oil exports, but a vulnerability to slowdown in external demand.
- Tripling of foreign direct investment to nearly US$5 billion in the three years to 1989.
- Some good signs of deregulation and reform, as well as the liberalisation of markets and recent widespread reduction in import tariffs.
- Far greater political stability than is generally appreciated and a relatively high degree of economic growth in 1990.
- The world's largest producer of liquefied natural gas.
- The fifth largest population in the world.
- Import and consumer spending growth expected to remain high throughout the 1990s.

The country's weaknesses

- The succession crisis. Will Suharto stand yet again for re-election at term end in 1993?
- An immature industrial and commercial base.
- Infrastructure limitations, but these are being overcome with private sector establishment of industrial estates.
- Social tension from uneven income distribution and a young population.
- 'Poor rich country' blessed with too many medium-term opportunities and too many shorter term high priority needs.
- Manageable, but massive, external debt.
- Political tension with the transition of power from President Suharto to a new order.
- Relatively high market entry costs due to the regulatory and licensing system, decreasing over time.
- Corruption: the Attorney-General of Indonesia publically endorsed a new 'shame culture' campaign to expose officials wanted on extortion and other charges.
- Large-scale unemployment. Estimates run between an official figure of around three per cent to anywhere as high as nine per cent in the next five years. The present size of the work-force is around 75 million people out of a population of 188 million. Over half the work-force continues to be employed in agriculture and under ten per cent in manufacturing.

Goals

Indonesia would like to achieve NIC status by 1994. At the moment, however, there is a vicious circle it has yet to break out of in order to begin to reach such status. On the one hand, foreign investment is attracted by opportunities to export low value-added processed raw materials. On the other hand, it needs to increase the value-added content locally without frightening away foreign capital.

Politics

The forthcoming elections should have few surprises in store but have nevertheless been raising the political temperature in Indonesia. The election of the DPR, for 400 elected members and 100 army appointees, was a foregone conclusion and the government faction Golkar was expected to win, as it has in the last three elections. Other parties are gaining in prominence, especially the Indonesian Democratic Party (PDI) in Jakarta, but the PPP, a Moslem-orientated political party is gaining an increasing share of the vote. The government, in true liberal fashion, has already issued an instruction that mass rallies and motorcades are to be banned during all elections. Over the course of the next twelve months, the key players in the race for the vice presidential slot will emerge but it goes without saying that the support of the army is fundamental for any would-be president.

Election platforms include Press freedom, the dissident 'Group of 50' and the combined force of some retired army officers whose intention it is to join ranks with the PDI. Regardless of whatever incarnation opposition presents itself in, so far Suharto's position still appears very strong. Nevertheless there are some rumours doing the rounds that certain elements in the army would prefer him to step down in 1993. Presidential hopefuls will have to become very adept at second guessing Suharto who remains a master of the political scene.

Suharto's main political vulnerability lies increasingly in the active role of the presidential family in a number of spheres of public and commercial life. The newly established clove marketing monopoly, for example, which was set up by the business group Humpuss is owned by one of Suharto's sons. More generally his family's prominent involvement in telecommunications, toll roads, television and petrochemicals has raised concerns. Also causing concern is the affluence of ethnic Chinese businessmen which has led to calls for a greater distribution of the benefits of Indonesia's economic development. Something will have to be done, by Suharto and his men, to put down these increasing rebellions before they put him down.

Domestic economy, current economic policy and forecasts

The per capita GDP of Indonesia is nowhere near as high as that of the other embryonic tigers in the Asian-Pacific Rim, but there is no doubt that her high rate of growth (around six per cent per annum, exceeding the five per cent minimum growth targeted in the current Five Year Plan) will continue to ensure that while she may never really catch up she will certainly be no laggard.

Where other economies were sharply disrupted by the Gulf conflict, Indonesia, with her vast reserves of oil was one of the few countries to 'benefit' from the crisis with a sharp increase in oil prices and a salutary effect on the economy. The windfall profits over and above the allowed for average oil price of US$16.50 per barrel will probably be used to pay off some of the country's external debt and contribute to national coffers for conservative but much-needed expansion of the infrastructure. With her vast reserves of people, largely unskilled but ripe for training, she may now take advantage of the slow but steady increase in investment from both home and abroad to march along the road to becoming an industrialised economy of the future. The vast increase in the number of capital goods being imported in the rush towards modernisation suggests that this is a country in a hurry to catch up with the rest of the Asian-Pacific Rim.

The economy is now in altogether a better position, it is felt, to withstand the challenges of the ambitious budget introduced last year which called for an 18 per cent increase in expenditure. There is continued control of inflation and even though there was a pay rise last summer at long last for the public sector, wage demands are being kept comparatively low. The collection of taxes is being streamlined and generally made more efficient.

The rupiah, the Indonesian currency, has undergone regular depreciation to the good effect that both the private and the financial sector have begun to become increasingly aware of its potential as a good buy and so invested more and more. Since price rises were threatening to be disruptive, the government introduced a tighter monetary policy whose effects have begun to be felt in terms of controlling the country's inflation which had runs of between nine and ten per cent.

For the last couple of years, Indonesia has received significant foreign aid, coming to around US$4.5bn, the largest sum of which was provided by Japan (US$1.8bn) who is undoubtedly looking forward with great eagerness to Indonesia's 'arrival' in modern economic and infrastructural terms. The swarms of Japanese businessmen, and not a few Koreans and Singaporeans not only in Jakarta but in outlying areas of Indonesia as well, attest to this high degree of expectation. Few can doubt the country's potential when her vast pools of labour and resources are coupled with technical and management expertise. The Inter-Governmental Group on Indonesia (IGGI) in The Hague which organised the ODA funding were sufficiently impressed with the Indonesian Government's use of the money that they commended the country on its macro-economic management and the infrastructural uses to which the money was applied. The UK Government offered an initial concessional loan of £240m, of which £183m was put to project use. In the second phase, Britain pledged £18m to new aid, mostly as technical co-operation. The money will be used for forestry education, energy and public administration.

This brings the total amount pledged for the year ending 1992 to US$4.75bn, of which US$1.82bn will come from Japan. This last figure also includes sums of money pledged outside the programme from the The Hague.

Indonesia, like Malaysia, Thailand and the Philippines, has witnessed remarkable growth, especially since the transformation of the stock-market in 1989, with a surge in inward investment prompting a shift away from primary products towards manufacturing. There has been a further consolidation by the Indonesian economy in promoting the growth of its export-orientated industries.

At present the domestic economy dominates Indonesia's GDP al-though in five years' time the domestic component is expected to be matched by export demand. With Australia, China, and Japan, Indone-sia is one of the least exposed economies in terms of dependency upon global economies and specifically on the US market.

Lower oil prices following the end to the Gulf crisis impacted on Indonesia by reducing the value of oil exports. Export growth in 1991 halved from 16 per cent growth to just seven per cent. Indonesia of course has a high dependence on oil exports, but seems at last to be moving towards a sustained level of economic growth which is not entirely oil-based. This is attracting more investors, banks and insurance companies. Japan's slowing economy has had an effect, accounting as it does for 40 per cent of Indonesia's exports. Exports should recover strongly in 1992 to around the 13 per cent figure, with the export of manufactured goods reaching 20 per cent.

Mounting deficit is a concern – 4.6 per cent of GDP. This is due to heavier than expected imports of plant and equipment as well as rising consumer demand.

Further substantial progress in reforming the economy can be ex-pected. A package of trade deregulations announced just ahead of the IGGI conference in June 1991 will liberalise the palm oil industry and lead to greater competition in the auto sector. More such packages can be anticipated.

The capital market is seen as having a vital role to play in attracting investment capital, the appetite for which, especially for project finance, remains very strong. A privatised exchange, better managed supporting agencies and more active involvement by domestic institutions in the stockmarket are all part of government policy. Political manoeuvrings are not expected to alter the fundamental direction of these policies.

Banking and finance, equity market outlook, stockmarket

The banking system in Indonesia could be said to have almost busted itself in its rush for expansion, with increased foreign currency dealings and other heightened business, in the past couple of years. The undue haste was probably in a desire to prepare for what was seen as the coming boom times but everything was undertaken, as if often the case in Indonesia, in a haphazard fashion and without sufficient control and management of the structure. The result has been confusion at best. In 1990, the country's fourth largest bank, Bank Duta Ekonomi reported very heavy losses and was 'rescued' by being placed under the control of Bank Indonesia, the state bank. Then, a short time later, another bank, Bank Umum Mojopahit closed its doors. If the same had happened in Hong Kong, the result would have been social chaos. Life is not quite so daunting for foreign banks, it would seem, since a few of them (including Standard Chartered with a new branch in the textile centre of Bandung, and a number of Japanese entitities) are pressing on in the market regardless taking advantage of the windows of deregulation. Yet more are hard at work in setting up joint ventures to sell banking services, some of which are completely new to the market.

Following the Indonesian banking deregulation in October 1987, there was a major expansion in the number of bank branches. As a result the deposit base rose sharply, increasing money supply and therefore fanning inflation. The Indonesian government is determined to quell inflation and has allowed interest rates to rise to a level where real interest rates currently exceed 15 per cent. However there are definite signs that inflationary forces are now abating, so lower inflation is expected for the rest of this year. Interest rates have surged as high as 26 per cent in Indonesia in the recent past as the government aggressively sought to contain inflation. When inflation then fell interest rates started to drop quite sharply. However, as oil prices fell and the trade deficit widened, currency speculation forced the government to tighten liquidity once again.

The Indonesian stockmarket, which is expected to have over 200 new share listings this year up from just nine two years ago, has been relaxing restrictions on the foreign ownership of equities. Measures were introduced to strengthen the capital market and to privatise stock exchange operations, as well as to increase the protection afforded to investors. The government would very much like to see a major increase in the market's efficiency to attract new liquidity and so that new areas of business may be developed. In the recent past, the market has been drifting off around 15 per cent (17 per cent in US dollars), and trading has been down. This malaise has probably been due to low levels of domestic investor demand, as well as the uncertainty over the short term economic outlook, and lack of progress in improving the market infrastructure. The returns on bank time deposits with high interest rates and tighter credit controls have had a major negative impact on the market. The gross national savings ratio is quite high at around 29 per cent of GNP and inflation should gradually come down to a more manageable eight per cent.

The best-known banks are Bank Negara Indonesia 1946, Bank Bumi Daya, Bank Rakyat Indonesia, Bank Dagang Nagara, Bank Ekspor Impor Indonesia, and Bank Duta Ekonomi (controversial due to possible close association with Suharto. Currently being restructured due to alleged fraud).

Trade and industry

British exporters and potential investors should now be making determined steps to enter the Indonesian market, *en masse* if necessary, so that a great opportunity to take part in what will be a vibrant economy is not missed. The competition is already there in force. No one in the market, or indeed even with the slightest knowledge or it, pretends that breaking in is easy. Indonesia is one of the most difficult markets to tackle, without a doubt, but the potential rewards are also proportionately far greater in the long-term than in other markets in the region. The situation is, however, becoming easier gradually with all signs that deregulation is beginning to filter right through the economy slowly but surely. A great deal of grit, and some measure of social machination and ingenuity is required to tackle the challenge, but the key to success is, once again, local knowledge and presence and an empathy with and appreciation of the market's characteristics.

The Government of Indonesia in 1991 announced the removal of non-tariff barriers and also reduced tariffs on hundreds of commodities, as well as reopening several sectors to new domestic and foreign investors. These are all in the continuing stream of measures for reform introduced by the government over the last six years. Not a small part of the motivation is to further convince the aid givers in The Hague – IGGI – that the government is fully committed to restructuring and to increasing inward investment and the best possible use of ODA money.

The top five UK exports to Indonesia are specialised machinery, power generating machinery, industrial machinery, iron and steel and transport equipment. The top five UK imports from Indonesia are cork and wood, clothing, textiles, footwear and vegetable fat and oils. An analysis of Indonesia's imports shows that by far the largest sector is in machinery and transport equipment at 42.7 per cent of the total value of exports. This is followed by manufactured goods, chemicals, mineral fuels and lubricants, crude materials, food and livestock.

Indonesia will continue to attract a large amount of foreign investment, an estimated US$6.0bn for 1991, or 5.4 per cent of GDP. Moreover foreign investment in Indonesia for the coming year should continue to rise to US$7.5bn or 6.1 per cent of GDP, making Indonesia the most favoured area for foreign investment over the next couple of years. This is compared with Thailand whose foreign investment for 1991 is said to have been US$2.1bn or 2.2 per cent of GDP.

Buoyant foreign investment is boosting the Indonesian economy although excessive money supply in 1990 caused inflation to rise to 9.5 per cent last year. As a result the government imposed sharply higher interest rates not only to curb inflation but to stop recent currency speculation. Whilst it is believed the interest rates will soften, private consumption will be affected in the process. Being a net exporter of oil, Indonesia has been a beneficiary of developments on the oil front. Oil prices are still higher than before Iraq invaded Kuwait, although they have fallen. Higher oil revenus will allow the government to increase local infrastructure projects which will help to offset the negative impact of higher interest rates.

A recent cutting of import duties on 562 items is designed to encourage local industries to become more competitive and thus increasingly productive. These moves should help propel future economic growth and are viewed positively. Other reforms in the pipeline include the opening of the banking sector to foreign investors and allowing the pension funds greater access to the stock market.

Of particular interest to those with exports subject to potential trademark violations are new regulations which insist that those who use a mark on a product can prove that the mark is entirely theirs to display. It is hoped that, over a period of time, this will do more to get rid of the lingering counterfeiters. Not unrelated is a move that has come about owing to major criticism from foreign companies and governments about pharmaceutical companies in Indonesia. Now there are new regulations in Indonesia for the import of patented pharmaceuticals and for the registration of and application for patent rights. This will allow 50 identified patented pharmaceutical products to be imported by people other than the specific patent holders without infringing the new law.

The main industries in Indonesia are cement, chemical fertilisers, mining, palm oil, petroleum, textiles, timber and, increasingly, light manufacturing. Major exports include coffee and tea, copper, liquefied natural gas, palm oil, petroleum, rubber, timber and tin. Import requirements include cereals, flour, rice, wheat, chemicals, iron and steel products, machinery and transport equipment, as well as textiles,

The leading sectors, timber, rubber, garments and textiles seem set to continue good growth of up to 48 per cent. British exporters are tending to concentrate in the fields of petrochemicals, oil and gas, machinery, power generation and supply, pollution control, airport-related equipment, food processing, mining and railway equipment, as well as telecommunications and automotive components and accessories. Financial services and tourism also offer very good opportunities.

Companies of note

PT Astra International Inc (automotive)	PT Multi Bintang Indonesia
PT Barata Metal Works & Engineering	Pabrik Gula Rejo Agung Baru
	PT Pantja Niaga
PT Bayer Farma Indonesia	Pertamina
PT Batu Sepatu	Perum Perhutani
Biro Asri	Perusahaan Aspai Negara
PT British American Tobacco	PT Philips Ralin Electronics
PT Budidharma Daja Manunggal	PT Semen Cibinong
PT Dos Ni Roha	PT Sumber Matraman
PN Garuda Indonesian Airways	PT Supreme Cable Manufacturing Corp (SUCACO)
PT Goodyear Indonesia	PT Teijin Indonesia Fiber Corp
Gudang Garam (tobacco)	Tijiwi Kimia (paper and pulp)
PT Indah Kiat Pulp & Paper Corp	PT Tjipta Niaga
Indocement	TMS (cable)
PT Industri Sandang	PT Unilever Indonesia
PT International Nickel Indonesia	PT United Tractors
JAPFA Comfeed (animal feed)	PT Waskita Karya
Marison NV	PT Wijaya Karya

A thorough study of the history, as well as of both the annual and stockbrokers' reports (where available), of the companies of note will give you a good idea of the commercial 'inner game' psychology of the countries in which you plan to do business.

Agriculture

Indonesia relies on agriculture, forestry, fishing and mining to produce nearly 25 per cent of its gross domestic product, 85 per cent of export earnings and 55 per cent of its total employment. The main agricultural products of Indonesia are rice, sugar, coffee, rubber and copra. Currently rice is in surplus production to about one million tonnes per annum. Only some 14 per cent of the total land mass is cultivated and 67 per cent is under forest. Indonesia has some of the world's largest remaining reserves of tropical hardwoods, estimated in 1987 at around 191m acres.

Tourism

1991 was 'Visit Indonesia Year' and while it is still too early to measure the real benefits, great efforts were made to boost Indonesian tourism in the international market-place and to create awareness of destinations other than the ever-popular Bali. The rewards in terms of foreign currency earnings for Indonesia are too important to make their efforts anything other than worthwhile, although the country is in fairly dire need of expertise from abroad to train top-level management and local staff to work in the four- and five-star hotel environments that are springing up.

Some 16,000 new hotel rooms are coming onstream nation-wide this year, adding to well over 400 existing hotels with over 30,000 rooms, and focusing on Jakarta itself, as well as Jogjakarta and East and West Java, and to a lesser extent in Sumatra and Sulawesi. Bali, which quite rightly is considered overdeveloped and saturated with tourists, has been given a development reprieve. A programme is in place for a total of 77 new hotels to be built altogether by the end of 1993 and infrastructural investment to date totals around US$553m. The government is working towards a goal in 1994 of 3.5 million tourists per annum.

Infrastructure

A number of infrastructural developments are still under discussion. However, one of the main projects which has just recently been finished is the pan-island bridge that will link Java with Madura. Other new projects have included the Citayam-Nambo Railway line at a cost of £23m, new forestry communications systems (£37m) and national short-wave radio transmitters (£29m) to improve communications throughout the disparate islands of Indonesia.

The Indonesian Government has now authorised the private sector to develop oil and gas processing facilities with the state-run company Pertamina under the auspices of the Foreign Contractors' Guidance Board. Indonesia is now eager to add value to its oil and gas products and is trying to shift away from the export of crude to processed goods. All gas stations in Indonesia are being privatised over the next few years so that a programme may be effected whereby all pumps will produce high octane, low leaded petrol. Studies are under way to establish a nuclear power station on Java and possibilities for alternative energy sources, such as solar and geothermal, are also being investigated.

With regard to the environment, the minister reponsible, Prof Emil Salim recently announced that the Government will, in an effort to get them to clean up their acts, sue some 500 firms who are said to be polluting the environment. Offenders are being given two years to install liquid waste water treatment systems to cut down on the amount of liquid toxic waste going into Indonesia's rivers.

Communications

According to statistics from AT&T International, Indonesia at present has about five phones per 1,000 head of population and a cellular network will shortly be set up in Jakarta. Nowadays, cable and telex facilities are widely available and used and the use of fax machines is fast on the increase throughout the business community.

Transportation

Transportation is still the weakest link in Indonesia's developmental chain. Nevertheless, the country's national airline Garuda which connects cities throughout Indonesia with daily services from Jakarta to Bali, Medan and Surabaya, is of a moderately high standard. Main roads are fine in the city but outside are generally not surfaced, making life very difficult in the rainy season. Trains are more or less confined to Java and parts of Sumatra and Madura and apart from the main, well-maintained express trains, can be erratic and uncomfortable.

There is an extensive if piecemeal bus service throughout the country and vast numbers of boats, both scheduled and unscheduled which ply their way across the inter-island channels.

Conferences, conventions and trade fairs

An increasing number of trade fairs are being held each year in Jakarta, with the largest number being held in the technical, scientific and medical sectors.

Taxation

A sales tax was introduced about five years ago and reforms have been undertaken in the income system to ensure that the burden of tax is distributed more equitably, as they see it, through the general wage-earning population.

Exchange rates and currency's posititioning relative to US$

The currency of Indonesia is the Rupiah (100 sen).

The people, their languages, education and religion

There are five main ethnic groups in Indonesia, the largest group, the Javanese, make up nearly half the population, but there are some 300 minorities. These include the Sundanese, the Madurese and the Coastal Malays.

The official language is Bahasa, not an impossible language – compared to Cantonese or Mandarin – for the serious businessman to pick up to some degree of useful ability. Bahasa is a dialect of Malay, but since there are altogether some 200 different dialects and there is as yet no spoken standard, a Malay speaker from Indonesia and one from Kuala Lumpur are unlikely to understand each other. English is common for commercial activities and some older Indonesians still speak Dutch from colonial days.

Illiteracy is much higher amongst Indonesian women than men, with over 30 per cent of the female population unable to read. Men fare better with about 20 per cent of all males unable to read. The total literacy is estimated to be about 70 per cent of the population. There are about 41.5 million school students in both primary and secondary schools, and about 1.5 million in the country's colleges and universities.

Publications of note

English publications include the daily newspapers, *The Indonesia Times*, *The Indonesia Observer* and *The Jakarta Post*.

The most important domestic publication is *Kompas* which is published in Jakarta. Other well-read publications include *Tempo*, *Bisnis Indonesia* and *Editor* all of which are in Bahasa.

A business publication worth more than a passing interest is the bilingual *Indonesian Commercial Newsletter* published every two months.

Visas and health requirements

All visitors need a valid passport but no visas are required for US, and EEC citizens and several other countries, such as Thailand and Australia, for a stay of less than two months. Please note however that this period may not be extended. Visitors without visas can enter Indonesia through Jakarta, Bali, Medan, Manado, Biak, Ambon, Batam, Surabaya and Pekanbaru and will be issued with the usual tourist visa which cannot be extended. Businessmen who anticipate a longer stay in the country should apply for the five-week business visas which may be extended subject to the normal bureaucratic checking procedures.

Visitors coming into Indonesia from infected areas are required to have smallpox, yellow fever and cholera shots.

Domestic success boosts optimism

It is a reflection of confidence in Indonesia's sound macroeconomic management that top business executives consistently showed enthusiasm for the country's economic prospects. Respondents gave Indonesia a confidence vote of 85.

Their optimism can be traced partly to opportunities for growth in the domestic market which is expanding rapidly as government deregulation takes effect.

About 74% of the respondents said the local market is expanding, which is just as well, since only 32% said they believe the export market is growing. No surprise there – Indonesia's largest export market is the US, which is currently in bad shape.

Some 46% of the respondents regard the US as the most important export market, followed by Japan (31%) and China (23%).

With foreign investment hitting record levels, about 63% of the respondents feel the government ought to be looking to Japan for further investment. Interestingly, about 12% think China should also be wooed for investment, only just behind the 16% who favour the US.

Indonesia confidence index: 85

Asian Business provides readers with a Confidence Index for each country surveyed. To compare the results of confidence surveys conducted around the region, we process the data from each survey and (in conjunction with Frank Small & Associates) arrive at a numerical rating for each country. This Confidence Index measures the following six criteria used in the survey: local market, export market, turnover, profits, company prospects and economy.

ECONOMIC/POLITICAL

National economy: Are you more optimistic about the national economy than you were six months ago? Less? About the same?

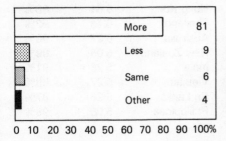

More	81
Less	9
Same	6
Other	4

0 10 20 30 40 50 60 70 80 90 100%

Local market: During the last six months, has your company been operating in an expanding, a static, or a contracting local market?

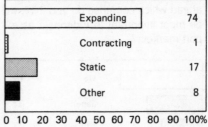

Expanding	74
Contracting	1
Static	17
Other	8

0 10 20 30 40 50 60 70 80 90 100%

91

Hunting with the Tigers

Export market: During the last six months, has your company been operating in an expanding, a static, or a contracting export market?

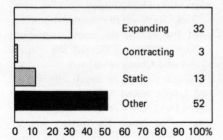

Expanding	32
Contracting	3
Static	13
Other	52

0 10 20 30 40 50 60 70 80 90 100%

Foreign investment: From which countries do you think Indonesia should try hardest to attract investment in the year ahead?

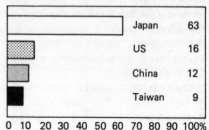

Japan	63
US	16
China	12
Taiwan	9

0 10 20 30 40 50 60 70 80 90 100%

Starting out: In the year ahead do you expect it to become easier or harder than it is now to become a successful exporter from Indonesia?

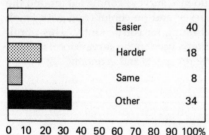

Easier	40
Harder	18
Same	8
Other	34

0 10 20 30 40 50 60 70 80 90 100%

Important export markets: In the year ahead which countries do you think will be most important to Indonesia as export markets?

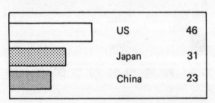

US	46
Japan	31
China	23

0 10 20 30 40 50 60 70 80 90 100%

Economic prospects: On a scale of one, for very poor, to 10, for very good, how would you rate the likely economic performance of the following economies in the next 12 months?

	Average Rating	Proportion who gave a rating
Japan	8.37	100%
South Korea	7.47	98%
Singapore	7.35	100%
Indonesia	7.27	100%
Taiwan	7.25	99%
US	7.12	97%
China	6.98	94%
Malaysia	6.87	97%
Hong Kong	6.81	98%
Thailand	6.73	99%
Australia	6.27	90%
New Zealand	6.05	89%
India	5.28	91%
Vietnam	5.27	86%
Sri Lanka	5.26	87%
Philippines	5.08	98%

CORPORATE

Company prospects: Would you say you are more optimistic, about the same, or less optimistic about your company's prospects than you were six months ago?

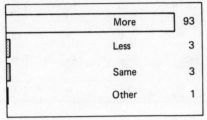

More	93
Less	3
Same	3
Other	1

0 10 20 30 40 50 60 70 80 90 100%

Company performance: Overall, would you say that your company is doing well, badly, or neither?

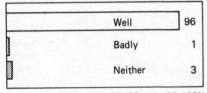

Well	96
Badly	1
Neither	3

0 10 20 30 40 50 60 70 80 90 100%

Gross profits: During the last six months, has the trend of your gross profits been up, down, or the same compared with the same period last year?

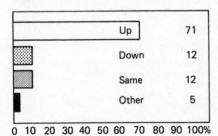

Up	71
Down	12
Same	12
Other	5

0 10 20 30 40 50 60 70 80 90 100%

Turnover: During the last six months, have your company's turnover/billings compared with the same period last year gone up, stayed the same or gone down (i.e. in real terms excluding the effects of inflation)?

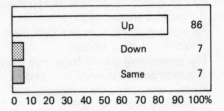

Up	86
Down	7
Same	7

0 10 20 30 40 50 60 70 80 90 100%

Staffing levels: Do you expect employment levels in your company over the next six months to rise, decline or remain unchanged?

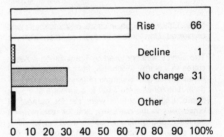

Rise	66
Decline	1
No change	31
Other	2

0 10 20 30 40 50 60 70 80 90 100%

Concern for company future: Which of the following areas do you expect to be your main business concern during the next six months? (Multiple responses possible)

Tight competition	49
Cashflow	10
High interest rates	9
Industrial unrest	6
Speed or service or deliveries	4
Insufficient demand	4
Fixed asset capacity	2
Devaluation	2
Labour supply	1
Others	7

Hunting with the Tigers

Attitudes towards foreign firms: Do you agree with the following statements?

	Agree	Disagree	Don't know	No answer
Foreign companies make an important contribution to Indonesia's economy	80	10	9	1
Foreign companies provide an important source of employment	74	15	10	1
Foreign companies stimulate local firms to become more efficient	86	8	5	1
The government should encourage more foreign firms to operate in Indonesia	51	28	20	1
Foreign companies are necessary to generate economic growth	78	12	9	1

Note: 'Other' category in charts refers to those who answered 'Don't know' or declined to answer.

The survey was compiled by Frank Small & Associates in Jakarta, Indonesia, from telephone interviews with a quota sample of businessmen. Business directories were used to conduct a sampling frame. Eligibility criteria were set for number of employees in the company, and for respondent's seniority, and company quotas were set for different company types. Interviewing took place between Dec 4 and 20. A response rate of 42% among eligible companies was achieved.

Respondents had the following company titles: President 2; vice president 5; director 48; general manager 3; manager 36; controller 1; accountant 2; executive 1; others 2. In terms of their companies' activities, 25% are in manufacturing; 22% in banking, insurance or finance; 28% in imports, exports or trading; and 25% in other sectors. The number of staff employed by the companies broke down as follows: 25-100 employees, 59 companies; 250-499, 18 companies; 500-999, 11 companies; 1,000-4,999, 8 companies; More than 5,000, 3 companies.

Investment risk: Indonesia 57

The prospects for stable growth in Indonesia are promising. The economy has received a boost from higher oil prices following the Gulf crisis, and from massive foreign capital inflow last year.

The government actively wooed tourist dollars under the banner of 'Visit Indonesia Year', so higher tourism receipts should help improve its finances further, provided the infrastructure can be improved. All this will cushion the Indonesian economy from a weakening external demand for its non-oil exports.

With better than expected revenue earnings, debt servicing will be less of a burden, and the government can be expected to meet demands for better income distribution.

In the short term, a major challenge for Indonesia is to bring the inflation rate down to a more acceptable level of between 5% to 6%.

Indonesia scored as follows:

1	Inflation	6
2	Interest rate	0
3	GDP growth	7
4	Infrastructure	5
5	Labour: Strife and shortages	8
6	Bureaucratic impediments	4
7	Government intervention	4
8	Threat of armed aggression (internal and external)	8
9	Political volatility	6
10	Business confidence level	9

Investment risk: 57
Last year's score: 51

Reproduced by courtesy of *Asian Business*

REPUBLIC OF KOREA

Nominal GNP: US$237.9bn
GDP real growth: 9.0 per cent
Exports: US$63.1bn (+ 2.8 per cent)
Imports: US$65.1bn (+ 14.6 per cent)
Net foreign debt: US$4.9bn
Trade deficit: US$2.0bn
Population: 43.5m
Work-force: 62.5m (1988)
Unemployment: 2.4 per cent
Inflation (annual CPI): 8.6 per cent
Savings rate: 35.3 per cent
Overseas visitor numbers: 2,728,054 (1989)
Head of State: President Roh Tae-Woo
Head of Government: Prime Minister Chung Won Shik
Ruling party: Democratic Liberal Party (DLP),
    formed from merger of Democratic Justice Party and
    Reunification Democratic Party, Feb 1990.
Other political parties: Party for Peace & Democracy (Kim Dae
    Jung), New Democratic Republican Party (Kim Jong Pil).
Capital city: Seoul (GMT+9 hours)

(Figures for year ending 1990, except where stated)

Membership of international organisations: African Development
Fund, Asian Development Bank, ASPAC, CCC, Colombo Plan, EC
Trade and Co-operation Agreement, ESCAP, FAO, G-77, GATT, IAEA,
IBE, IBRD, ICAC, ICAO, ICCAT, ICMMP, IDA, IDE, IFAD, IFC, IFDF,
IHO, ILO, IMF, IMO, INTELSAT, International Whaling Commission,
Interpol, IOC, IPC, IPU, IRC, ISO, ITU, IWC, UNCTAD, UNDP,
UNESCO, UNIDO, UN Special Fund, UPU, WACL, WHO, WIPO,
WMO, World Bank, WTO

Republic of Korea

(*Source*: DTI)

Brief history

South Korea has recently faced what it believes to be a momentous and long-awaited event in its political history; the simultaneous entry into the United Nations General Assembly by South and North Korea together (largely orchestrated by Mikhail Gorbachev). There now seems to be at least some real possibility of a new openness on the part of northern half of the peninsula and there is much talk of South Korean investment in a proposed free trade zone in the North. If the North shows a 'good' response to recent overtures, some already-tabled proposals such as the reconnection of broken railway links and roads through the demilitarised zone and the joint development of natural resources may well soon come to fruition.

At the moment, Seoul maintains that the two sides should work towards restoring mutual trust through various cultural and economic projects before broaching complex and difficult political and defence issues. South Korea has definitely had its eye for some time on the pools of cheap labour in North Korea which it so desperately needs to avail itself of. Factories set up by South Korea in the North, would also they believe, afford various linguistic and cultural advantages over alternative offshore locations such as those in Latin America.

There is little question that over the past 30 years, South Korea has been the economic miracle of Asia. When Park Chung-Hee seized power in a military coup in 1961, per capita income was well under $100. In 1991 it topped the $5,000 mark for the first time and the country's growth rate is among the highest in the world. This has been achieved not through the exploitation of natural resources, but by hard work and a determination to export. The capital of Korea is Seoul, but other cities accorded 'special' national status are Pusan, Taegu, Inchon and Kwangju.

In 1987, just before it hosted the Olympic Games, South Korea carried out a long overdue democratic revolution as a result of which Roh Tae-Woo was directly elected as President in February 1988 for a five-year term with the inauguration of Korea's sixth republic. The Korean's tendency to factionalism and their unwillingness to compromise have meant that political reform has proved unsettling. In recent months the main cities have been rocked by demonstrations triggered by the deaths of students in police custody. Meanwhile, North Korea has been quick to capitalise on the democratic growing pains of the South by suggesting that the government is unrepresentative and oppressive.

Through his Nordpolitik, President Roh has established diplomatic relations with all the former Soviet satellites in eastern Europe and in April 1991 had an historic meeting in Cheju with his then Soviet counterpart Mikhail Gorbachev. It was Gorbachev who promised to support Korea's application to become a member of the United Nations. Roh is now hoping to achieve an equally amicable state of relations with China and Korean investment in China is certainly accelerating. However, the government in Seoul still has to face a heavily armed rival across the demilitarised zone which bisects the peninsula, while the people's desire for reunification, strengthened by the example of Germany, grows. President Roh has predicted that unity will be achieved by the end of the century. The trouble is, there are forces both within his country and to the north who just might not wait that long.

The country's strengths

- A falling unemployment rate for four out of the last five years, currently 2.6 per cent.
- Nearly 60 per cent of the population is under 60.
- A new (the seventh) Government ten-year plan to strengthen the manufacturing sector with intensive technical training
- A shift from export-led growth to domestic development.
- Increased consumer spending levels.

The country's weaknesses

- The appreciation of the 'won', the Korean currency.
- Rising wage rates, a growth of 20 per cent annually for the last three years.
- Growing trade tensions internationally.
- A national power supply problem, insufficient energy resources with an unremitting increase in demand.
- Heavy investment in R&D equivalent to 3.5 per cent of the GNP necessary to try to catch up or even keep up with the Japanese.

Goals

- To achieve democracy and political maturity.
- A concrete, plausible plan to tackle the trade deficit.
- Measures to cool domestic demand and curb the money supply growth rate.
- To restrain domestic unrest and dissatisfaction – often resulting in street protest and violence.
- To engage in a mutually satisfactory peace pact with North Korea.
- To resolve the reunification, if it is to come about, as peaceably and with as little economic disruption as possible.

Politics

South Korea is largely an authoritarian state, whose trade (and some would say very existence) is dominated by its 'chaebols' (general trading companies) such as Samsung and Hyundai. It can only be said that Korea is at the moment going through a learning process of combined policy formulation and implementation in what we are led to believe is a far more democratic environment than has been previously known. The push for more democracy internally is largely resulting in more expressions of anti-Western, specifically anti-American sentiment.

However, the juggle between immediate concerns, such as the civil unrest of students and farmers in particular, and longer-term issues does not always result in a perfect balance. Far from it. The situation is more of a push-me-pull-you one, with all the disadvantages that such instabilities bring. In the near future Korea will have no choice, if it is to continue on its chosen economic path, but to allow more political freedom as well as far more political accountability.

Domestic economy, current economic policy and forecasts

Korea is currently characterised as a 'little dragon', an aggressive manaufacturer and exporter, and her import/export figures continue to bear this out. Most Japanese executives take the potential Korean threat very seriously, expecting her to be their greatest competitor by the end of the century. The projection is that Korea's total export and import volume in the middle of this decade will more than double that of 1990 to about US$270bn on a customs clearance basis, making the country one of the ten largest trading powers in the world.

That is what the Ministry of Trade and Industry very much hopes will happen for Korea if all their interventionist economic planning bears fruit. The reality may look slightly different, however, by the time 1996 comes around.

Korea, Hong Kong and Singapore all recorded trade deficits in 1991 and Korea has been chalking up record current account deficits of late largely due to soaring imports and all-time high trade deficits with the US. Some government officials have a fairly phlegmatic approach to the whole situation.

One in particular, Kwon Ki-Sung, director of Export Division II at the Ministry of Trade and Industry, as well as the author of a new book outlining the latest developments in global trade, says: 'It is an inevitable trend for global trading partners to face friction in view of the fact that more than US$4 trillion worth of goods are traded annually among 151 countries and 5.1 billion people. That is the situation, and yes, the government will sit back and take the flak while still taking measures to reduce the number of direct hits. It is, after all, the Korean Government's belief that all NICs suffered a setback in their exports to the US and that, despite such nagging problems, the economy will grow by an average 7.5 per cent between 1992 and 1996'. This was stated recently in the seventh five-year plan by the Economic Planning Board (EPB). The plan aims to make the country a net creditor nation by 1995 with a zero net external debt figure in 1994, and a GNP figure of US$492.6bn in 1996, that is up US$272.7bn on the current figure.

Wage hikes brought about by trade union activism, severe manpower shortages in the manufacturing sector and little movement upwards in production and quality have for a long time been compromising Korea's better efforts. The government has announced a number of measures including incentive schemes to tackle the quality problem, encouraging companies to manufacture and market high value-added products and world-class brands abroad, to improve Korea's image as an exporter of relatively inexpensive, low-end goods.

The main stumbling block in the economy has to be the recent growth in Korea's imports. This has far exceeded that of imports, and to compound the problem, the worsening international balance of payments has created what the government now sees as a serious bottleneck to improved export performance. The picture is not a particularly pretty one. Domestic demand must urgently be cooled down (despite the fact that a restrictive import policy cannot be adopted in the face of cries calling Korea 'protectionist') and strict measures will have to be taken to control the money supply. Just how far these succeed will remain to be seen in the coming 24–36 month period. The much called-for opening up of Korea's distribution market to foreign products will, of course, only serve to exacerbate the problem.

On the plus side, the Korean economy's growth can hardly be said to be slow and some sectors, particularly motor cars, food and beverages, petrochemicals and shipbuilding, are still booming. The catalyst to the whole Korean phenomenon though, the electronics sector, is going through adolescent problems.

Banking and finance, equity market outlook, stockmarkets

All banking in Korea comes under the direct control of the Bank of Korea and the Ministry of Finance. By the mid 1990s, Korea should be in a position to export capital and to start to play a larger role in world affairs but firm measures will have to be taken to privatise the Korean commercial banks and to eliminate exchange and interest rate controls.

The truth is that Korea's banks are still in a mess, with hopeless inefficiency in some cases. There had been a failure to pay attention to future requirements in the financial services sector while Korea was rushing ahead with rapid growth throughout the rest of the economy. The deregulation of interest rates has been mooted often enough, only to be frozen recently by the Ministry of Finance. Foreign banks have played a key role in financing trade and in providing funds for capital projects. Joint venture banks, merchant banks and leasing companies have now been established in South Korea with varying degrees of success.

The insurance markets can be said to be opening up graudually as are the opportunities for foreign stockbrokers.

Moves are now said to be afoot to establish a 'north-east Asia' bank to expand regional trade, but to be of particular benefit to South Korea in its dealings with North Korea. According to a recent report in the national economic daily *Seoul Kyungje Shinmoon*, the bank is to be internationally funded and would aim to promote economic exchanges between the two Koreas. The bank will also, it is thought, help in the setting up of special economic zones in both the North and the South and possibly even in the Russian port of Nakhodka. Also planned are industrial parks in south-east Asian countries such as Malaysia, Indonesia and Thailand for the exclusive use of South Korean manufacturers.

The best-known banks are Bank of Korea, Bank of Pusan Ltd, Korea Exchange Bank, Korea Development Bank, Bank of Seoul & Trust Co, Cho Heung Bank Ltd, and Commercial Bank of Korea.

The stockmarket

The Seoul stockmarket, currently capitalised at around $100bn (1991) and around the fifth largest in Asia, was one of the few in the world to remain largely untroubled during the financial upheavals of October 1987. It was not exposed to foreign investment patterns as share ownership by non-Korean interests was still prohibited. For some time Korea has been enjoying a period of high savings and that money has been flowing into the stockmarket which up until recently was relatively small and completely closed. Now it is said that the Korean stock exchange will become the fourth largest in the world by the year 2000.

The situation is now one of major changes in the market, with large measures of deregulation and liberalisation being finally introduced. Some are now expecting a large inrush of money into the stockmarket, mainly from the expatriate financial community.

There are, however, still major conditions attached. From this year, foreign ownership of shares will be allowed up to the level of ten per cent in any one company, but some 70 per cent of companies specified by the Government that are currently listed on the market are subject to yet further restrictions.

At the moment, the main conduit for investment into Korea remains the various 'Korea Funds' and unit trusts. These, together with limited direct investment between them already account for as much as 3.5 per cent of the market, leaving little take-up available up to the ten per cent maximum.

Trade and industry

The Korean market was officially opened to foreign wholesalers and retailers on 1st July 1991 causing the entire domestic industry to shudder at the idea of facing fierce competition in their home market. For the first time ever, foreigners can now set up their own retail outlets for direct marketing in Korea. Now foreign businesses can operate up to ten retail stores, each with an area of no more than 1,000 square metres, up 300 square metres from the previous limit. The items foreigners are still not allowed to sell however (of course, the items they would most like to sell and would probably have the most success in) are tobacco, antiques and works of art, grain, meat, vegetables, fruit, other unclassified food and beverages, pharmaceuticals, books, oil stations, gas stations, cosmetics, coal briquettes and oil and gas retailing. The Japanese did not rush headlong into the market, wary as ever that antipathetic sentiments lie only just below the surface for them and their products. Ironically, foreign importers into Korea are being accused of 'dumping' their products by resorting to excessive price cutting to gain long-term market shares.

While businessmen in the West who missed the boat last time around with Japan now get very excited about the potential of Korea and 'how they will get it right this time', it should be borne in mind that South Korea's market is substantially smaller than Japan's and that the Korean consumers have a much lower per capita income than the Japanese. There is also still not as much market access as all the laws for 'liberalisation' would have us believe.

Until comparatively recently, Korea used to sell its products into overseas markets through a network of small and frequently under-capitalised firms with a sort of 'some you win, some you lose' approach. Today Korea, like Japan, has its 'sogo shosha' or General Trading Companies, but whereas the Japanese entities date back to the late 1870s, the 'chaebol', as they are called in Korea, were created only as recently as 1975 spurred on largely by the government's realisation that it had to take some concerted action to meet head on the oil crisis of the early 1970s.

These new groups were able to take advantage of subsidised trade financing and the easing of restrictions, for them specifically, on the transfer of both funds and personnel in the export drive. More than 15 years on, these giants have gone on to play a major part in turning the country's long-running trade deficits into surpluses. Now the eight

GTCs which remain – Yulsan, Hanil Synthetic Fibre Industry Co Ltd, Samwha Corp, Kum ho and Kukje Corp dropped by the wayside – from the original inception of the programme, such as Samsung, GoldStar (Lucky-Goldstar), Daewoo (pronounced 'tay-oo') and Hyundai are household names all over the world. The others are Sunkyong Ltd, Ssangyong Corp, Hyosung Corp Ltd and, finally, Korea Trading International Inc which is slightly different in that it acts as a clearing house for smaller concerns. The latter remains state-owned while all the others are listed on the stockmarket. Between them they account for about 40 per cent of Korea's total outward shipments in a vast range of goods, from textiles to semiconductors, machinery and automobiles.

While Korea's GTCs may have been inspired by the 'sogo-shosha' there are a number of important differences between them, the main one being that till very recently Korea's have concentrated almost entirely on exports. Japan's on the other hand, were set up to diminish the importance of and dependency on foreign trading companies on whom Japan had relied so heavily for imported goods.

External political pressures resulting from Korea's fast economic growth, and from a general fear in the West (from the EEC and USA) and no less in the East (from ASEAN) that Korea may well become another economic goliath like Japan, are now causing Korean companies and their government to re-appraise their policies. Domestic problems, too, such as the appreciation of the won and rising wage rates are forcing them to rethink their policies and actions.

The emphasis these days, they believe, must change to a renewed drive for imports, as well as the sourcing of vital new raw materials which at present they pay for heavily in foreign currency. Diversification is the key to the survival and growth of the 'chaebol', and must include broader product portfolios and wider market exposure. The companies that are learning the lesson well include Samsung, Sunkyong and Ssangyong. Surprisingly, although Daewoo and Hyundai are present-day giants, their economic future must be somewhat hampered in the long-term by their inherent inability to take on very large-scale natural resource projects overseas.

Many companies in Korea, both large and small, are now seeking to remain competitive by moving their sources of supply of light industrial products away from the high wages environment of Korea to other markets. These include Mexico and other parts of Latin America, as well as China, the former eastern European bloc and other destinations in the Asian-Pacific Rim, such as Saipan, where Korean industry and infrastructural investment and development are welcomed.

The picture is not altogether uncloudy, though, since many of the GTCs have a history of low profitability, unbalanced sales, and hampering by bureaucratic internal administration. Indeed, during the last five years, since the balance of trade moved into surplus and many restrictions on overseas trade were gradually eroded, the predominance of the GTCs has been diminished.

Foreign companies seeking to prise a way into the Korean market should make full use, in the first instance, of the Korea Trade Promotion Corporation (KOTRA). A non-profit state-invested organisation, KOTRA was established in 1962 to carry out government policy relating to foreign trade promotion, and to act as a conduit and liaison office for companies interested in doing business with Korea. They operate a branch network of Korea Trade Centres spanning 69 countries and 80 cities world-wide, as well as the 11 domestic branches and the 55-floor World Trade Centre in Seoul.

The Consultation Office for Overseas Companies will offer informal consultancy on trade and investment procedures and problems and general advice on doing business in Korea. They will also explain trade and industrial policy guidelines and regulations and will act, when necessary, as a government liaison and help with foreign firms' participation in trade exhibitions.

It is said that the average worker is losing his taste for having his nose to the Korean grindstone. He is not sure any more, that an increase in Korea's national wealth will benefit his own personal lifestyle even if it does add to his pocket. Many are said to be disenchanted by the Japanese example which for all its wealth and putative power has made very little real difference to the life of ordinary working folk over the last 15 years.

With the Korean won appreciating ever upwards against the US dollar, domestic manufacturers are getting worried. The combination of the appreciation coupled with eternal wage increase demands make life very difficult for a country that is determined to reach the status of an advanced economy as quickly and surely as possible. The erosion of trade competitiveness in labour-intensive industries is causing Korean manufacturing operations to look elsewhere because they fear that, if they do not, their operations simply may not survive. The militancy of some Korean workers is making offshore production look increasingly attractive.

Nevertheless the domestic market has been relatively strong, some economists would say too strong, and industry in Korea, particularly in the food and beverage, automobiles, shipbuilding and petrochemical sectors has been enjoying a boom.

During the next five-year plan, some 30 or so industrial complexes will be established across the country for small and medium-sized enterprises as well as 35 apartment-style factories for smaller concerns. The government is also hoping to encourage the General Trading Companies to devolve some parts of their production processes to these smaller firms. The manufacturing sector in Korea is expected to grow 9.8 per cent annually during the five-year plan providing that state-of-the-art technology is applied and that the export figures pick up. Employment in manufacturing is expected to increase from 27.4 per cent last year (1991) to 29 per cent in 1996.

South Korea's major industries are automobiles, chemicals, clothing, food processing, electronics, shipbuilding, steel and textiles. Her major imports are grain, machinery, oil, organic chemicals, steel, textiles and transportation equipment. Her major exports are motor cars, clothing and textiles, electrical machinery, fish, footwear, ships and steel. Korea has plentiful resources of coal, graphite, limestone, iron ore and tungsten.

The textile and footwear sector, which may well both soon be faced with a general oversupply in the world market, has in the recent past enjoyed brisk business with exports to the EEC, Hong Kong, and south-east Asian countries, even though they have not fared particularly well in North America generally, or in Japan. Like a number of other industries, textile companies are chronically plagued by labour shortages and lack of investment. Korean businessmen recently launched a homegrown version of British retailer Burberry which is reportedly sweeping the outer garments market. Early last year, perhaps as a reflection of a pro-European buying spree, even for low ticket items, Korea was for some months the largest importer of confectionery from the EEC.

The pharmaceuticals sector is gaining increasing prominence and one company, Samchully Pharmaceutical is said to be producing AZT, the only real medical breakthrough so far in the treatment of AIDS.

The paper industry has been booming but demand is expected to exceed supply soon because of a number of new production lines. Cement has been strong in production, sales and profitability even though some efforts were made by the government to dampen down the construction boom (some 5.7 per cent of the work-force is employed in construction). The oil refining sector boomed, partially as a result of greater demand created by the dramatic increase in the number of cars in the country. Both the steel and petrochemical sectors, however, are facing at best mixed demand and pricing fluctuations.

It is in her electric and electronics sectors, that Korea has the most problems. Sales have been quite sluggish of late and foreign sales of audio equipment and telephones have been stagnant, drastically affected by the cutback in consumer spending all around the Western world. Most electronic makers have been dependent on foreign sales as part of OEM, that is Original Equipment Manufacturing, arrangements. For example, about 30 per cent of Korea's total computer exports are in the OEM category. The semiconductor market has been troubled by the EEC investigation into Korean semiconductors.

Car exports are stagnant at best and auto makers have the burden of having to pay higher wages to their work-force than the rest of the industrial market and this is one of the main reasons for diversification of production into overseas' markets. Hyundai's *Excel* recently became Korea's first car to cross the historic two million unit production mark. In the US this car was marketed as a Japanese car under its own name, the Mitsubishi *Precis*, exactly what it is despite the fact that it is made in Korea. Foreign competition has been threatening the domestic tyre market somewhat since the market opened in July of 1991. The French company, Michelin, the world's largest tyre manufacturer is to open 15 shops in Seoul and other major cities and the Japanese company Bridgestone Tire Co Ltd will open independent retail outlets soon.

Of particular interest is the liberalisation of the production of alcoholic beverages from 1st September 1991 with the issuance of new licences for beer, whisky, brandy and rice wine. Requirements for entering the market vary but capital of 30 billion won is required for beer, five billion won for whisky and four billion for 'soju' rice wine and other refined liquors.

Korea has also become a major exporter of industrial plants since its first venture in 1971 – US$1.0m worth of equipment for a textile plant in Pakistan. This developed into the export of electrical and petrochemical plants, and then into transportation, steel structures, desalination, paper-making and telecommunications. These exports peaked at around US$1.38bn in 1985 but have since then marked a downward trend to around US$500m a year.

The defence industry is blossoming and Western powers are expressing concern more often these days about Korea having a nuclear industry with potential for offensive capacity. Some believe that South Korea may well emerge as a major arms supplier before Japan does. It is certainly looking at the moment to gain great freedom to export, without the present restrictions. A fighter aircraft project is in progress, and many kinds of military equipment have been in production for several decades.

Korea's brand new 'technopolis', Taedok, is in central Korea, just two hours' drive from Seoul in the town of Taejon and is now home to the Korea Advanced Institute of Science and Technology (KAIST). The literally intelligent city aims to attract 3,000 'brains' to work day and night in its chemistry, energy, machinery, resources, telecommunications, electronics and, believe it or not, ginseng research institutes, trying to promote Korea's leading edge. The equivalent, it is supposed, of Japan's Tsukuba, Taejon will be the site of *Expo '93*.

Companies and businessmen of note

Daewoo Corp (pronounced 'tay-oo')
Hyosung Corp Ltd
Hyundai Corp (Chung Ju-Yung, founder and honorary chairman)

Hyundai Motor Co Ltd
Korea Electric Co
Korea Trading International Inc
Lucky-Goldstar (trading company)
Pohang Iron & Steel Co Ltd
Samsung Co Ltd (trading company)
Samsung Electronics Co Ltd
Ssangyong Corp
Sunkyong Ltd
Yukong Ltd (oil)

A thorough study of the history, as well as of both the annual and stockbrokers' reports (where available), of the companies of note will give you a good idea of the commercial 'inner game' psychology of the countries in which you plan to do business.

Agriculture

Alongside Korea's main five-year economic plan is a plan for the agricultural sector which currently employs some 23.6 per cent of the work-force when combined with those employed in fisheries. This plan is designed to ensure a more balanced economic profile through the construction of small-sized farming industrial zones across the country, with medical facilities, roads, piped water supply and sewerage systems in rural areas. These measures it is hoped will help to increase farmers' incomes and, as a whole, give a major shot in the arm to the sector.

However, while Korea, along with Japan and other food importing nations, would like to keep at least what they see as minimum protection for their farming sector, the major world food exporters are continuing, of course, to push for full market liberalisation in agricultural products as was seen at the Uruguay Round multilateral trade talks. The US is insistent that agriculture and fisheries, like intellectual property rights and services, should be subject to GATT trade regulations. Koreans are worried particularly that this will leave their rice sector defenceless in an open market and would therefore usher in the demise of rural Korean life as they now know it. Nevertheless 131 agricultural, forestry and fisheries products will between 1992 and 1994 become open to foreign competition, including frozen fruit and molasses in the first year. The US and the EEC are also insisting that frozen fowl and squid, as well as fresh and processed cheese, honey, oranges, grapes and apples also be deregulated.

The government-subsidised agricultural output of Korea still comes mostly from the country's smallholders whose crops are mostly barley, rice, sweet and regular potatoes and a number of kinds of vegetables and fruit, most notably pears. It is anticipated, however, that a number of these punitive import tariffs and outright bans on some consumer foods will be removed in the not too distant future. Animal feed is not produced in sufficient quantity for the burgeoning livestock production (cattle, pigs and poultry) so mostly has to be imported.

Korea's fisheries industry, constrained as it is by international boundary limitations, is nevertheless an important source of export earnings for the country, providing more than US$1.2m per annum. The deepsea fishing industry has set its sights on the northern Pacific waters near the Siberian coast and after an initial Korea-Soviet fishing co-operation pact was concluded three years ago, a number of joint ventures have been established in the region.

The forestry sector is enjoying growth with production of plywood and other materials for export as well as newsprint.

Tourism

South Korea has now greatly relaxed travel restrictions for its citizens but it also now positively encourages people to go abroad to set up businesses or to make other investments. Where the Japanese go, the Koreans will surely follow and, like the Japanese, the Koreans have begun buying into foreign property in North America, Australia and New Zealand.

Infrastructure

Half a dozen or more infrastructural construction projects are now either underway or on the drawing board.These include development of the port of Pusan in the south, a third international airport at Chongju and an expansion of the main international gateway to South Korea, Seoul's Kimpo Airport.

Communications

The entire telecommunications network in Korea falls under the jurisdiction of two main bodies, the state-run Korean Telecommunication Authority (KTA) and the Data Communications Corporation of Korea (DACOM). Until comparatively recently the government owned a 51 per cent controlling stake in DACOM which it has now sold, while some 30 per cent was owned by the KTA and the rest is privately owned. There is a great deal of external pressure being applied from both the US and the EEC to ensure that South Korea does open this lucrative market to foreign competition. Since there is a large measure of liberalisation taking place in other sectors, it is not that unlikely that the government will keep its word and open up the telecommunications sector within the next two years or so.

ISDN is currently undergoing a trial operation in Korea by the Korean Telecommunication Authority and is expected to be fully commercialised with the necessary digitalised phone lines available in Seoul in 1992. It is expected that the network will be extended to all major cities by 1996 and throughout the country by 2001. As it is, the country currently has some 15 million or more domestic phone lines alone with a staggering 14.5 per cent increase over the period 1989-90. That means that one out of every three Koreans now has access to a home phone.

Extensive research and development has been underway by many companies and major universities for some time into new phones and products for the ISDN service. These herald the dawning of what the government hopes will be 'the welfare telecommunications era'. The ideal is that all homes and offices should have a phone and linked PC, whether networked or stand-alone, for the transmission and reception of all information whether oral or visual. Services such as cordless phones and linking to overseas data networks have been available for some years.

Transportation

Seoul and other major cities throughout Korea are linked by modern roads of superior international class, some of them four-lane highways. Elsewhere, however, their condition is often very unsatisfactory. All towns are linked by the railway network and buses are plentiful and cheap. Korean Air Lines operates on a daily basis to most major domestic cities. There is a daily ferry service from Pusan in the south to Shimonoseki, Japan.

South Korea's main ports are Pusan, Inchon, Masam, Ulsan, Mokpo, Kunsan and Yosu. Her once heavily protected shipping industry is now facing liberalisation in exactly the same way as other parts of the domestic economy. In-country branch offices and joint ventures by overseas shipping lines have been permitted since 1989 and deregulation of the inland container trucking market has also started. By 1992, so-called 'outsiders' will be allowed to compete on long-haul sea routes, and on South-Korea/Japan and other inter-Asian routes from 1995. The Korea Shipowners' Association figures show that the market share of South Korean-owned ships slipped in 1990 to 36.3 per cent from 45 per cent just over five years ago. With the Shipping Industry Rationalisation Plan, the Korean Government dealt with the bankruptcies and losses from the global shipping recession in the early 1980s by the pruning and merging of lines.

Conferences, conventions and trade fairs

A large number of conferences, conventions and trade fairs are held in Korea each year mostly organised by the new Korea Exhibition Center (KOEX) which opened just three years ago and is part of the World Trade Center in Seoul (tel 02-553 7907, fax 557 5784). Of particular interest is the CAD/CAM and Graphics Exhibition (formerly the Korea International Computer Graphics Exhibition), organised by the Korea Exhibition Center in conjunction with the Ministry of Trade and Industry and the Ministry of Science and Technology. Others worth noting include the Seoul Instrument exhibition, KOAMI (the Korea Association of Machinery Industry), and KOFAPS, (the Korea International Factory Automation/Precision instruments show) which is held every two years to introduce factory automation products and related technologies. The last KOFAPS drew 68 companies from six countries and attracted around 200,000 visitors.

Taxation

Visitors who stay in Korea for longer than 183 days must pay tax at a rate somewhere between 36 and 55 per cent on assessed earned income and on allowances which arise both in Korea and overseas. A tax clearance certificate must be presented when leaving the country after a stay exceeding this duration.

Exchange rates and currency positioning relative to US$

The currency is the 'won' (KW, ie Korean won) which is split into 100 'chon' and converted to the US dollar at about 715 won to the dollar. The local currency is not convertible outside Korea and foreign currency must be declared on arrival and on departure.

The people, their languages, education and religion

The people are 100 per cent Korean and the main language is Korean. This is based largely on Chinese vocabulary but is also of Mongolian origin. The phonetic written script is called 'Hangul'. Japanese is quite widely spoken and the use of English, especially in business circles, is on the increase. The main religions of Korea are Confucianism, Sheminism and Buddhism.

Korea's literacy rate is among the highest in the Asian-Pacific Rim at around 93 per cent. There are nearly ten million primary and secondary school students and just over one million people in full-time tertiary education.

Please note that South Korea is officially still at war with the North, so air-raid practices are still held every month on or around the 15th when everyone has to clear the streets for one hour. Occasionally, you may also hear a very loud thud or din in the distance which is nothing more than a sonic boom from supersonic planes flying way over head and some 35 miles away patrolling the Demilitarised Zone some 35 miles away.

The children of expatriates in Seoul have three English-language schools from which to choose, The Seoul Foreign School (grades 9-12), The Seoul International School (kindergarten to last year of high school), and The Seoul British School (from kindergarten to high school).

Publications of note

The two English-language daily newspapers in Korea are *The Korea Times* and *The Korea Herald* and there are altogether more than 70 published in the native language six days of the week. A useful new business publication, *The Korea Economic Journal*, has also started publication.

The main English-language broadcasting services for both radio and television are provided by part of the US Armed Forces, the Far East Network, specifically the Armed Forces Korea Network. This service is generally available in most Western-style quality hotels. There are 30 or more Korean television stations. Recently three new FM stations started up including a Buddhist station, a Catholic station and a state-of-the-traffic station. Experimental cable television and private channel television operations are also in progress.

Visa and health requirements

Non-business visitors do not usually need visas providing they have a ticket showing confirmed onward reservations. If, however, you plan to stay for more than 80 days you must have a letter of invitation from a local Korean business and demonstrable means of financial support.

Hepatitis is said to be on the rampage in Korea so be sure to take all the usual precautions by not drinking water of unknown quality or eating dubious vegetables. A certificate for a cholera jab might be a good idea.

A slightly brighter view

South Korean executives are cautiously confident about business. Their overall optimism is reflected in the *Asian Business* confidence index, which was 69, up from 63.

In particular there is a marked improvement from last year in the way they perceive the economy and their own companies' prospects. No less than 42% of the respondents were optimistic about the country's economic prospects; last year the figure was only 30%. And this year 63% were enthusiastic about prospects for their own companies compared with 55% last year.

One reason for the greater optimism, the survey shows, is the improved labour supply situation. Last year, labour supply topped the list of executives' concerns. This year it was relegated to second place, overtaken by worry about tight competition.

But the outlook is by no means all rosy. One revealing statistic is the way Korean businessmen perceive economic prospects vis-à-vis other countries: They rate Korea behind Australia, New Zealand and the US, all of which have considerable economic problems, and see themselves on a par with anxiety-ridden Hong Kong.

One specific problem is indicated by the high number of respondents worried about the possibility of greater US trade protectionism. Four out of five say they are concerned, which may indicate more strenuous efforts will be made to diversify South Korea's markets.

South Korea confidence index: 69

Asian Business provides readers with a Confidence Index for each country surveyed. To compare the results of confidence surveys conducted around the region, we process the data from each survey and (in conjunction with Frank Small & Associates) arrive at a numerical rating for each country. This index measures the following six criteria used in the survey: local market, export market, turnover, profits, company prospects and economy.

ECONOMIC/POLITICAL

National economy: Are you more optimistic about the national economy than you were six months ago? Less? About the same?

Local market: During the last six months, has your company been operating in an expanding, a static, or a contracting local market?

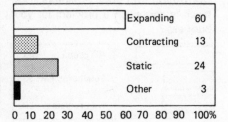

More	42
Less	30
Same	22
Other	6

0 10 20 30 40 50 60 70 80 90 100%

Expanding	60
Contracting	13
Static	24
Other	3

0 10 20 30 40 50 60 70 80 90 100%

Hunting with the Tigers

Export market: During the last six months, has your company been operating in an expanding, a static, or a contracting export market?

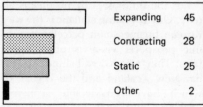

Expanding	45
Contracting	28
Static	25
Other	2

0 10 20 30 40 50 60 70 80 90 100%

Education: How good is the South Korean education system at producing enough graduates with the technological skills required by the business?

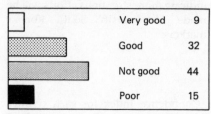

Very good	9
Good	32
Not good	44
Poor	15

0 10 20 30 40 50 60 70 80 90 100%

North Korea: Will a more liberal policy in North Korea help or hinder your business?

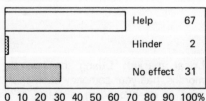

Help	67
Hinder	2
No effect	31

0 10 20 30 40 50 60 70 80 90 100%

Corruption and your business: How much is corruption a problem for your business?

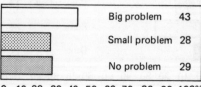

Big problem	43
Small problem	28
No problem	29

0 10 20 30 40 50 60 70 80 90 100%

Corruption and the economy: How much is corruption a problem for the economy?

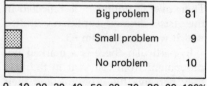

Big problem	81
Small problem	9
No problem	10

0 10 20 30 40 50 60 70 80 90 100%

US Protectionism: Are you concerned about current trends of US protectionism?

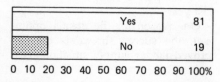

Yes	81
No	19

0 10 20 30 40 50 60 70 80 90 100%

Financial liberalisation: What will be the effects of financial liberalisation on the local market?

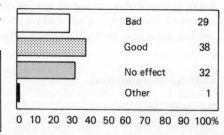

Bad	29
Good	38
No effect	32
Other	1

0 10 20 30 40 50 60 70 80 90 100%

Manpower shortage: What effect will a shortage of manual or technical manpower have on your business?

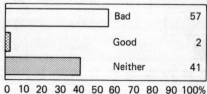

Bad	57
Good	2
Neither	41

0 10 20 30 40 50 60 70 80 90 100%

114

Economic prospects: On a scale of one, for very poor, to 10, for very good, how would you rate the likely economic performance of the following economies in the next 12 months?

	Average Rating	Proportion who gave a rating
Japan	7.7	100%
Taiwan	6.5	100%
Australia	6.5	99%
US	6.4	100%
New Zealand	5.9	97%
Hong Kong	5.8	100%
South Korea	5.8	100%
Singapore	5.7	100%
Malaysia	5.6	100%
China	5.6	99%
Thailand	5.4	100%
Indonesia	5.4	100%
Philippines	4.8	100%
India	4.7	99%
Sri Lanka	4.3	99%
Vietnam	4.1	99%

CORPORATE

Company prospects: Would you say you are more optimistic, about the same, or less optimistic about your company's prospects than you were six months ago?

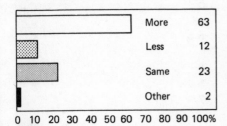

More	63
Less	12
Same	23
Other	2

0 10 20 30 40 50 60 70 80 90 100%

Company performance: Overall, how would you say that your company is doing?

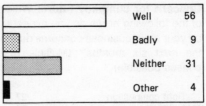

Well	56
Badly	9
Neither	31
Other	4

0 10 20 30 40 50 60 70 80 90 100%

Gross profits: During the last six months, has the trend of your gross profits been up, down, or the same compared with the same period last year?

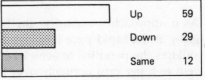

Up	59
Down	29
Same	12

0 10 20 30 40 50 60 70 80 90 100%

Turnover: During the last six months, have your company's turnover/billings compared with the same period last year gone up, stayed the same or gone down (i.e. in real terms excluding the effects of inflation)?

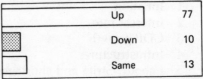

Up	77
Down	10
Same	13

0 10 20 30 40 50 60 70 80 90 100%

Staffing levels: Do you expect employment levels in your company over the next six months to rise, fall or stay the same?

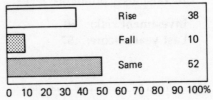

Rise	38
Fall	10
Same	52

0 10 20 30 40 50 60 70 80 90 100%

Concern for company future: Which of the following areas do you expect to be your main business concerns during the next six months? (Multiple responses possible).

Tight competition	27
Tight labour supply	20
Industrial unrest	13
Cashflow	8
Insufficient demand	7

High interest rates	6
Availability of cost of raw materials	5
Political instability	5
Devaluation	3
Fixed asset capacity	2
Other	4

The survey was compiled by Frank Small & Associates in Seoul, South Korea, in April 1991, from telephone interviews with a quota sample of businessmen.

Note: 'Other' category in charts includes those who answered 'Don't know' or declined to answer.

Investment risk: South Korea 60

As it approaches maturity, the South Korean economy clearly cannot grow at the rapid pace it enjoyed in the mid-to-late 1980s. That said, it still has the potential to achieve a stable, relatively high growth of 7 per cent to 8 per cent annually over the next five years.

The main challenge for Seoul is economic management. The government of president Roh Tae-Woo has a tendency to stand policy on its head in order to achieve short-term objectives.

Unless the government can display greater consistency in its policy making and management, it risks doing more harm than good to the economy.

South Korea scored as follows:

1	Inflation	5
2	Interest rate	3
3	GDP growth	8
4	Infrastructure	8
5	Labour: Strife and shortages	5
6	Bureaucratic impediments	5
7	Government intervention in business	6
8	Threat of armed aggression (internal and external)	8
9	Political volatility	5
10	Business confidence level	7

Investment risk: 60
Last year's score: 57

Reproduced by courtesy of *Asian Business*

FEDERATION OF MALAYSIA

Nominal GDP: US$42.6bn/M$115.1bn
GDP real growth: 10 per cent
Exports: US$28.9bn (+ 16.6 per cent)
Imports: US$27.2bn (+ 30.1 per cent)
Net foreign debt: US$15.3bn (35.9 per cent of GDP)
Trade surplus: US$1.7bn
Population: 17m (1989)
Work-force: 6,662,000
Unemployment: 6.0 per cent
Average factory wage (US$): 260
Inflation (annual CPI): 3.1 per cent
Savings rate: 30.9 per cent
Overseas visitor numbers: 7.9m (1988)
Head of State: (The King) Yang di-Pertuan Agung –
  HM Sultan Azlan Muhibuddin Shah Ibni Al-Marhum,
  Sultan Yussuf Izzuddin Ghafarullahu-Lahu Shah (Sultan of Perak)
Head of Government: Dr Mahathir bin Muhammad
  (formally, Hon. Datuk Seri Dr Mahathir bin Muhammad)
Ruling party: National Front Coalition (Barisan Nasional).
Other political parties: Democratic Action Party
  The ruling party is a coalition of UMNO (United Malays National
  Organisation), Malaysia Chinese Association, Malaysian Indian
  Congress, and others. Dr Mahathir bin Muhammad is the
  president of UMNO.
Capital city: Kuala Lumpur (GMT+8 hours)
            (Figures for year ending 1990, unless otherwise stated)

Membership of international organisations: ANEPC, ASEAN, Asian
Development Bank, Association of Tin Producing Countries, CCC,
Colombo Plan, The Commonwealth, Economic and Social Commission
for Asia and the Pacific, The EC Trade and Co-operation Agreement,
FAO, G-77, GATT, IAEA, IBRD, ICAO, IDA, IFC, ILO, IMF, INTEL-
SAT, Interpol, IPU, IRC, Islamic Conference, Islamic Development
Bank, ITC, ITU, NAM, OIC, UN, UNESCO, UPU, WHO, WMO, World
Bank, WTO.

Peninsular Malaysia

Brief history

Strictly speaking, Malaysia is a hereditary monarchy, but is composed of a federation of 13 states, which are collectively 'ruled' by the constitutionally elected King of Malaysia.

This ruler, who serves a five-year term, is the Yang di-Pertuan Agung, who is chosen in conjunction with the rulers from all the other 'kingdoms'. A council of ministers is also appointed, made up of members of both the House of Representatives and the Senate and others, and chosen by the king. All the sultans of Malaysia are allowed to favour their chosen retainers with titles, if they so wish, and seem to live, as far as publicity and nationalist sentiment is concerned anyway, with all the ceremonial trappings of The Sun King.

Each of the federated states has autonomy to a degree in that it has its own federal constitution and legislative assembly. Some well-known areas of Malaysia, however, specifically Penang and Malacca, as well as Sabah and Sarawak, do not happen to have hereditary rulers. They have governors.

Malaysia covers a total area of some 127,581 square miles and is divided into two distinct areas, peninsular Malaysia and eastern Malaysia. The capital, Kuala Lumpur – or KL as it is more commonly called – is on the western plain of the peninsula. The main towns in Malaysia apart from KL, are Johor Baharu, Georgetown, Ipoh, Kota Kinabalu, Kuching, Malacca, Miri, Sandakan, Shah Alam, and Alor Setar.

The country's strengths

- One of the highest average annual growth rates in income per head in the world for the last two decades.
- The country is resource-rich in commodities, has a well-established business infrastructure and an educated population. It is the world's largest producer of rubber (26 per cent of world output), palm oil (61 per cent) and tin.
- The government approved record £2bn foreign manufacturing investments in the year ending 1989, and as of end of 1991, that figure was running at around 25 per cent of GDP.
- There is good expansion potential with a shift to manufactured exports in the economy, an increased demand for discretionary consumer purchases and countrywide development of rural markets.
- The electronics sector dominates manufacturing employment with some 100,000 workers and 200 companies. Of these nearly one half are US or other foreign companies.
- Imports rose by 40 per cent in 1989 owing to rapid growth and internal infrastructural development. Malaysia is the world's third

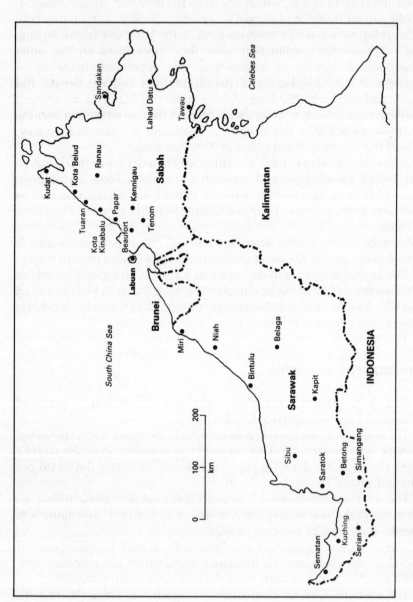

Sarawak and Sabah

Celebes Sea

Sandakan

Lahad Datu

Tawau

Sabah

Kalimantan

Ranau

Kota Belud

Kennigau

Kudat

Tuaran

Papar

Kota
Kinabalu

Beaufort

Tenom

Labuan

Brunei

South China Sea

Belaga

Miri

Niah

INDONESIA

Bintulu

Sarawak

Kapit

200

Simangang

100

Betong

km

Sibu

Saratok

Kuching

0

Sematan

Serian

largest importer of transistors, tubes and valves (after the US and Germany).
• Malaysia is a net oil exporter, underpinning its impressive economic performance, with GDP growth of ten per cent.
• Malaysia is now offering itself as a viable alternative location to both Singapore's capital and technologically intensive industry, and to Thailand's labour-intensive manufacturing and its congested capital, Bangkok.
• The country attracted more direct investment from Taiwan and Korea than any other Asian-Pacific nation in 1989.
• Most economic forecasters predict that it is on the verge of joining the ranks of the NIEs.

The country's weaknesses

• Small domestic market and limited population.
• Malaysia's society is vulnerable to national rivalries and jealousies with strong racial overtones.
• Creeping inflation, now around 4-5 per cent.
• The long-term prospects for reliance on non-oil commodities are not encouraging, but seem to be improving.
• Continued dependence on Singapore as Malaysia's entrepôt is a source of potential weakness.
• The national economic policy seems to be predicated on a high degree of social engineering rather than the best principles of economic management.

Goals

Malaysia is endeavouring to create national competitive advantages over Thailand and Indonesia on its road to achieving national harmony and synchronisation. Its main problem lies in its relatively small domestic market. The vulnerability of its economy to the looming shadows of Islamic fundamentalism and the lingering new economic policy must be eradicated.

Politics

Malaysia may be a monarchy, constitutionally speaking – albeit a collection of diversified monarchies – but great pains are taken in daily and national political life to ensure that everyone understands that the men who really have their hands on the reins are, like Dr Mahathir

Muhammad the Prime Minister, from UMNO. The New United Malay's National Organization has been in power as part of the coalition, the Barisan Nasional, which is the ruling party, since independence in 1957.

The country is governed as a parliamentary democracy with a constitutional monarchy. Under the surface, political matters are more fragile even though in the last general election, October 1990, the ruling coalition retained the two-thirds majority which was needed to be able to effect constitutional amendments. There is continuing resentment between the majority Malays, or Bumiputras (indigenous Malays), and the more economically successful Chinese community. There is also the problem of accommodating the growing Islamic fundamentalism, and there are tensions between peninsular Malaysia and the Borneo states of Sabah and Sarawak.

In his ten years as Prime Minister, Dr Mahathir Muhammad has promoted rapid industrialisation and tried to better the lot of the Bumiputras. In the process, some say he has ridden roughshod over opponents, the Press and the judiciary but he now approaches his second decade in power determined further to increase the Malay stake in the economy and to raise the country's profile as a champion of Third World economic interests.

Domestic economy, current economic policy and forecasts

Malaysia's economic advisers are intent on developing the export-led economy by expanding the manufacturing sector. Special attention will be paid to the expansion of the leading edge or technological capabilities. The commodity-rich sectors of timber and rubber will be finessed with high value-added products, so that they are a little more sheltered from the hazards of simple exposure to the world's commodity prices.

Malaysia is richly diverse. Commodities such as oil, natural gas, tin, rubber, cocoa and a thriving electronics industry, have all contributed to growth of more than eight per cent in 1988 and 1989 and around ten per cent in 1990. A recent blueprint from the Prime Minister calls for the economy to double by the year 2020.

During 1987–90, foreign investment in Malaysia quadrupled to M$33.2bn, up from M$7.6bn in the seven-year period ending in 1986. It is now at about 25 per cent of GDP. This investment is creating jobs and reducing unemployment, and wholly foreign-owned projects in Malaysia consistently generate more jobs than if those projects were established under the auspices of local companies. It is recognised by the government as an important contribution to technical and manufacturing know-how, and to capital and export markets. Today there are investments from more than 30 countries in more than 2,000 joint-venture projects covering a broad range of industries.

This growth in foreign investment was attributable to the Malaysian Government's relaxation of foreign equity ownership in 1986 and has allowed a complete transformation in the economy from a predominantly agrarian base to one that is export-led. The relocation of industrial plants by Japanese and Asian NIE manufacturers, for cheaper labour and currency advantages, has turned the manufacturing sector into an unstoppable machine growing at the rate of 13.7 per cent annually, compared to 6.8 per cent for the economy as a whole. The Japanese Government, for example, intends to relocate half of its labour-intensive consumer electronic firms abroad by 1994 and Malaysia is proving to be a very suitable location. This massive foreign investment has led to the creation of a large urban middle class and is now producing a consumer boom which has started to spread throughout the country to other states.

One of the central themes of current government policy is privatisation, around which all other factors and political concerns must pivot. A master plan was prepared for the government by bankers J. Henry Schroder Wagg & Co Ltd. The programme now includes plans for the privatisation of airport facilities (excluding air traffic control), electricity, railways, ports and telecommunications.

For the third consecutive year, Malaysia's outstanding national debt has fallen and now stands at approximately M$42bn. However, the external debt increased nearly three per cent, partially as a result of the ringgit weakening against the US dollar.

Banking and finance, equity market outlook, stockmarkets

Malaysia believes it now has a full range of domestic and international banking services with about 38 commercial banks in the country including Bank Negara Malaysia and Bank Islam Malaysia. Of these, 22 are locally incorporated and 16 are headquartered in the USA, Europe, Japan and other capital and technology exporting countries. Government development banks offer medium and long-term loans for industry.

US or European banks or financial institutions who may have been considering opening up a branch in Malaysia in the near future are in for a disappointment. No new bank licenses will be issued for the time being to either domestic or foreign financial institutions. The only other course of action open to those interested would be to buy into an existing bank that already has a license and is looking to expand. Potential in the insurance sector, which is regulated by Bank Negara, is just as bleak with little scope for new or start-up business in Malaysia.

On the positive side however, it is now clear from the recently published new Five-Year Plan that Malaysia will be undertaking a large number of fairly major infrastructural projects over the course of the next few years, most of which will need project financing in some form or other from investment bankers. Banks will continue to benefit from the investment inflow into Malaysia and will benefit from the strong loan demand which will result from a requirement that at least 60 per cent of loans for foreign investment projects must come from domestic banking concerns.

Malaysia now has an official offshore financial centre at Labuan (an island off the coast of Sabah) although the physically remote location and haphazard communications are serving as an unwitting deterrent to all but the most enthusiastic against running operations out of there. There is no question in the Government's mind that Labuan must take off, both internationally and domestically, and they are making their best efforts to draw as much attention to its creation and inception as possible.

As far as commodities are concerned, the Kuala Lumpur Stock Exchange is one of the world's most important exchanges.

It was revitalised in December 1989 when it was formally separated from the Singapore Stock Exchange. Trading increased dramatically with volume in 1990 reaching 13.1bn share units, up nearly 30 per cent on the 1989 figure. The value of shares traded in 1990 also went up to M$29.5bn, a 60 per cent increase over 1989. A number of foreign brokerage houses are very active in Malaysia, including W I Carr Sons & Co from the UK, as well as Baring Brothers & Co, Barclays de Zoete Wedd, Smith New Court and Jardine Fleming Securities.

During 1991, the Malaysian stockmarket performed dismally, 'punished' as it was, not for lack of growth as in some countries, but for the effects of too much uncontrolled growth over the last few years. After GDP growth of nearly 10 per cent in 1989 and 1990, the juggernaut has only recently begun to slow with the rate for 1991 still up around 8.5 per cent. Even for 1992 it is not expected to fall below seven per cent. The problems that have hit the equity market have clearly come about as a result of this hyper growth which Bank Negara has only belatedly addressed. Specifically, the symptoms of overheating have been rising inflation, an acutely deteriorating current account and severe labour shortages.

Inflation has risen steadily from around 2.5 per cent in 1989 to its current level between five and six per cent. More spectacular, and more damaging, has been the chronic worsening in the current account. The minor deficit in 1989 of M$0.4 bn blew out to M$4.7bn in 1990 and to around M$14bn in 1991, more than ten per cent of GDP. The bullish analysts who are expert in Malaysia believe that the problem with the current account should begin to sort itself out by 1994 at the latest. This is because, they say, exports should grow rapidly as more foreign investment comes into play.

In the meantime, however, the government clearly had to act and therefore introduced a number of tightening measures including higher interest rates, controls on consumer credit and direct intervention in the domestic money supply. The base lending rate has been pushed up from 7.5 per cent in 1990 to between nine and ten per cent and is expected to continue on and up as the central bank's rather tardy measures take time to bite. The prime objective of these actions is to curb the excessive consumer spending that lies at the heart of both the inflation and current account problems and, concurrently to arrest the decline in gross national savings which, as a percentage of GNP, fell significantly in 1991 from 31 to 26 per cent.

One further additional measure recently became necessary in order to complete the tighter monetary stance. As Malaysian inter-bank rates rose, and US rates eased, banks increasingly exploited this widening differential by borrowing US dollars and lending out ringgit. These swap transactions resulted in a sharp increase in short-term monetary inflows (M\$4.6bn in the 12 months to June 1991) which prompted Bank Negara to impose statutory reserve and liquidity requirements on such foreign liabilities. The government's tougher approach is expected to be continued and indeed extended possibly with the addition of higher import duties, a sales tax, the abolition of withholding tax on savings interest and increased Employer's Provident Fund contributions.

Although Malaysia was late to the Asian-Pacific party, so to speak, in terms of dynamic growth, it is nevertheless fast joining the elite club of 'tigers'. Central to this achievement has been the successful diversification of the economy away from its traditional agricultural base. Some 20 years go, nearly 30 per cent of the country's GDP was in the rural sector and less than 14 per cent in manufacturing. Today, only about 18 per cent is accounted for by agriculture and over 27 per cent by manufacturing. By the end of the decade, these ratios could be approaching ten per cent and 40 per cent respectively.

The massive industrialisation and urbanisation programme will continue to generate stresses and strains on capacity, infrastructure and labour (despite unemployment of five per cent plus, shortages of skilled and unskilled workers are being experienced). However, it will also underpin the corporate sectors whose earnings should continue to grow at a rate of 15 per cent plus in 1992. What is more, after three years of strong profits and numerous rights issues, most companies' financial positions are in a much healthier position. Two years ago, companies on average had net debt amounting to 25 per cent of shareholder's funds. Now they have net cash amounting to seven per cent. With a yield of nearly three per cent and prospective PER of about 15x, Malaysian equities are not historically expensive and once the present situation eases, could perform well. They will therefore once again attract the attentions of international investors.

The disappointing market behaviour of the last 18 months is not irredeemable. Malaysia certainly does not have to fight some of the chronic problems of other countries in the Asian-Pacific. Nor are the problems it does have of such magnitude that investors should remain indefinitely deterred.

The best-known banks are Ban Hin Lee Bank Bhd, Bank Bumiputra Malaysia Bhd, Bank Buruh (Malaysia) Bhd, Bank of Commerce Bhd, Bank Utama (Malaysia) Bhd, Hock Hua Bank Bhd, Malaysian French Bank, Orient Bank Bhd, United Asian Bank Bhd, and United Malayan Banking Corporation Ltd

Trade and industry

The share of capital goods in the country's trade composition has surged dramatically, changing the overall picture, while manufactured goods have overtaken commodities as the country's major exports.

UK exports to Malaysia grew by over one third to £600m in the year ending 1990 (up 36 per cent on the previous year), whilst UK imports from Indonesia grew by nearly one fifth to £780m.

The five top exports to Malaysia from the UK are electrical machinery (18 per cent), transport equipment (17 per cent), road vehicles (eight per cent), general industrial machinery (six per cent) and metalworking machinery (five per cent). Britain's five largest exports are electrical machinery (40 per cent), telecommunications equipment (11 per cent), clothing (eight per cent), cork and wood (seven per cent), road vehicles (five per cent).

The government-run export Credit Refinancing Scheme offers concessionary financing to exporters with the maximum interest rate under this facility currently running at four per cent per annum.

In many ways, Malaysia, of all the Asian-Pacific Rim countries is perhaps the easiest for most Western businesses in which to set up industrial operations. The Malaysians know exactly what they want and are going the right way about getting it. Many of the priority operations they have targeted are well within the technological capabilities of numerous companies in the UK and the EEC, as well as in North America. The Malaysian Industrial Development Authority (PO Box 10618, 50720 Kuala Lumpur; fax 603-255 7970; see Appendix for other addresses) keeps a registry of investors and contractor manufacturers who are looking for joint-ventures with overseas partners.

Malaysia's Industrial Master Plan provides what the government believes will be the thrust for further industrialisation for the next decade and has clearly identified 12 priority industries where foreign investment opportunities are plentiful.

These sectors are:
- In the rubber products industry, where the priority is for the development of such items as radial ply steel-belted passenger car tyres, latex products such as toys, medical latex and fashion footwear.
- In the palm oil sector, where oleo-chemicals and processed palm kernel oil have been designated as priority products.
- In the food processing industry, opportunities exist in meat processing and preparation, cocoa processing and related products, tropical fruit preparation, aquaculture, animal feeds, and the use of agricultural waste and by-products.
- For the wood-based industry, there is considerable scope for the production of decorative mouldings for picture frames, for example, door and window frames,etc.
- In the industrial machinery sector, the priorities include the manufacture of precision machine tools, metal-working and woodworking machine tools, lathes, drilling and boring machines, polishing machines, etc.
- In the non-ferrous metal industry, priority products designated are tin plate, solder, and pewterware.
- In the non-metallic mineral product industry, priority items include ceramic tiles, marble products and high grade calcium carbonated powder.
- In the iron and steel arena, they need the production of steel bars, wire rods, angles and flats.
- The textile industry, the production of yarn and textile products and quality apparel products for export is sought after.

As has already been stated the Japanese and others, particularly Asian NIEs, are relocating their plants to Malaysia to make good use of the cheaper labour and the currency advantage with the result that the manufacturing sector is now growing at a rate of 13.7 per cent per annum. This engine of growth has brought particular benefits to three specific sectors: electrical and electronics, chemicals and textiles. The largest share of Malaysia's manufactured exports belongs to electronic component goods (29.8 per cent), then to textiles (8.2 per cent) and then to chemicals, transport equipment and wood products. The country is a world leader in the export of a number of goods including semiconductors, room air-conditioners, rubber gloves and catheters.

Malaysia is bountifully rich in resources and produces 26 per cent of the world output of natural rubber, and 61 per cent of the world output of palm oil. It is also a leading producer of tropical hardwoods, pepper and cocoa, as well as a net exporter of crude petroleum and natural gas.

Under the Promotion of Investments Act (PIA) 1986, tax incentives are offered by the government for those wishing to invest in the manufacturing, agriculture and tourism sectors. These include Pioneer Status, ie a tax holiday, ranging from five to ten years, as well as an investment tax allowance, export incentives and grants for R&D and training.

More than 140 developed industrial estates and free trade zones have been set up to cater for the needs of export-orientated and other high-tech operations. The price of industrial land ranges from about M$5.00 to around M$161 per square metre, depending upon the location.

Companies of note

Amalgam & Steel Mills
Associated Pan Malaysian
  Cement
Boustead Holding Bhd (trading
  company)
Chemical Company of Malaysia
Consolidated Plantations
Esso Malaysia Bhd
Federal Flour Mills
Genting Associated (casinos and
  leisure)
Harrisons Malaysian Plantations
Magnum Corporation
Malaya United Industries
Malaysia Airline Systems (MAS)
Malaysian International Shipping
  Corp Bhd

Malaysian Mining
Malaysian Tobacco
Multi-Purpose Holdings Bhd
  (conglomerate)
Nali Industries
Palmco Holdings
Perlis Planatations
Petronas
Selangor Dredging
Shell Refining Co (F of M) Ltd
Sime Darby Holding Ltd
Sime Darby Plantations Ltd
Tan Chong Holding Group
Telekom
UMV Corporation
UMW Holdings Sdn Bhd
  (vehicles)

A thorough study of the history, as well as of both the annual and stockbrokers' reports (where available), of the companies of note will give you a good idea of the commercial 'inner game' psychology of the countries in which you plan to do business.

Agriculture

This sector's share of the GDP has fallen further to just 19.4 per cent and low prices for Malaysia's main commodities, cocoa, palm oil and rubber have not helped the situation either.

Rice is the main subsistence crop and the latest technology is being employed to improve yields. Other produce includes cocoa, pepper, coconuts, sugar-cane, pineapples, tobacco, vegetables, sago, tapioca, coffee, tea, maize and groundnuts. Malaysia is also a major producer of timber and timber products including hardwoods.

Tourism

The Government of Malaysia is making diversification of the economy a key point of its policy. As part of this trend, tourism is a main player and has become the sixth largest earner of foreign exchange earnings. This was especially noticeable during 1990 which was dubbed 'Visit Malaysia Year'. The potential for ever-increasing employment of its people is also considered vitally important, as well as the sector's ability, hopefully, to forge stronger bonds of national cohesion and identity in an ethnically diverse population. In keeping with another key government policy, privatisation, funding and input from the private sector is vigorously encouraged with not insignificant incentives. The Fifth Five-Year Plan, which formally came to an end in 1990, specified particularly the development of accommodation, convention centres, resorts, transport, training and duty-free shopping.

Infrastructure

There is a clear realisation amongst key members of the government of Malaysia that unless considerable effort and expense is applied to improving the country's infrastructure, it will be increasingly difficult to attract the high volume of overseas investment it will continue to require. The prime task is to keep infrastructural expansion at such a pace that the continuing development will not necessarily result in worse urban congestion. This is especially important if Malaysia wants to stay competitive as a vehicle for investment with Thailand and Indonesia, who on the face of it, have better facilities.

On present form, the authorities appear to be on top of the task. During the first nine months of 1990, the Malaysian Industrial Development Authority (MIDA) approved investment proposals totalling M$21.3bn (half of them from overseas interests), a 127 per cent increase over the previous year. The largest number of these foreign proposals came from Taiwan, followed by Japan, Indonesia, Iran and then the UK.

A new 800km north-south expressway, due for completion by 1993 at a cost of some M$6.0bn, is being co-ordinated for construction by PLUS, the consortium with 30-year operating rights on the road. A number of British interests are involved in the project including Taylor Woodrow, Sir William Halcrow and Acer/Freeman Fox, as well as financial consultants for the project, Morgan Grenfell.

The demand for power has drastically increased in Malaysia, due of course to the country's rapid economic growth. Long-term energy guidelines were set out in the Fifth Malaysia Plan which ended in 1990 and focused on reducing the country's dependence on oil by diversifying energy resources to hydroelectric, gas and coal. Tenaga National

129

Bhd, the main power company, is to be privatised within the next two years. In the long-term natural gas is likely to become one of Malaysia's main sources of energy since large fields have recently been discovered around the coasts.

Communications

Malaysia's national telecommunications company, Telekom Malaysia is undergoing privatisation and nearly a quarter of its shares have been sold in the stockmarket. Under the Sixth Malaysia Plan, some M$5bn has been allocated by the government to ensure that the telecommunications industry in Malaysia is brought up to par with some of the very best in the Asian-Pacific Rim. The increased consumer demand for, and use of, modern communications gadgetry, such as faxes, cellular phones and the growing array of business communications is making the considerable update crucial. Malaysia otherwise cannot hope to compete as a seriously viable location for running and operating interna-tional businesses.

Transportation

The government is currently working towards a fairly ambitious programme of massive upgrading, including new signalling and communications, as well as the entire electrification of the Peninsular Railway network. This will be operated by KTM (currently being advised by UK company, Transmark) and will significantly improve rail travel. The system will use overhead power lines and the first tranche to be tackled is in the Klang Valley.

Privatisation for Malaysia's airports has been mooted but, as yet, no firm plans are in place. It is envisaged that, in a multi-billion dollar investment programme, plans will be put into action to upgrade KL airport, as well as to develop and upgrade other airports in Penang, Sibu (Sarawak), Kuantan, Terengganu and, of course, the offshore financial centre of Labuan.

Conferences, conventions and trade fairs

Several international trade fairs are held each year, among them are specific fairs for the Defense Asia Exhibition, Industrial Development Technology, Machinery and Equipment.

Taxation

Malaysia has double taxation agreements with 24 countries.

Exchange rates and currency positioning relative to US$

The unit of currency is the ringgit (Malaysian dollar) which is made up of 100 sen and there are about five dollars to one pound sterling.

With regard to foreign exchange regulations, all payments abroad, including the repatriation of capital and the remittance of profits are completely without hindrance and may be made in most foreign currencies.

The people, their languages, education and religion

The people who are considered to be of greatest importance in Malaysia, especially to Dr Mahathir Muhammad, the prime minister, and most other fundamentalist politicians, are the 55.3 per cent who are 'bumiputras' (sons of the soil) or indigenous Malays. The combined population of the whole of Malaysia is about 17 million people, with three million of those on Sabah and Sarawak made up mostly of ethnic peoples. (Both Sabah and Kelantan, incidentally, have opposition-run state governments.) Other significant groups include the Malay Chinese (about 33 per cent) and the Indians (about ten per cent). Both of these groups were brought in as indentured labourers in the nineteenth century to work in the mines and plantations, but the Indians very quickly turned to the professions, most notably the law. Acutely aware that such a small population will never constitute the vital force of an NIC, the Prime Minister is doing all he can to encourage a national population boom and it looks as though he may be succeeding. The current population growth rate runs at a high 2.2 per cent annually.

English is very widely spoken throughout Malaysia, being an old member of what some elderly colonels refer to as the 'pith helmet brigade'. Britain has traditionally had historical ties with Malaysia and today such companies as ICI, Newey Group Ltd, Multitone Electric, Blue Circle Industries, Cadbury Schweppes, and Guinness are in operation in the country.

Nevertheless, Malaysia takes pride in its own official language, Bahasa Malay. A number of Chinese dialects are also widely spoken including Cantonese, Hokkien and Mandarin), and Punjabi and Tamil are spoken by the members of Malaysia's Indian community. The ethnic Malays on Sabah and Sarawak, the Kadazans, the Ibans, the Land Dayaks, the Bidayuhs and the Melanaus, speak a variety of dialects.

Just under one in three citizens in Malaysia is reputed to be illiterate although this is improving. There are 3.3 million children currently in primary and secondary schools and nearly 34,000 in the tertiary sector at universities and colleges.

The country's official religion is Islam and all Malays are Muslims. Islam is not the state religion since the constitution guarantees freedom of religious belief for all Malaysians, whatever their ethnic group. Most of the Chinese are Buddhists, Confucians or Taoists and a few are Christians. Most of the ethnic Indians are Hindu but some are Muslim, Christian or Sikh.

Publications of note

Malaysia has (apart from Hong Kong's *South China Morning Post*) one of the best English-language newspapers in the Asian-Pacific Rim, *The New Straits Times*. There are also four other English-language newspapers including the well-known *Malay Mail* and *The Business Times*. It is worth remembering that all the news you are digesting will have been channelled through the government-controlled news agency Bernama, so is 'politically correct' according to their particular sensibilities along Islamic fundamentalist lines.

There is one main English-language radio station, as well as Kuala Lumpur's Federal Capital Radio station. Some English-language programmes are shown on both the commercial television station and on the two government-run broadcasting stations.

Visa and health requirements

Passports are required but entry visas are normally granted to visitors on arrival in the country. The visitor passes handed out on arrival do not allow for travel to Sabah and Sarawak. All Commonwealth citizens, citizens of Japan, the US, EEC countries and Korea need no visa for visits of up to three months. ASEAN member country's citizens may stay for up to one month. Citizens of Israel and South Africa are not allowed to enter, or even to transit, Malaysia.

If travelling from an area infected by yellow fever, it is essential that you have a valid certificate of vaccination. Inoculations against cholera, typhoid, hepatitis and polio are recommended, as are anti-malaria tablets, though none of these is mandatory.

Worries about labour supply

Malaysia's economy has boomed so fast that demand is now running ahead of supply. What worries businessmen in Malaysia, and is reflected in the country's confidence index of 81, slightly below last year's figure of 83, though still high in comparison with other countries.

One particular concern is the labour shortage, up sharply this year. This is shown in the higher percentage of respondents who say they are very concerned about the shortage of skilled workers – 73% compared with 61% last year.

By contrast, business executives believe infrastructure will strongly improve with privatisation of public utilities.

One issue which has been resolved is the shape of government economic policy. With the more liberal National Development Plan replacing the New Economic Policy, stressing growth ahead of equity distribution and ditching racial quotas, business executives have given a stunning vote of confidence in Kuala Lumpur's long-term plans. A high 88% of respondents say Malaysia's target – to become a developed country by the year 2020 – is likely to succeed.

Malaysia confidence index: 81

Asian Business provides readers with a Confidence Index for each country surveyed. To compare the results of confidence surveys conducted around the region, we process the data from each survey and (in conjunction with Frank Small & Associates) arrive at a numerical rating for each country. This Confidence Index measures the following six criteria used in the survey: local market, export market, turnover, profits, company prospects and economy.

ECONOMIC/POLITICAL

National economy: Are you more optimistic about the national economy than you were six months ago? Less? About the same?

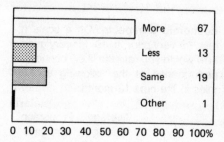

More	67
Less	13
Same	19
Other	1

0 10 20 30 40 50 60 70 80 90 100%

Local market: During the last six months, has your company been operating in an expanding, a static, or a contracting local market?

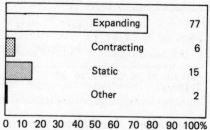

Expanding	77
Contracting	6
Static	15
Other	2

0 10 20 30 40 50 60 70 80 90 100%

Export market: During the last six months, has your company been operating in an expanding, a static, or a contracting export market?

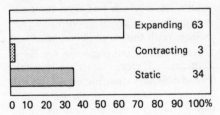

Expanding	63
Contracting	3
Static	34

0 10 20 30 40 50 60 70 80 90 100%

2020 vision: The Malaysian government has announced its vision of Malaysia being a developed country by the year 2020. How likely is this plan to succeed?

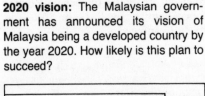

Likely	88
Not likely	3
Other	9

0 10 20 30 40 50 60 70 80 90 100%

Privatisation: Do you expect the infrastructure to become more efficient, or less, as the government privatises more state functions such as postal services, railways and energy?

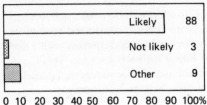

More	92
Less	3
No change	5

0 10 20 30 40 50 60 70 80 90 100%

Infrastructure constraints: Do you feel that the government is placing sufficient emphasis on its effort to ease supply constraints in infrastructure?

Too much	1
Just right	57
Not enough	41
Other	1

0 10 20 30 40 50 60 70 80 90 100%

Levy on foreign workers: The government has proposed a levy on foreign workers. Would such a policy be good or bad for your investments?

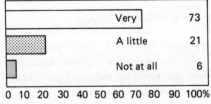

Good	18
Bad	15
Neither	66
Other	1

0 10 20 30 40 50 60 70 80 90 100%

Labour shortage: How concerned is your business about the labour shortage for skilled workers?

Very	73
A little	21
Not at all	6

0 10 20 30 40 50 60 70 80 90 100%

Economic prospects: On a scale of one, for very poor, to 10, for very good, how would you rate the likely economic performance of the following economies in the next 12 months?

	Average Rating	Proportion who gave a rating
Japan	7.3	95%
Singapore	7.2	95%
Malaysia	7.1	97%

134

Taiwan	6.8	94%
Korea	6.8	96%
Thailand	6.7	94%
Hong Kong	6.1	94%
Indonesia	6.0	95%
US	6.0	95%
China	5.2	91%
Vietnam	4.6	92%
New Zealand	4.5	93%
Sri Lanka	4.0	89%
India	3.8	93%
Australia	3.7	93%
Philippines	3.6	95%

Gross profits: During the last six months, has the trend of your gross profits been up, down, or the same compared with the same period last year?

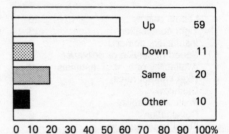

Up	59
Down	11
Same	20
Other	10

CORPORATE

Company prospects: Would you say you are more optimistic, about the same, or less optimistic about your company's prospects than you were six months ago:

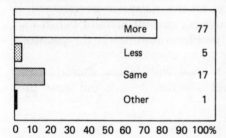

More	77
Less	5
Same	17
Other	1

Turnover: During the last six months, have your company's turnover/billings compared with the same period last year gone up, stayed the same or gone down (ie, in real terms excluding the effects of inflation)?

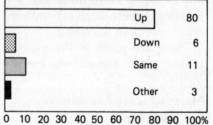

Up	80
Down	6
Same	11
Other	3

Company performance: Overall, would you say that your company is doing:

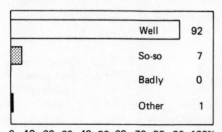

Well	92
So-so	7
Badly	0
Other	1

Staffing levels: Do you expect employment levels in your company over the next six months to rise, fall or stay the same?

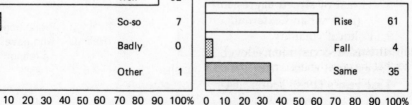

Rise	61
Fall	4
Same	35

Concern for company future: Which of the following areas do you expect to be your main business concern during the next six months? (Multiple responses possible)

Labour supply	36
Tight competition	18
Insufficient demand	8
Speed of service or deliveries	5
Availability or cost of materials	6
High interest rates	6
Cashflow	3
Political instability	2
Devaluation	2
Fixed asset capacity	1
Other	10

The survey was compiled by Frank Small & Associates in Kuala Lumpur, Malaysia, from telephone interviews with a quota sample of businessmen. Business directories were used to construct a sampling frame. Eligibility criteria were set for number of employees in the company and for respondent's seniority, and company quotas were set for different company types. Interviewing took place between July 12 and July 24. A response rate of 43% among eligible companies was achieved.

Respondents had the following company titles: director 25; general manager 16; manager 45; assistant manger 6; accountant 3; executive 1; company secretary 1; controller 3. In terms of their companies' activities, 27% are in manufacturing; 25% in banking, insurance or finance; 24% in imports, exports or trading; and 24% in other sectors.

Note: 'Other' category in charts includes those who answered 'Don't know' or declined to answer.

Investment risk: Malaysia 70

Domestic demand, the main engine of growth, remains strong and investment sentiments are bullish as investors are happy with the more liberal policies of the newly released National Development Plan which replaced the New Economic Policy.

But there are immediate challenges for the Malaysian government. It has to tackle rising inflation, a widening current account deficit and growing government expenditure, problems that reflect the country's rapid economic success.

There are plans in the pipeline to deal with labour shortages and infrastructure constraints, but it will take time to iron out these problems.

Malaysia scored as follows:

1	Inflation	8
2	Interest rate	6
3	GDP growth	9
4	Infrastructure	7
5	Labour: strife and shortages	4
6	Bureaucratic impediments	6
7	Government intervention in business	5
8	Threat of armed aggression (internal and external)	9
9	Political volatility	8
10	Business confidence level	8

Investment risk: 70

Last year's (1990) score: 64

Reproduced by courtesy of *Asian Business*

REPUBLIC OF THE PHILIPPINES

Nominal GDP: US$43.9bn/Peso 1.066.3bn
GNP real growth: 2.1 per cent
Exports: US$8.2bn (+4.7 per cent)
Imports: US$12.2bn (+17.2 per cent)
Net foreign debt: US$28.8bn (65.7 per cent of GDP)
Trade deficit: US$2.7bn
Population: 60,097,000 (1989)
Work-force: 23m (1989)
Unemployment: 17 per cent
Average factory wage: US$87.1
Inflation: 12.7 per cent
Savings rate: 34 per cent
Overseas visitor numbers: 1.2m (1989)
Head of State: President Corazon Aquino
Ruling party: Presidential Party (Lakas ng Bansa) – a coalition of
  the PDP-Laban, Lakas ng Bayan, National Union of Christian
  Democrats, Liberal Party and Bandila.
Other political parties: Grand Alliance for Democracy (UNIDO),
  Partido ng Bayan, Kilusang Bangong Lipunan.
Capital city: Manila (GMT+8 hours)

(Figures for year ending 1990, except where stated)

Membership of international organisations: ASEAN, ASPAC, Asian Development Bank, CCC, Colombo Plan, EC Trade & Co-operation Agreement, ESCAP, FAO, GATT, G–77, IAEA, IBRD, ICAO, IDA, IFAD, ILO, IMF, INTELSAT, Interpol, IPU, IRC, ISO, ITU, UN, UNESCO, UPU, WFTU, WHO, WIPO, WMU, World Bank, WTO.

Brief history

Between the South China Sea and the Pacific Ocean lies a vast archipelago made up of 7,090 islands which constitute the country that is

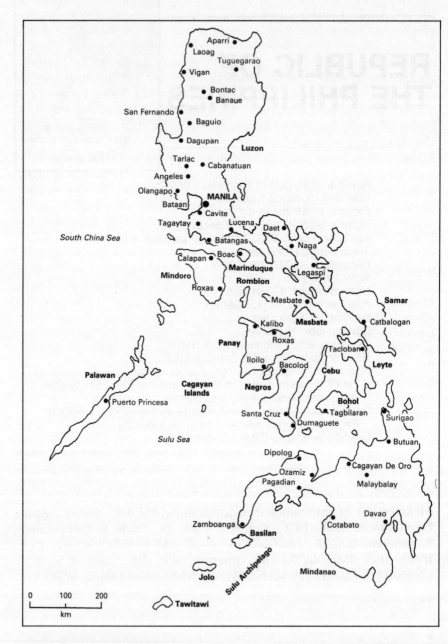

Republic of the Philippines

the Philippines. The eleven largest of these islands combine to make 94 per cent of the entire country's land mass. The interior of the country varies from coastal plain and valleys to marshlands to mountainous, volcanic-rock plateaus. For the most part, the climate is tropical with the hottest months being April and May. The rainy season (in the north of the country mostly) runs from June to November. Humidity varies in the range 65–90 °F.

The capital of the Philippines is Metropolitan Manila on the island of Luzon. It is the most congested conurbation in the country averaging 198 people per square kilometre, and includes Manila, Quezon City, Makati (the banking and financial district), Pasay City, Caloocan City and Pasig. Combined Metro Manila makes for a total population of eight million people. It is here that you will find the centre of government and the industrial and commercial headquarters of the country. The other major population centres are Cebu on Visayas, Davao and Iligan on Mindanao, and Iloilo on Panay. Some 42 per cent of the population live in the urban areas and Mindanao, Negros and the other southern islands are sparsely populated.

The Western world first stumbled across the Philippines during Magellan's voyages of discovery in 1521. It took Spain just 44 years to colonise the country (in 1565) under King Phillip II. It was not until the late nineteenth century that the country was ceded to the United States in 1898 after the Spanish-American War. During the Second World War the Japanese brutally occupied the country and independence was eventually granted on 4th July 1946. Ever since, many Filipinos have lived in the not-so-secret hope that they would somehow or other be magicked into becoming nationals of the fifty-first state of the USA.

The country's strengths

- An inexpensive and very trainable English-speaking work-force.
- A proven track record for successful foreign investment.
- A wide range of opportunities in plantation agriculture and mining.
- An upturn in underlying economic performance evident in recent years.

The country's weaknesses

- Economic and political uncertainty due to the fragile nature of the country's democracy.
- The danger of rapid population growth – consistently exceeding fluctuating economic growth and exacerbating income disparities.
- The need for radical land reform to stem communist insurgency.

- Low agricultural and industrial productivity due to past inefficient investment, arising from protectionism and vested interests.
- High dependence on imported oil and gas (and repatriation of foreign earnings).

Goals

To embrace a policy of complete stabilisation in every aspect of domestic life, but especially in politics and the economy. To pull up the GNP growth rate, to overcome the foreign-debt crisis and to restructure exports towards those which are less import-dependent and can be made value-added using local skills.

Politics

'Cory' Aquino's miraculous ascent to power in the tumultuous events of 1986, in what had largely been a 'guns, goons, and gold' political climate, saw the final downfall of that wicked double act, Ferdinand and Imelda (of the shoes fame) Marcos.

The widely publicised presidential elections responsible for the ousting were held on 7th February 1986. Till then, Marcos had ruled largely unchallenged, with the full blessing of the United States, for the previous 20 years. He had begun his rise as leader of the Nationalist Party and had ruled with martial law for much of the time since 1972. Now, however, the United States was giving him a way out, to an idyllic Hawaiian refuge safe from a political lynching, where he was eventually to die.

The Marcos's removal and the 'yellow power' revolution of the people led by Cory Aquino was supposed to mirror an equally miraculous revitalisation of the economy. Her ascent to the throne of Filipino power was given a strong vote of confidence for a new constitution of February 1987. This was reinforced by elections in May of that year, when she received a large majority in both the senate and the congress. Local elections which finally restored full democracy to the country, rather than the virtual dictatorship under Marcos, were held in January of 1988.

With the demise of Marcos there was supposed to be an instant eradication in the Philippines, as if by magic, of the widespread and endemic vice that is corruption. In its place was to be a time of great peace, stability and supreme justice for people who had known only chaos, disintegration and fear for far too long. Seven or more coup attempts later, the stumbling economy looks remarkably the same fundamentally, despite some strength from fresh capital inflows and lower interest rates and the communist insurgency which continues to thrive throughout much of the countryside.

With an ostensibly more enlightened military leadership in the Philippines with the policy of gradual construction that the government is pursuing, the Communists and their military arm, the New People's Army, are probably not the force they once were. Other rebels have been rounded up, especially those who took part in the 1989 coup, and even the cashiered leader Gregorio Honasan. 'Gringo' as he is familiarly known, steers the 'Reform the Armed Forces' movement from deep 'underground'. These days he is constantly reported to be about to give himself up, despite which there is always coffee-shop talk of yet another coup on the horizon.

Cory Aquino, the wife of the publicly slain former opposition leader Benigno, who dared to challenge Marcos, is now in the final stretch of her six-year presidency. She has not quite turned out to be the Virgin Mary that many people hoped she was going to be. She did manage to introduce a fairly ambitious development plan, currently in progress, that is meant to alleviate poverty, create more work, promote equality and social justice and stabilise the economy to encourage long-term growth. Regardless of whatever she may have achieved, her term will always be seen perhaps as a period of transition from the Marcos dictatorship and the abuses of his cronies to an as yet unknown future rather than something that was substantive on its own merits. The 11th May 1992 will see the nation's 30 million voters choose a successor and nearly a dozen candidates are already lined up. Aquino has declared that she has had enough of politics. She will not seek a second term, that is unless compelled to do so by the 'people power'.

Now the woman who once could do no wrong in the eyes of her people, only has a popularity rating of around 20 per cent and even that is sorely threatened with the showbiz return of Madame Marcos, rosary in hand, to the scene. Imelda went back, without the remains of the late president, to face corruption charges on 80 different counts of defrauding the government out of millions of dollars and of secreting the booty in the elite vaults of Switzerland's private banks. (One charge was of defrauding a special scholarship fund out of money which was supposedly collected to send young people abroad for study.)

She could go to jail for over 400 years if found guilty on all counts but the legal case could take years and cost the government millions. Imelda, of course, will apparently have no trouble meeting her litigation costs with the endless source of hard cash that has been squirreled away. Not so secretly, she is also making it extremely plain that either she or her son, Bong Bong, the Marcos heir apparent, will make a political challenge. Criminal charges, she knows, just rev up the Marcos PR campaign.

One of the other leading contenders in the succession from the ruling Lakas ng Demokratikong Pilipino party (LDP) is Defence Secretary, Fidel Ramos, a full general who took part in the final coup against Marcos and subsequently supported Aquino. Others include Salvador Laurel, Aquino's vice president (but a Marcos man if there ever was one), the House of Representatives Speaker, Ramon Mitra, and the Aquino favourite, Oscar Orbos.

While Filipinos are seeking consolation for their national woes in their favourite pastime, politics, there have in fact been major changes in the form of government. The monolithic business elite has been fragmented slightly and there now seems to be a new sense of political conscious-ness and a slow growth in the middle class.

There is a certain religious influence in the way votes are cast in all the country's elections and the Catholic Bishops Conference of the Philip-pines has been spelling out to congregations the exact qualities that they should seek in candidates. Ramos is not a Catholic which may prove to have been rather inconvenient for him at the final count.

Aquino may be finishing a great deal stronger than anyone might have reasonably predicted. There is still no getting away from the political reality that she has avoided tackling a number of the reforms that might have made a real difference to the country. One example is that of agrarian reform in general and land distribution in particular, perhaps not a surprising omission as she is herself, hypocritically, a substantial landowner. She was always too weak to brave taking certain factions on this and other issues, for fear of alienating those she most needed for support.

During her political tenure there have been a number of attempts by right-wing forces, the most serious in December 1989, to overthrow her and her government. During this nadir, even a great many interested, committed outsiders shook their heads and agreed to virtually write the country off. Such extremes of negativity were unwarranted, it now seems, but even though God and the bishops may have been on her side (in that she has succeeded in surviving so far in one piece), the inherent corruption and greed of those in positions of long-held power still count against her.

Despite the creation of the Philippine National Police (which finally separated the military from the civilian justice system) there are real fears that, with her gone, there may be a reversion to the patronage-style politics of old, or worse. No attempt has really been made to flesh out the merely skeletal democratic framework that Aquino will leave behind her. At the moment the supposed democratic system still clashes at each and every election contest with violence and corruption on a scale unmatched almost anywhere.

The question of US bases in the Philippines has always been a thorny one. They have the largest American military presence away from home. In an ideal world, the US, who prized the locations for their strategic importance would have wanted to keep Subic into the next century and to have gained a seven-year extension on Clark. It was not to be.

In a preliminary vote, the Philippine senate denied the ratification of the Subic Bay US naval base agreement which would have extended its lease for another ten years. The US Defense Secretary Dick Cheney stated that for its part the US would on no terms pull out. Filipino senators voting against the treaty, which would have given their country US$203m in annual compensation, plus US$2.3bn in debt relief, trade concessions and other assistance, cited the end of the Cold War, the presence of nuclear weapons on Philippine soil and the 'one-sidedness' of the treaty as grounds for rejection.

The nationalist bloc in the Philippines has long wanted the US military banished from the bases, while the moderates wanted a more gradual disengagement. Nevertheless, as a result of the decision to deny Subic a further ten-year extension, as well as the closure of Clark through the devastation of Mount Pinatubo, a great many Filipinos will lose their jobs and incomes. (The country's highest still active volcano is not Pinatubo, but Mount Apo in Mindanao at 2,965 metres.) The two bases combined provided a 'market-place' of 20,000, both servicemen and their families, and their demand for products and services will be missed, especially in Olongapo City for whom the base was the *raison d'etre*.

The total US Government expenditure in favour of the Philippines that was at stake was in the region of US$300–400m, with a not dissimilar amount spent by the service people and their dependants. The loss of the bases will cause a putative loss in the Philippines of nearly three quarters of a billion dollars and many now ask themselves if the point of pride is worth such a cost.

The only ray of hope now is that the two countries might sign an assistance agreement to allow the Philippines to receive benefits by way of a financial and technological package whereby the bases could be metamorphosised into industrial centres. For the moment, Clark has been literally stripped of everything worth two pesos. The Philippines was known to be drawing up a US Bases Conversion Plan to achieve this, with export processing zones and commercial and transport hubs as part of a grand scheme. Most people, sadly, are immensely sceptical that such ambitions could have any hope of realisation under the present political and economic clouds.

Domestic economy, current economic policy and forecasts

The economic story of the Philippines is one of fluctuations and uncertainty, far more so than anywhere else in the Asian-Pacific Rim, largely because of political factors. The saddest point is that the cheeriness and affability of the people would make them amongst the most ideal of long-term business partners for foreigners looking to develop Asian-Pacific Rim business interests.

Even now, the favourite point of Filipino debate, is whether or not their country has in fact seen an economic turnaround. As this book goes to press, however, the situation is certainly not looking as bad as it has in the recent past. Foreign investment is increasingly significant, the trade deficit seems to be decreasing around five per cent year on year, export earnings have been growing slightly, the balance of payments showed a US$1bn surplus, and the current account deficit has narrowed nearly 100 per cent.

Since 1986 there has been an increase in economic activity that has allowed a more or less continuous period of stability. It was this stability that helped to create a new breed of Philippine entrepreneurs who should be sought out for the best opportunities of the future.

Aquino believes that the next government now has the building blocks in place which will finally allow the country to turn the corner. Filipinos, for their part, believe they have swallowed enough bitter medicine and the rewards must be imminent. No one knows how long, or if, this so-called stability will last. Such is the nature of the Filipino economic game.

The flip side of this cheery coin are the unwelcome reminders that the gap between rich and poor has, if anything, widened. The three million squatters who now crowd into Manila's ever-extending slums are economic refugees from the ravaged economies of the Filipino countryside which offer little hope of real sustenance for their inhabitants. The rich in the Philippines come from the oligarchy of the Chinese-Filipino moneybags and landowning businessmen. They are said to contribute to the country's ever-growing underground economy through their gambling and other illicit business interests. These interests, which amount to a sort of economic dualism show up nowhere in the country's economic statistics. An enormous amount of tax revenue is being lost and in 1984 only 827,000 tax returns were filed out of a labour force of 19.8 million. It is these Chinese-Filipinos also who are the most significant and vocal supporters of the seemingly nationalist political leaders.

Aquino has always been very proud that the 1988 census showed that poverty had been sharply reduced, from hitting 59 per cent of households to just 49 per cent. In all six million fewer people are now said to no longer live below the poverty line, but this is not a lot of help to those who still do and who feel nothing is being done to alleviate their appalling conditions.

After Cory Aquino's accession to the political throne, the Philippines's economy staged a somewhat surprising (given the odds) but gentle recovery during the period 1986–90. In the relatively calm political environment, real optimism in the business sector stimulated strong domestic demand for goods and services and there was a consequent growth in the country's GNP. The forecast for the coming year from most quarters is a daring five per cent. Nevertheless, inflation has been increasing and reached 19 per cent, year on year in August 1991 the highest level since 1987.

Coupled with these problems there is the seemingly indomitable trade deficit which as of September 1991 stood at US$1.7bn. It is diminishing slightly (around 5 per cent year on year) but constitutes a constant budgetary headache. The previous year had witnessed at one stage an increase of over 100 per cent year on year, a situation that looked as though at one stage it was about to run away with itself to the brink of doom. External debt, though, has dropped slightly to about US$27.2bn.

Many in the region thought that one of the first victims of the Gulf conflict might well be the fragile economy of the Philippines' which could have been side-swiped completely by the fallout. The worst, thankfully, never happened. The key to control now must lie in stabilisation (single-digit inflation) and in getting some kind of growth pattern back into the economy. Policies are beginning to bite. The country even now is still digesting the effects of other measures imposed by the Government such as petrol price hikes, increases in bank reserve requirements (making less funds available in the market) and higher interest rates.

The IMF recently granted the Philippines a new 18-month credit facility (first tranche was US$458m from the IMF and US$174m from Japan's Eximbank) and this together with the recent falling off in a recent domestic demand and the lowering of oil prices has saved the country from a troublesome foreign exchange crisis. The regulations for foreign exchange transactions have now also been loosened up so that letters of credit are allowed for imports of non-essential items. The controversial nine per cent import levy has been reduced to five per cent as of August 1991. While many thought that it was unlikely that alternative sources of revenue would be given congressional approval, the loss was made up by Finance Secretary Jesus Estanislao's imposition of an additional tariff averaging one peso per litre on imported crude oil. Crude oil and petroleum imports have encouragingly risen less than one per cent in the past year.

The official unemployment picture has dramatically declined from 11.1 per cent in 1985 to around eight per cent. This figure is influenced by the source and is probably a long way from the real truth since there are vast pockets of the countryside where there is severe underemployment and people survive only a subsistence level. These people are often entirely dependent on the income of one member of their family who is employed overseas and who remits all his earnings back home to support them. The total amount of money remitted to the Philippines from its overseas nationals is now around US$680m a year. The 7-8 million contract workers who have been through the Middle East and elsewhere are beginning to return sporadically and play a huge part in influencing opinions back home.

Another part of the unemployment problem must lie in the number of domestic businesses going under through financial problems. The number of dissolved companies in the Philippines grew 100 per cent in just one year, according to the Securities and Exchange Commission who pointed out that in June alone last year, 21 firms folded. Unemployment in the manufacturing sector has nevertheless decreased from around 10.9 to 10.4 per cent, but the 'service industries' (which includes low paid work such as working in bars and hawking) had risen to 34.9 per cent by 1989 from 10.9 per cent.

For the near future, the Philippines is desperately making an attempt to encourage funds from abroad up to more helpful levels but many will now want to take a wait-and-see attitude because the instability that has plagued Aquino will not necessarily disappear overnight. Net foreign investments in the country fell by 45 per cent to US$469m in 1990. For 1992, a 125 billion peso target has been set and Japan and Taiwan are particularly targeted to help meet it. Of all the countries that Japan choose for direct investment in the Asian-Pacific Rim, the Philippines has traditionally been the least favoured. Of the total US$14.1bn in Japanese foreign direct investment in Asia during the period 1985–88, the Philippines received only US$288m, just two per cent of the Asian total and seven per cent of the US$4.1bn invested in ASEAN countries. There is nevertheless a renewed Japanese interest in the country as an offshore manufacturing base and at least four major industrial estates have sprouted in conjunction with Japanese interests.

Many of the biggest Japanese enterprises in the Philippines have linked up with powerful political figures or with the business aristocracy. Jose Laurel III, ambassador to Japan in the early 1970s, for example, sits on the board of three Japanese-controlled firms. Now those who remember the pre-war 'pro Japanese' nationalists believe with renewed vigour that, if the Philippines can jump on the Japanese economic bandwagon in this way, they will be able to significantly enhance their very poor business and economic reputation in the region and even in the world. There were always those who said that the Philippines has been fixated by the US for far too long. Just how many of them will be happy that, despite the short-term economic impact of new jobs and investment, this fixation has instantly transferred itself to Japan remains to be seen.

Meanwhile the Filipinos are coming to terms with the devastation caused by the volcanic eruption of Mount Pinatubo which has forced the US to abandon the nearby Clark Air Base. The ethnic Aetas in the area swore that the eruption was a deified ancestor in action, stirred out of his slumber by the incursions of outsiders. Some said that the real blame was on the National Power Corp which was prospecting for geothermal sources of energy. This caused them to drill into the volcano, creating a well which was then plugged up only to subsequently explode. Whatever the cause, paranormal or otherwise, the volcano spewed out around two cubic kilometres of debris destroying crops and causing widespread fatalities. Clouds of ash were deposited over half the country affecting Metro Manila, Palawan and Cebu and as far afield as Cambodia across the South China Sea. Roofs and buildings collapsed and mud flows destroyed roads and bridges. Unfortunately, the Philippine Institute of Vulcanology and Seismology believes that a new phase of eruptions is just beginning, so be warned. Japan has an economic community that prospers in the shadow of volcanoes so maybe the Philippines could take a few leaves out of their book.

This was the third natural disaster to hit the Philippines in less than a year following the earthquake that hit northern Luzon in July 1990 and typhoon *Mike* which swept through the Philippines in November of the same year. Official damage was estimated at around three billion pesos but, given the devastation caused to property and farming areas, was probably much higher. When *Mike* hit Cebu Province, the national Government gave the area only modest economic help for reconstruction and rehabilitation and yet the private sector put in the money that was needed to restore its normal levels of activity and production. The result was that, with a kind of Keynesian pump-priming of the economy, just a short time later everything is back to a relatively normal state. The people are flexible and hardworking and know how to deal with the ever-present threat to them of disaster, from any quarter political or natural.

Banking and finance, equity market outlook, stockmarkets

The Asian Development Bank gave a loan to the Philippines Securities and Exchange Commission of US$200m to improve the transition towards a unified stock exchange (there are two, Makati and Manila, all stocks being listed on both), as well as to develop a capacity for gold and silver futures. A great many of the problems of the Philippines are believed to lie in the infrastructure for capital markets which, by comparison with similar countries in the region, is not a little backward.

It is fairly surprising then, many would think, that just recently some ten foreign brokerages, with heavy research capabilities, have started up operations in this somewhat esoteric and dangerous stockmarket. You would be forgiven for wondering if in fact the market really warrants such attention, given the apparent chaos, but the truth is it probably does. There is real money to be made for those aficionados who have

147

taken pains to study and really know what they are doing. It is not a market for experimentation, however.

The Securities and Exchange Commission of the Philippines declared recently that overall foreign capital invested in local business ventures rose nearly ten per cent year on year in 1991. Since 1987 there has been a rapid listing of new issues and the last year of the Aquino regime has seen total offerings valued at around 15.6bn pesos. This is a real breakthrough given the turbulence of the domestic scene and the fact that the Philippines has the thinnest market in the whole of the Asian-Pacific Rim, some would say not without justification.

Great moves and reorganisations are afoot in the banking sector, such as the privatisation which will take place of some 30 per cent of the Development Bank of the Philippines. A couple of years ago, stock in the government-owned Philippine National Bank was at 170 pesos (in June 1989). Those same shares closed in May 1991 with a 254 per cent appreciation at 432.50 pesos. There is no doubt that low money-market yields and declining interest rates have forced more money out of banks and into the stockmarket. A stockbroker expert in the market now estimates that foreign participation in the two exchanges is now around the US$300m level. Even those most conservative of British institutional fund managers are now said to be dipping their toes in, just in case they miss out on something big.

The Central Bank of the Philippines' statistics show that recently total domestic liquidity has been increasing as have the total money supply and savings and time deposits. The Bank has also rolled over US$100m worth of Treasury Bills to raise extra money to finance the reconstruction of the areas devastated by the eruption of Mount Pinatubo.

Trade and industry

The domestic government is trying to maximise foreign interest through the introduction of more liberal foreign investment laws, with a provision for a transition period allowing unregulated entry (and up to 100 per cent ownership of an entity) to all industries unless they are specifically exempted in the constitution. Priorities for investment have been established in areas with incentives that will give overseas interests higher new rates of return on their money. The Board of Industry has said that approved projects are now well on the rise with those in the manufacturing sector showing the greatest increase.

The Government of the Philippines would like to boost exports by 14 per cent to 9.7bn pesos per annum. The leading export products are in the clothing and textile sector, while the biggest export earners for

Britain in the Philippines are in electrical machinery (£32m), power generating machinery ((£18m) and specialised machinery (£10m).

The country's import expenditure has been increasing gently but export earnings have been growing with electronics accounting for the largest income. Of significant interest is the production of coconut oil (with European prices for this commodity climbing steadily) but the export of coconut products and coconut-based chemicals have been falling.

There is a very active European Chamber of Commerce of the Philippines (3rd Fl, Electra House, 115 Esteban Street, Legaspi Village, Makati, Metro Manila; tel 85-47-47) which represents the common interests of European countries in the Philippines. They will also provide general trade information, business contacts, market reports and investment advice. There is no dedicated Chamber of Commerce for British interests in Manila but the British Ambassador does have an informal advisory group made up of a number of leading businessmen who are active and successful on the local commercial scene.

Companies and businessmen of note

Atlas Consolidated Mining & Development Corp
Ayala Corporation (conglomerate)
Ayala Land
Benguet Corporation (mining)
Lepanto Consolidated Mining
Marsman & Co Inc (trading company)
Metro Drug Corp (pharmaceuticals)
Philex Mining Corp
Philippine Long Distance Telephone Co (PLDT) (telecommunications)
San Miguel Corp (food and beverages)

A thorough study of the history, as well as of both the annual and stockbrokers' reports (where available), of the companies of note will give you a good idea of the commercial 'inner game' psychology of the countries in which you plan to do business.

Agriculture

Cory Aquino's greatest failure, the consensus maintains, has been her total inability to get to real grips with one of her country's most pressing needs, that of agrarian reform. Nevertheless legislation to dilute some of the massive landholdings of multinational corporations, associations

149

and some super-rich individual interests was introduced with great razzmatazz in 1988. A department was duly created whose sole purpose was to tackle the 'comprehensive' redistribution of all public and private agricultural land throughout the country to farmers and farm workers within ten years. The oligarchy of the tiny group of very powerful and tyrannical landowners was to be broken up.

Managed basically through the Land Bank of the Philippines, in conjunction with the department of agriculture and the Agrarian Reform Council, the programme has so far turned out to be anything but comprehensive because progress has been so very slow. In future, the revolutionary scheme stipulates that landowners will only be able to keep a maximum of five hectares, plus three hectares extra each per child aged 15 years or over.

Putative reform apart, however, forestry and agriculture combined are the only sectors in the recent past that have managed to score gains in their share of the economy of nearly four per cent. Manufacturing only moved marginally upwards over the same period. Agriculture, the dominant sector of the economy, had seen its share decline previously from 29.2 per cent in 1985 to around 27 per cent of GNP. It would be wrong to assume, however, that this was as a result of increased industrialisation. Part of the real growth though must to some extent lie in the external demand for aquaculture products which caused a 4.23 per cent growth in the fishery subsector and there seems also to be increased demand for wood and wood products.

The most obvious problem last year was the major eruption of Mount Pinatubo which caused severe dislocation in the agricultural sector where the two main crops are rice ('palay') and corn. Coconuts from the Philippines, the world's largest producer, provide well over eight per cent of the country's export earnings but production is on the way down. Sugar-cane and the growing of coffee also feature strongly and more land is being turned over to bananas, pineapples and mangoes than ever before in order to diversify into new areas to broaden the export base.

The fears of major food shortages never really materialised since rice crops were not threatened as they had already been harvested and yield had been substantially improved anyway by the rice enhancement programme of 1987. Other producing areas in the country were some-how or other able to make up for much of the loss, but the total damage to agricultural lands and crops and stock on a national scale was said to total 3.5bn pesos. The knock-on effect might well turn out to be more serious, however, since planting was naturally delayed and more importantly the ash fall was highly acidic. Even though this has a certain nutritive quality, vast amounts of lime will be needed to stabilise the soil. It will probably be some time before any kind of real equilibrium is restored.

Tourism

The political situation domestically has played havoc with tourism in the Philippines. Enough people from overseas have been caught mid-coup at one time or another for the word to get around that visits to the Philippines, either on business (16 per cent of visitors) or for pleasure, are unwise. Having said that, the country did quite recently manage to achieve over one million visitors a year, the same sort of fairly high levels as a decade ago before the Marcos demise when the country was supposedly at the height of its 'stability'. Fires in major hotels – maybe arson, maybe accident – have not helped keep the figures up though and occurred in some of the newest and very best hotels in the country. Infrastructure still leaves a lot to be desired and there is great scope for tourism development in terms of both provision of buildings and facilities and expertise.

Communications

The majority of the country is covered for telephone services by a network of small companies. Metro Manila is serviced by just one private company for the whole region. Full satellite communications are operational as are telex lines and microwave relay stations.

Transportation

The national carrier of the country is Philippine Air Lines which flies to North America, Europe and throughout the Asian-Pacific Rim and domestically serves 50 cities. A new, second airline will be introduced in the near future following an application made to the Aeronautics Board by Aerolift Corporation.

There are nearly 1000 miles of track along the Philippine National Railways' lines in Luzon. Manila recently saw the opening of the new railway transit system from Monumento in Manila to Baclaran in the south.

Only one quarter of the 150,000 kilometres or so of road in the Philippines is asphalted and the best-known trans-national highway is the Maharlika Road from Cagayan in the north to Davao in the south which was finished at the beginning of the 1980s. Taxis are plentiful and inexpensive but the most popular form of transport is probably the rather hazardous jeepney.

The Philippines has well over 750 ports both public and private up and down the country and there is a fine network of boats and ferries connecting the islands.

151

Taxation

The UK has a double taxation agreement with the Philippines as well as an agreement on Investment Promotion and Protection. World-wide income is taxable in the Philippines for all citizens as well as for resident aliens. Personal income tax is levied on wages up to a maximum, for earnings over 500,000 pesos, of 35 per cent. Corporate income tax is also applied at a standard rate of 35 per cent and resident foreign businesses in the Philippines pay tax on net income. Non-resident aliens who are not working in a profession or running a business but who live in the Philippines for more than 180 days in a year are also liable for tax.

There is ten per cent VAT charged domestically on most goods and services (except for medical and dental care and a few other items), but exports are free from VAT.

Exchange rates and currency positioning relative to US$

The national currency is the peso (100 centavos) and there are roughly 25 pesos to one US dollar.

You are required by law to declare any sum of money brought in greater than US$3,000 as a business visitor or tourist and you are not allowed to take out of the country more dollars than you brought in. You are not allowed to leave with more than 500 pesos.

The people, their languages, education and religion

The people of the Philippines come basically from the same racial group as Malays, but there is very extensive ethnic mixing with Chinese, Indian, Spanish and American influence prevalent throughout its peoples.

The official language of daily use is Tagalog, spoken by more than 40 per cent of the population in the Philippines but English is very widely used. There are dozens of regional dialects and Filipinos can sometimes only talk to each other through the medium of English. There was a time when Spanish was in common currency (a legacy of the colonial past) but now it is very rarely found.

The country is predominantly Roman Catholic, making it the only country in the Asian-Pacific Rim where a majority of the population is Christian. Protestant churches are quite common too in larger cities. Less than 15 per cent of the population is Buddhist and, in the southern regions of the country, specifically Mindanao, there are large numbers of Muslims waging a long-fought battle for secession. Following a referendum held in November 1989, four provinces elected to become autonomous regions.

There is an American International School (from kindergarten right up to the end of high school) in Manila where most of the children from the expatriate population study and there is also a British school for children aged five to 11. Fees for both are relatively high. You must obtain the necessary study permits from the authorities before your children can be enrolled in these schools. Younger children, pre-nursery and kindergarten, are well catered for only in the Makati district where most of the foreign population live and work.

Large luxurious properties to rent in Makati (the most popular expatriate district) are not quite in such demand of late and can be reasonably priced. Hard bargaining can pay dividends.

The traditional Filipino shirt or 'barong' is worn outside the trousers and is the nearest thing the country has to national dress. It is considered smart enough to be worn for business meetings and special ones may be worn for formal occasions. The highland areas of the country do get cool, so a sweater may occasionally be required.

Publications of note

There are eleven main newspapers published in English, including the best known, *Manila Bulletin*, as well as the *Manila Chronicle* and the *Philippine Star*. Apart from these there are about nine other papers in the local Filipino tongue, Tagalog. The Press is generally considered to be amongst the freest, if not always the most responsible, in Asia. Apart from the newspapers themselves, there is a vast stable of specialised publications covering most sectors of industry and commerce, as well as local interest publications.

Economic problems overshadow politics

Poor economic management rather than political instability was the main concern of Philippine business executives interviewed for this *Asian Business* confidence survey. This translates into a low vote of confidence in the economy as reflected in the index score of 60, down from 81.

A high 70% of the respondents being optimistic about the government's capability to put down any further coup attempts, compared with 17% who are pessimistic, shows that political instability is not the main preoccupation.

Many respondents cited import liberalisation and the peso devaluation as having negative effects on the economy, despite the fact that the measures were taken to conform with the IMF requirements on which depend loans essential to preventing the economy from collapsing.

Rather than seeing Manila tied to the IMF's apron strings, the majority of the respondents say the government should take more independent – and drastic measures – such as declaring a moratorium on loan interest payments. No less than 68% of the respondents are in favour of this measure, compared with 21% who are against a moratorium.

At the micro level, the good news is that respondents seem to have a better grasp of corporate management. A high 82% of the respondents say their company is doing well while only 10% recorded bad performance.

Philippines confidence index: 60

Asian Business provides readers with a Confidence Index for each country surveyed. To compare the results of confidence surveys conducted around the region, we process the data from each survey and (in conjunction with Frank Small & Associates) arrive at a numerical rating for each country. This Confidence Index measures the following six criteria used in the survey: local market, export market, turnover, profits, company prospects and economy.

ECONOMIC/POLITICAL

National economy: Are you more optimistic about the national economy than you were six months ago? Less? About the same?

Local market: During the last six months, has your company been operating in an expanding, a static, or a contracting local market?

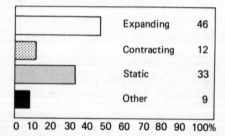

More	18
Less	65
Same	7
Other	10

0 10 20 30 40 50 60 70 80 90 100%

Expanding	46
Contracting	12
Static	33
Other	9

0 10 20 30 40 50 60 70 80 90 100%

Export market: During the last six months, has your company been operating in an expanding, a static, or a contracting export market?

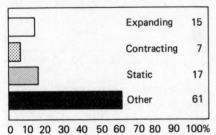

Expanding	15
Contracting	7
Static	17
Other	61

0 10 20 30 40 50 60 70 80 90 100%

Loan payments: Some say that, considering the country's present economic problems, the government should declare a moratorium on interest payments on international loans to the Philippines. Are you for or against such a moratorium?

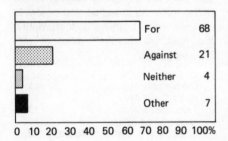

For	68
Against	21
Neither	4
Other	7

0 10 20 30 40 50 60 70 80 90 100%

Import liberalisation: Would you say the effects on the economy of the import liberalisation policy have been positive or negative?

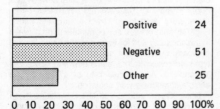

Positive	24
Negative	51
Other	25

0 10 20 30 40 50 60 70 80 90 100%

Political stability: How optimistic are you about the government's ability to withstand another coup attempt?

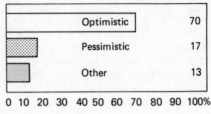

Optimistic	70
Pessimistic	17
Other	13

0 10 20 30 40 50 60 70 80 90 100%

Economic prospects: On a scale of one, for very poor, to 10, for very good, how would you rate the likely economic performance of the following economies in the next 12 months?

	Average Rating	Proportion who gave a rating
Japan	8.7	93%
South Korea	7.5	92%
US	7.4	92%
Singapore	7.3	92%
Taiwan	7.3	91%
Malaysia	6.6	92%
Thailand	6.6	92%
Indonesia	6.4	91%
New Zealand	6.3	82%
Hong Kong	6.3	92%
Australia	5.8	85%
China	5.8	87%
Vietnam	4.5	89%
India	4.2	89%
Philippines	4.2	95%
Sri Lanka	4.0	84%

CORPORATE

Company prospects: Would you say you are more optimistic, about the same, or less optimistic about your company's prospects than you were six months ago?

Hunting with the Tigers

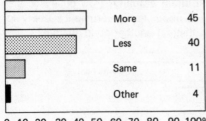

More	45
Less	40
Same	11
Other	4

0 10 20 30 40 50 60 70 80 90 100%

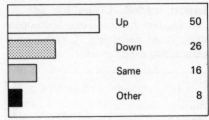

Up	50
Down	26
Same	16
Other	8

0 10 20 30 40 50 60 70 80 90 100%

Staffing levels: Do you expect employment levels in your company over the next six months to rise, fall or remain the same?

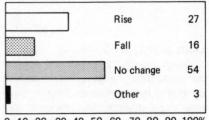

Rise	27
Fall	16
No change	54
Other	3

0 10 20 30 40 50 60 70 80 90 100%

Company performance: Overall, would you say that your company is doing well, badly, or neither?

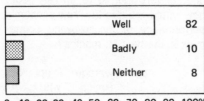

Well	82
Badly	10
Neither	8

0 10 20 30 40 50 60 70 80 90 100%

Gross profits: During the past six months, has the trend of your gross profits been up, down, or the same compared with the same period last year?

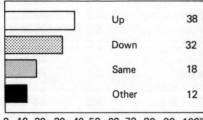

Up	38
Down	32
Same	18
Other	12

0 10 20 30 40 50 60 70 80 90 100%

Turnover: During the last six months, have your company's turnover/billings compared with the same period last year gone up, stayed the same or gone down (ie, in real terms excluding the effects of inflation)?

Concern for company future: Which of the following areas do you expect to be your main business concern during the next six months? (Multiple responses possible)

Devaluation	21
Political stability	17
Tight competition	13
High interest rates	10
Availability or cost of materials	9
Industrial unrest	6
Cashflow	6
Insufficient demand	5
Speed of service or deliveries	4
Fixed asset capacity	1
Labour supply	1
Other	5

The survey was compiled by Frank Small & Associates in Manila from telephone interviews with a quota sample of businessmen. Business directories were used to construct a sampling frame. Eligibility criteria were set for number of employees in the company and for respondent's seniority, and company quotas were set for different company types. Interviewing took place between November 13 and 18. A response rate of 47.4% among eligible companies was achieved.

Note: 'Other' category in charts includes those who answered 'Don't know' or declined to answer.

Investment risk: The Philippines 41

Slower growth is forecast for the Philippines this year, and there is the prospect of overseas Filipino workers being forced home at a time of high unemployment.

Although Manila has devalued the peso to conform with IMF demands, the effect should not be immediate because trade orders are generally placed months in advance. In addition, any increase in demand for Philippine goods is likely to be limited by the global slowdown.

The news is not all bad, however. The economic growth rate of just under 3% may not be exactly spectacular but it is better than the contractions of 1984 and 1985. Also, political stability has much improved over the last year.

The Philippines scored as follows:

1	Inflation	2
2	Interest rate	0
3	Growth	3
4	Infrastructure	4
5	Labour: Strife and shortage	8
6	Bureaucratic impediments	4
7	Government intervention in business	6
8	Threat of armed aggression (internal and external)	3
9	Political volatility	5
10	Business confidence level	6

Total investment risk: 41

Reproduced by courtesy of *Asian Business*

REPUBLIC OF SINGAPORE

Nominal GDP: US$35.9bn/S$62.7bn
GDP real growth: 8.3 per cent
Exports: S$91.9bn (+ 8.9 per cent)
Imports: S$101.1bn (+ 13.5 per cent)
Net foreign debt: negligible
Trade deficit: S$9.3bn
Population: 3,002,800
Work-force: 1.3m
Unemployment: 1.7 per cent
Average factory wage: US$550
Inflation (annual CPI): 3.4 per cent
Savings rate: 44.6 per cent
Overseas visitor numbers: 4.83m
Head of State: President Wee Kim Wee
Head of Government: Prime Minister Goh Chok Tong
Ruling party: People's Action Party
Other political parties: Singapore Democratic Party, Workers' Party.
Capital city: Singapore City (GMT+8 hours)

(Figures for year ending 1990)

Membership of international organisations: ASEAN, Asian Development Bank, Colombo Plan, The Commonwealth, EC Trade and Co-operation Agreement, ESCAP, FC, GATT, IAEA, IBRD, ICAO, IDA, IFAD, IFC, ILO, IMF, IMO, INTELSAT, Interpol, SPF, UN, UNIDO, UPU, WHO, WMO, World Bank, World Energy Conference.

Brief history

Singapore, a small island republic about the size of England's Isle of Wight and not much bigger than Manhattan, has long been convinced that in order for its multi-racial society to survive and thrive, everyone must live in complete social harmony providing the right atmosphere for intense hard work and growth. 'The Lion City', as it likes to be known in

158

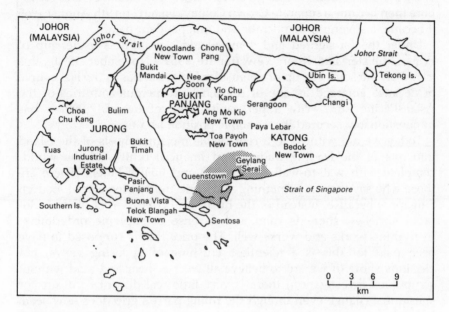

Republic of Singapore

English (the literal translation of its name), really has very little apart from its wits as far as natural resources are concerned to secure its survival. Nevertheless it is fiercely independent and feisty. The deep pride felt by its people that such a small and seemingly defenceless state could overcome not only colonial rule but also the Japanese imperialist tyranny during the occupation, is still never far from the surface.

With one of the best strategic vantage points in the Asian-Pacific Rim, (at the western entrance to the South China Sea), Singapore has its earliest origins in a trading centre, 'Temasek' or 'Sea Town', which was part of Sumatra's Srivijaya empire. Many of Singapore's modern-day government-affiliated corporations bear witness to these early influences with the name 'Temasek'. A Malay prince is once said to have landed on the island and, thinking he saw an exotic red-bodied animal perhaps like a tiger, named the place Lion City or Singa Pura.

The Asian-Pacific regimes throughout the ages thereafter warred over the island, with Java and Siam (Thailand) battling over it and then the Indians, and finally, the British. Sir Stamford Raffles in 1819 finally concluded a treaty with Sultan Hussein of Johore, the local ruler of the Malay Peninsula and Singapore, the 'Temenggong', to set up a trading post at the mouth of the river. Singapore was then occupied by the Japanese from February 1942 until 21st August 1945, when British warships returned and the Japanese finally surrendered. On 1st April

159

1946, the Straits Settlements given to Raffles was dissolved and Singapore then became a separate Crown Colony. Finally, on 9th August 1965 it became a soverign, democratic and independent nation.

Under the far-sighted and some would say ruthless leadership of Prime Minister Lee Kuan Yew (tenure 1959 – November 1990), this island off the southern tip of peninsular Malaysia, has in the last couple of decades emerged as one of the most prosperous countries of the Asian-Pacific Rim. With a per capita GNP of over $12,000, it has unquestionably secured its economic position as a tiger.

Today we are witness to a remarkable metamorphosis of the island into one of the leading trading and financial centres of the world, complete with wall-to-wall skyscrapers and luxury hotels. There are those who say there is something antiseptic and soulless about modern Singapore because, instead of the hustle and confusion of other multiracial societies, there is calm and a sense of supreme orderliness. Everything works and works well. The price that is supposed to have been paid for this is a relentless crushing of opposing views, but elections show (if we are to believe all we see, hear and read without scrupulous investigation) there is very little real dissent or desire for substantial change even though the ruling party's grip does now seem to be slipping very slightly over time.

Lee's successor as Prime Minister, Goh Chok Tong has, probably very wisely, developed a more open style of government and not without comment from his predecessor behind the scenes. He still, however, has to contend with Lee as a cabinet member and secretary-general of the ruling People's Action Party. It is also expected that Lee will succeed to a newly strengthened presidency when the incumbent retires in 1993. Lee's son, Brigadier-General Lee Hsien Loong, is one of the country's two deputy prime ministers and is regarded as Goh's likely successor. There is nothing that would give Lee Kuan Yew more political and personal pleasure than the creation of an indomitable dynasty in Singapore.

The country's strengths

- No corruption.
- Political stability for 26 years.
- Its banking, legal and accounting practices are wholly compatible with standards in both the US and Europe.
- An open economy that is highly attractive to foreign firms and investors, with meaningful incentives.
- An efficient and competitive business infrastructure.
- A position as the regional node for business operations.

- The world's best airport, busiest seaport – used by more than 600 shipping lines – and swiftest container turn-around.
- Unrestricted movement of personnel and goods.
- The hub of financial communications and logistics for the Asian-Pacific Rim.
- A highly educated and hard-working nation of people who are exceptionally computer literate and have the highest standard of English in the Asian-Pacific Rim.

The country's weaknesses

- A small country, physically, with very limited resources, work-force and economy.
- A high exposure to world trade fluctuations.
- Proportionate decline in its economic fortunes compared with the continuing rise of its revitalised neighbours.
- A paternalistic political structure.

Goals

Singapore must concentrate on creating and sustaining its competitive edge over its fast up-and-coming neighbours in order to consolidate its position as regional capital of the Asian-Pacific Rim.

Politics

Structurally speaking, Singapore has a total of 21 registered political parties but most of them do not really seem to count, except as tokens of so-called democratic expression. In the battle for seats in parliament, it is only the People's Action Party, the political incumbents, who call the shots with 77 out of the 81 total seats. The PAP lost four seats to opposition parties in 1991's autumn election and its share of the vote has declined about two per cent. Most believe though that these factors are very unlikely to affect either foreign investment or Singapore's financial markets in any significant way.

The other party with representation is the Singapore Democratic Party who, with just one seat, have their political hands tied behind their backs. A political amendment in 1984 does allow, however, for one other unelected representative, a candidate from the Workers' Party. He may take his seat as an MP but he is not allowed to vote.

Prime Minister Goh Chok Tong has emphatically stated during a recent press interview that he intends to remain in his position as leader of the country for the next decade. There are no indications as yet, however, that Lee Kuan Yew has given up forever because he is always standing in the wings with his son by his side.

As far as Lee's candidacy for the elected presidency is concerned, Goh Chok Tong refuses to acknowledge any position or influence the former prime minister may have, saying that the position is supra-political as it is not directly involved with, or dependent upon, any one political party. The fact remains that Lee is nevertheless the secretary-general of the ruling People's Action Party and therefore very much still in a position of having a firm and unrelenting grip on the reins whenever he wants to yank people back into place.

Parliament is elected for a five-year term and voting for those over 21 is compulsory. The constitution obviously allows for political change but has very little bearing on the reality of Singapore politics. Significant opposition to Lee Kuan Yew's rule when he was prime minister, and even now with him out of so-called 'power', is not tolerated out of a concern for 'internal security'. The PAP has jailed legions of dissidents without regard for habeas corpus, whenever and wherever it chose. As far as business is concerned, political shenanigans, visible or otherwise, have very little bearing in the matters of real concern, the big wheels of commerce and trade.

Domestic economy, current economic policy and forecasts

The tension between Hong Kong and Singapore as they vie with each other for regional supremacy, especially since 1984 and the Joint Declaration Treaty on Hong Kong, is almost palpable. Hong Kong is determined to hang on to is position of pre-eminence come what may, PRC or no PRC, while lion-hearted Singapore is equally gritty in its single-minded ambition to wrench the dominance away for itself. Hong Kong is suffering from the destabilising political and economic uncertainty in the run-up to 1997, while Singapore has enjoyed political stability for a great many years and will apparently continue to do so for the foreseeable future. The authoritarian government which gave birth to Singapore as a newly industrialised country (NIC) will not be sustained forever, as everyone realises both within and without. The transition to Western-style democracy will come and is worrying President Wee Kim Wee in the process. He is said to dread what the future may bring. It may be a painful process, a political and socio-economic catharsis, but most feel that the sane and sensible Singaporeans are unlikely to throw their economic baby out with the bathwater for the sake of political expediency. Time is money, but so is stability.

Singapore with a per capita GDP of more than $12,000 can claim to be the richest country in the Asian-Pacific Rim (that is, after Japan and

Brunei, which are not included for discussion in this book). Over 60 per cent of that GDP, however, is dependent on the outside business which is conducted through the medium that is Singapore and is therefore extremely vulnerable to world recessions. However, the factors that continue to work in Singapore's favour are the record levels of manufacturing investment and a continuing steady growth in trade, as well as a recently renewed growth in the manufacturing sector. Exports to Europe and ASEAN countries have offset the sluggishness in sales to the US export market and regional growth recently hit a ten-year high. The main problem for the economy, then, is how to stage-manage the growth and energy into a sustainable, long-lasting feature of Singapore's existence.

The inner secret of this flourishing domestic economy for the last 20 years has lain primarily in its extensive port and entrepôt facilities. It is a hub in Asia through which a great deal of international business must inevitably flow. The pleasant surroundings of the city, its superb telecommunications and banking infrastructure and its convenience as an East-West jumping-off point were all factors that made it seem, at one time, as though Singapore could never fail. In the mid-1980s, however, a slump moved in to flood out the good times and the government turned to construction projects as a vehicle to create employment and pull out of the gloom. The trouble is that this resulted in an oversupply of new office and hotel space which had been encouraged by all manner of incentives given to the builders and construction consortia.

Inflation is now sufficiently under control in Singapore, down to between three and four per cent, that the fears that many had of overheating in the economy are fading. The main factors that will keep the Singapore economy strong and stable are the strength of the Singapore dollar, a stabilisation in the price of oil and the resolution of the acute shortage of labour. The labour problem has been solved in the main through the implementation of a government policy to move as much of the labour intensive manufacturing industries as possible offshore and to allow service companies to double the number of unskilled foreign workers they hire. Simple expedients but ones that are working.

Singapore is also very much determined to hang on to its position as one of the trendsetters in leading-edge technology in the Asian-Pacific Rim, so it came as no surprise when the Deputy Prime Minister not long ago announced the National Technology Plan. This will allocate $2bn to be spent over the next five years on research and development, that is, some two per cent of the GDP by 1995.

Another, potentially very significant development for Singapore, is the emerging 'Golden Triangle' delineated as Singapore-Johor-Batam which only started to take shape a couple of years ago. It is, however, around ten years behind Hong Kong's integration with China, the model concept on which the triangle is loosely based. Nevertheless with its road connections to Johor in Malaysia and short sea links with Batam in Indonesia, the area will probably gradually strengthen over the coming years to become a region of greater economic clout. It will also provide a much-needed hinterland for Singaporean expansion. Even now many of the country's labour-intensive industries are being relocated into other parts of the triangle. Further down the road is the distinct probability that, as Indonesia develops its infrastructure and as its economy becomes increasingly dynamic, Singapore will become to Indonesia what Hong Kong has always been to China: its free trade, energy-giving life-support system.

Government expenditure currently runs at $13.3bn, or 24 per cent of GDP, and yet allows a budgetary surplus of more than $3bn. Reserves are said to stand at around $548bn on the official record, but are said by expert economists to run much higher. The wealth of these funds is in the main due to contributions, based on 23 per cent of earned income that all employees pay to the Central Provident Fund (like Britain's National Insurance Scheme). Employers pay a slightly lower 17 per cent. It is the very control of this sector in general by the government, that so far from stifling its growth, seems to have contributed most notably to its burgeoning strength.

Of vital importance to Singapore for economic policy planning and industrial growth is the think-tank that is the Economic Development Board (EDB) – the Singaporeans have a vast liking for acronynms – which was set up 30 years ago. Its aim is to plan and promote Singaporean industrial development by procuring land, arranging financing, luring the work-force and establishing the factories. The EDB (head office: 1 Maritime Square, 10-40 World Trade Centre, Lobby D, Singapore 0409; tel: 271-0844; fax: 274-7035; see Appendix for other offices) considers all incentives to encourage foreign investment and acts as a main information centre for those seriously considering major participation in the Singapore economy in practical terms. The Small Enterprise Bureau (SEB) may also be contacted through the EDB and is a service to help small businesses, once they are established in Singapore, to improve their financial, management, IT, training and other operations.

Banking and finance, equity market outlook, stockmarkets

Singapore is still vying with Hong Kong for the position of major financial centre of south-east Asia and British banks and other institutions, as well as major trading houses, have a significant presence there. A large number of consultancy firms, both financial and otherwise, operate in the region with Singapore as their base.

The financial services sector (some £3.8bn of Singapore's GDP), falls under the tight control of the Monetary Authority of Singapore. A decision was taken to allow some opening up of the sector and most notably it was intimated that more overseas stockbroking firms would be allowed to take a share of the local market. Consequently, the sector grew by 22 per cent in the year ending 1990.

Singapore now has 141 commercial banks with 422 offices. Of this total, the Hong Kong and British banks are well represented, led by the Hongkong & Shanghai and the Standard Chartered, as well as other major clearing banks with offshore operations. The vast majority of the work relating to mergers and acquisitions (M&A) falls to these two major banks. There are three types of banks in Singapore: full licence banks; restricted licence banks and offshore licence banks, all of which come under the same jurisdiction of the Monetary Authority of Singapore (MAS).

The best-known banks are Asia Commercial Bank Ltd, Bank of East Asia Ltd, Chung Khiaw Bank Ltd (80 per cent owned by UOB), DBS Bank Ltd, Far Eastern Bank Ltd, Four Seas Communications Bank Ltd (99 per cent owned by OCBC), Hongkong & Shanghai Banking Corp, Industrial & Commercial Bank Ltd, International Bank of Singapore Ltd, Overseas Chinese Banking Corp Ltd (OCBC), Overseas Union Bank Ltd, Standard Chartered Bank Ltd, and United Overseas Bank Ltd (UOB).

The stockmarket

Foreign firms are not yet allowed to be members of the Singapore Stock Exchange and all orders have to be placed indirectly through Singapore brokers. The management of funds comes under the auspices of a central authority, the Singapore Central Provident Fund. There has however been some relocation of asset management operations moving part of their business away from Hong Kong to Singapore, as a 1997 insurance policy perhaps. The regulatory authority, the Monetary Authority of Singapore, has issued 91 investment adviser licences in year end 1991, compared with 60 in the previous year and a mere 43 in 1989 and the estimate of money under management in the country is said to be around US$30bn. There are even some very limited opportunities for overseas asset management companies to run Singapore government funds although most of these functions are performed in-house by the MAS.

The Singapore Stock Exchange itself has 25 member firms acting as brokers and underwriters. Two kinds of companies are listed, First Trading and Second Trading. The former category lays down strict guidelines and regulations on share turnover, dividend policy and paid-up capital. SESDAQ is Singapore's Over the Counter exchange and is for companies which do not have a full listing perhaps being too tightly held. It is the equivalent of the United States' NASDAQ listing.

To date, Singapore has not shown itself to be liberal enough to encourage large numbers of foreign companies to actively participate in the country's stock exchange, for example by listing their shares. The repressive measures that are meted out with not irregular frequency, such as expulsions of press or financial personnel considered 'unfriendly', not suprisingly colour the Singapore financial community with more than a tinge of authoritarianism. While it is accepted that this undoubtedly makes for a most attractive and well-run city-state, it is not considered the most conducive of environments for freewheeling entrepreneurs and money men.

Debates rage constantly, both internally and within the Asian-Pacific Rim as a whole, as to whether or not Singapore will cut its authoritarian binds enough to let the blood course through its financial and business veins. It could be done. For the moment though, the odds are considered – by most people working in the sector – to be against any real chance that Lee Kuan Yew will allow true liberalisation while he is alive and kicking.

A steady stream of companies is expected to go for listings on the exchange during the course of the next few years and plans are in an embryonic stage for the privatisation of the Stock Exchange itself. IPOs, that is, Initial Public Offerings, by privately held entities are growing. The government's privatisation programme will also be bound to include such revenue-bearing icons as the Port of Singapore Authority and the Singapore Broadcasting Corporation. The programme itself will create a vast amount of work for the stockmarket to handle.

The major source of growth in the financial sector remains the Asian Dollar Market, established in 1968 as a key part of its strategy for financial hegemony in the region and in particular in the country's foreign exchange trading. The ADM, now worth several hundred billion dollars in trade annually, is an international money and capital market trading foreign currency funds, the most common of which is the US dollar. Closely linked to Eurocurrency market rates, the market is a way of achieving international deposit rates for Singapore-based funds. Banks can take part in the dealings of the Asian Dollar Market after approval from the Monetary Authority of Singapore and a separate entity dealing with Asian Currency Units. Singapore now constitutes the fifth largest Forex market in the world, bigger than Hong Kong.

The Futures Exchange, SIMEX, has proved to be a surprising success benefiting from its close links to the Chicago Mercantile Exchange. Foreign stockbrokers operate closely in partnership with local companies, such as Sassoons, and British insurance companies are faring well in this small market.

Trade and industry

The main government body in Singapore pushing forward the country's export drive with vigour is the Trade Development Board established in 1983. The Board (head office: 1 Maritime Square, 03-01 World Trade Centre, Telok Blangah Road, Singapore 0409; tel 271-9388, fax 274-0770, see Appendix for other offices) exists to engage in export promotion to increase Singapore's outward bound trade, to identify new markets and to build on existing market shares in overseas markets. It also acts as a conduit of information to the outside world's business community about business affairs, relating to both trade and industry in Singapore. It may also act in an advisory capacity giving informal consultations to foreign businessmen on exhibitions and trade fairs and on how to participate in them, on how to market your products and services in Singapore and on all regulatory requirements.

We have not yet seen large numbers of foreign individuals rushing to Singapore to start a business so, to date, most commercial activity by expatriates in Singapore has been in the form of representative offices, or joint ventures by foreign corporations in partnership with local companies. It is extremely competitive, with an open market that is ideally suited to European or American business operations and careful, not to say stringent, government control. The market is efficient and rewarding but the competition it offers should not be underestimated.

It is essential to establish and maintain a strong, inter-active local identity to deal with the main statutory boards who are usually solely responsible for most of the major projects undertaken in Singapore. These will not entertain the idea of giving significant business to people or parties who have no established presence in the country. Agents are not the answer. Carefully targeted investment and joint ventures, however, often lead to long-term success.

Singapore has always encouraged foreign investment and offers a comprehensive package of investment incentives (including tax holidays, help with capital investment and ready-built factories) and there are no barriers to investment. The interest in the country looks set to grow as consciousness of Singapore as 'The Gateway to The Pacific' hits Western businesses. To date, the largest single foreign investor country remains the US, closely followed by Japan. Britain remains in third position with exports growing at 35 per cent in 1990 to over one billion pounds.

Singapore would also like to attract large numbers of multinational corporations to its shores to add even further to its clout. To this end, a programme of tax incentives under the 'operational headquarters' scheme cuts corporate tax rates from 33 to 10 per cent on income generated in Singapore and allows tax relief on income from abroad.

167

This programme specifically encourages companies to, as it says, locate their headquarters (technical services, product development, distribution and other operations) in Singapore, but at the same time to take advantage of neighbouring countries' much larger human resources reserves for labour-intensive manufacture.

To date, Singapore has fewer than 20 international companies taking advantage of this programme (but these include both Sony and the Japanese construction firm, Kajima Corporation), but it has well over 300 multinationals successfully operating what former Prime Minister Lee Kuan Yew suggested would be the base of a 'total business location'. Few are disappointed with their achievements in the market, or the strategic advantage it gives them in the region for distribution, so far.

The Singaporeans are currently looking to attract high technology, value-added capital intensive industries. With her technologically minded and well-educated work-force, the entrepôt that is Singapore is the perfect springboard for companies seeking to expand their IT business in the Asian-Pacific Rim. Nevertheless the country is an expanding market in its own right. Export opportunities abound in technological and capital equipment (more than ever with the high yen making British goods more competitive) that will help the country to broaden her industrial base.

Singapore's main export markets are the US, Malaysia, Japan, Hong Kong and Thailand. The top five exports from Singapore to the UK (its eighth main export market, taking 3.18 per cent of total exports are currently, in order, office and ADP machines, electrical machinery and appliances, telecommunications and sound recording, miscellaneous manufactured goods and clothing. As of June 1991, exports from Singapore to the UK stood at a value of £510,175,000 whilst exports from the UK to Singapore stood at £495,481,000. The five leading sectors in the Singapore economy are construction (16 per cent growth in 1991), manufacturing (eight per cent), financial and business services (nine per cent), transport (7.8 per cent), communications and commerce. The slowdown in the growth of the manufacturing sector is said to be caused mainly by a changeover in the production lines of computer manufacturers as they regear for the output of 3.5in drives rather than the old 5.25in standard.

Singapore's top five imports world-wide are petroleum and petroleum products, electrical machinery, telecommunications equipment, office and data machines and general industrial machinery. Her top top five exports world-wide are drawn from exactly the same sectors.

Britain's share of both Singapore's exports and imports has been declining steadily in recent years, mainly due to the extensive diversification that the market has been undergoing and will continue to experience. There has, however, been a dramatic increase in imports into Britain of crude oil for refining and in basic foodstuffs such as rice, in areas therefore where we do not compete.

The service sector, growing 15 per cent, recently overtook the industrial sector for the first time. It is the former Prime Minister of Singapore's son, Lee Hsien Loong, who heads up the Ministry of Trade and Industry and with tight reins on the Monetary Authority of Singapore oversees most of the control systems through various regulatory authorities and the implementation of the Economic Development Plan, and a large number of programmes, industrial, economic and otherwise, seem to be organised through the previously mentioned 'Temasek' companies, ie quasi-official government commercial entities.

The Government cannot be ignored at any cost and working against the status quo would result in little business and a great deal of wasted effort. The best chances for orthodox market penetration, indeed, are through some of the largest Singaporean companies whose connections with government are the strongest and whose operations therefore are generally supported and approved of.

Bureaucracy in Singapore is a fact of life and the game has to be played precisely by the rules. With formal permission from the Singapore Trade Development Board, (see Appendix 1, page 279) you can set up a representative office to maximise your marketing and local liaison before creating the corporate entity that will officially trade. As time is invariably a factor in establishing a new business, most companies tend to take this option for the sake of expediency.

If and when you do decide to formally create a business entity, the forms that enterprise may take are either a Singapore incorporated company, a branch of an overseas corporation, sole trader status or, on a bigger scale, a joint venture. A private or public limited company would be constituted, for example, in the form of John Smith Trading Bhd (Malay for limited) or John Smith Trading Pte Ltd (Private Ltd). A private company would be one that limits its shareholders to no more than 50, a form which is unquestionably the most suitable for foreign businessmen who do not wish to raise share capital.

The Business Registration Act does not, however, cover some professions which are covered by specific statutes of their own. Most operations in the banking, insurance and general financial sector need careful attention in their exact formation. Other companies, most suitable for those in consultancy perhaps, would include unlimited or companies limited by guarantee. (The Registry of Companies and Businesses is at 1 Colombo Court 06-06116, Singapore 0617; tel 336-1293.)

The precise legal status of your operation in Singapore can be very complex with difference implications for tax depending on whether you are a branch or a subsidiary. It is essential that, having established a representative office, you take the fullest possible advice from accountancy firms experienced in Singapore, such as Price Waterhouse, Co-ward Chance, etc. There is no question that in the minds of the Singaporeans and the Singapore business community, a company is regarded in a better light and treated differently since it is felt that the commitment is more likely to be long-term and not predicated on the whims of a far-flung 'gweilo' (expatriate or 'foreign devil') head office.

Like Hong Kong there is no stipulation about local involvement in the equity of the company, but there is an important requirement about residency and the employment of a key local management executive. Singapore requires that at least one of the two minimum required corporate shareholders in the company must be resident in Singapore at the time of its incorporation. The ultimate responsibility is deemed to be in the hands of a manager of Singaporean citizenship whom you are obliged to employ from the outset. In most instances, this is very far from a disadvantage. Local staff are highly qualified for the most part, well educated to the tertiary level and keen to work for foreign operations, especially those of a more global or Asian-Pacific nature.

Foreign ownership of Singapore-based entities is not restricted up to a limited percentage except in the case of locally incorporated banks. Some newspaper publishing companies and enterprises like Singapore Airlines and certain shipping companies which affect the national interest do, however, limit foreign ownership of their shares.

It usually takes about a week after formal incorporation for the Registrar of Companies to issue the documents so that business may begin. The costs involved are around the S$3,000 level but can vary enormously of course depending on the complexity and intricacy of your structure as well as the predetermined sliding scale measured against share capital.

The Singapore Government has openly been encouraging foreign investment in the labour-intensive high-technology sectors and in all export-dominated trading operations for some time. Areas which have the best chance of long-term success would include projects in these fields with quick start-ups playing the industrial infrastructure to its best advantage.

Jurong Town Corporation (JTC) is the government entity responsible for all development and management of industrial estates. It also has a social welfare and philanthropic function in that is takes care of extra-curricular facilities for workers on their estates and of their families.

All computer and IT-related businesses, including media storage, find a natural home in Singapore with its leading edge bias. A government plan calls for the transformation of Singapore into the perfect 'IT Culture', where technical and technological literacy are a facet of everyday life. With around 1,200 computers per million head of population, very little persuasion will be needed to make the average Singaporean even more computer friendly than he already is.

Other possibilities include fund management (though most major international companies in this sector have based themselves increasingly in Tokyo and/or Hong Kong), marketing, product development and technical design. Other major industries include petroleum-refining, rubber-processing, electronics, food-processing, ship repair and the whole gamut of garment-related processes. The pharmaceuticals sector, together with medical equipment, has been designated an area of priority for new inward investment, together with industrial and laboratory equipment, luxury goods, aerospace, and industrial automation. The country's major imports are capital equipment, manufactured goods, crude oil, transport equipment and general consumer goods.

Those embarking on commercial projects in Singapore should bear in mind that the labour market is tight, so an inclination towards less labour-intensive projects would be wise if not essential. It is this acute labour shortage, amongst other factors, that has prompted the government towards a concentration in high-tech industries. Most people-intensive businesses of Singapore concerns are being located offshore in what is seen as 'the growth triangle', which we mentioned previously between Singapore, Johor in Malaysia and Indonesia's Batam Island. On top of last year's measure to allow service companies to double their unskilled foreign workers, a tendering system for foreign workers is also being considered.

The aerospace industry reached $1.2bn in 1990 and has strong participation from a number of major foreign corporations including Honeywell, Lucas and Pratt & Whitney. The government-owned Singapore Aerospace mostly services commercial aircraft using the hub and is engaged in component manufacture, R & D and software development.

Companies of note

Asia Pacific Breweries
Fraser & Neave (S) Pte Ltd
  (conglomerate)
Haw Par Bros International Ltd
  (conglomerate)
Inchcape Group (conglomerate)
Intraco Ltd (trading company)

Keppel Corporation
  (conglomerate)
Neptune Orient Lines Ltd
  (shipping)
Singapore Airlines Ltd
Times Publishing Bhd (media)
Wearne Brothers (conglomerate)

A thorough study of the history, as well as of both the annual and stockbrokers' reports (where available), of the companies of note will give you a good idea of the commercial 'inner game' psychology of the countries in which you plan to do business.

Agriculture

Only about six per cent of Singapore's 626 square kilometres is put to agricultural use and agriculture and fisheries combined account for the employment of less than one per cent of the labour force. The sector is worth about S$450m a year and is the focus of applied technology for intensive farming yields, or 'agrotech' as it has been called. An ambitious plan is currently underway by the Primary Production Department of Singapore which would like to see the country win the regional lead in the field.

Since most produce for domestic consumption is imported, the most common form of agriculture is small-scale subsistence farming of chickens for eggs, as well as of some vegetable and meat products. The most significant exports under the heading of 'agriculture' are, in fact, cut flowers, including orchids and plants. Also exported are about S$60m worth of aquarium fish. As far as is known, Singapore has no mineral or other resources.

Mainstream fishing, however, is far more important as you would expect from an island country and major port. The fishing industry is currently undergoing an extensive overhaul and infrastructural projects are underway to expand Jurong Port as part of this process.

Tourism

Perhaps one of the least complicated sectors for penetration into the Singapore market is tourism which accounts for around ten per cent of GDP. It is being given a brand new top priority status and those well-qualified and established in the field may reap rich rewards from the boom in travel in the Asian-Pacific Rim. The Singapore Tourist Promotion Board figures show the trend in hotel room revenues is distinctly upwards.

The main blow to Singapore's tourism trade, one of the best possible entrées for the Western businessman, has been an alarming decline in the bread-and-butter staple which is the number of Japanese visitors. The recent Gulf conflict impacted, obviously, to a significant extent on visitor arrivals and tourism receipts and the strong currency and high accommodation costs have affected Singapore's competitiveness as a tourism destination. Generally speaking, however, numbers on the whole have been showing a tendency to grow steadily. The tourism infrastructure continues to expand with nine new hotel projects coming onstream.

Infrastructure

Singapore has probably the best general infrastructure in the Asian-Pacific Rim, as well as a world-beating airport and airport facilities and fast computerised trade documentation, making it the best distribution centre for the Asian-Pacific Rim.

The Mass Rapid Transit System, the Central Expressway and the new airport terminal have all been completed, but the government is still committed to a number of further projects where there could well be room for participation. For example, new phases in the construction of generation plants and extensions to the MRT are always distinct possibilities.

New marine and tourist facilities are being built near Keppel Shipyard and the waterfront at Clarke Quay is the subject of renewal, as is the National Museum and colonial buildings near the city centre. There is to be a new Singapore entertainment complex at the marina and an upgrading of the World Trade Centre and the passenger vessel terminal. There will be a new performing arts centre and the new Suntec City exhibition, conference, commercial and retail complex. There are several container port redevelopments or expansions taking place at Jurong Port and Pulau Brani amongst others with the result that in the near future, Singapore will have one of the very best container ports in the world to add to its already first-class cargo-handling facilities. A number of major hospitals are undergoing refurbishment.

Communications

In 1989, the Singapore Telecommunications Authority stole the region's thunder by taking the very bold step of introducing a $15m cellular phone network for the Mass Transit railway system. A feasibility study was undertaken by a British accountancy firm to evaluate the advantages and disadvantages to the government of the privatisation of Singapore Telecom.

Fibre-optic cables have replaced old copper wiring and exchanges are going completely digital in 1994. Capital investment in the sector over the next five years is planned to be $2.7bn and will include ISDN (Integrated Service Digital Network), a Public Office automation system and VANs (Value-Added Networks). Coming in 1996 is the Broadband Integrated Systems Digital Network (BISDN) which will improve performance even over the ISDN by two and a half times the speed of transmission. Plans are being developed to introduce a cable television network to run on the same cables as those for telecommunications.

Also on the cards in conjunction with France Telecom is an optic-fibre 'rim' to link Asian-Pacific Rim countries with Europe. Viewtex services have recently been brought into the Singapore telecommunications environment through joint development with British firm GEC-Marconi for the service, 'Teleview'.

Transportation

Changi Airport is generally acknowledged, by airlines and business travellers alike, to be the most modern and efficient in the world. It handles 20 million passengers each year and is serviced by 55 different airlines operating a total of 2,000 weekly flights linking Singapore to cities in 54 countries. A major programme to upgrade Terminal 1 to match the newly built Terminal 2, in terms of handling systems and equipment is soon to be undertaken and tenders will soon be coming in for a third terminal. On the freight side the projected capacity for 1995 will be 1.3 million tonnes per annum.

Education

The general standard of education in Singapore is of the highest possible standard not only in the context of the Asian-Pacific Rim but in the world as a whole. Literacy is very high, pushing towards 90 per cent and all are encouraged to go on to tertiary education. Nearly half a million children are currently in primary and secondary schools and around 45,000 students are engaged in further study in the country's universities and colleges of further education.

It is, however, the 'education' aspect of Singapore that some outside find the most frightening. For example, the government has a core programme for a 'Three S's Productivity' plan for Social Responsibility, Social Attitude and Skill in order to keep everyone in a socially-conscious, community caring-and-sharing straitjacket. Higher birth rates among the better educated Chinese are fiercely encouraged and the Social Development Unit of the government indulges in 'matchmaking' top-level graduates with kindred spirits in an attempt to raise the IQ levels of generations of unborn children.

Conferences, conventions and trade fairs

As a reflection of her economic significance and central location in the Asian-Pacific Rim, Singapore has become a sophisticated international market centre, well served by exhibitions and seminars. Singapore receives a large number of outward missions each year sponsored by the

British Overseas Trade Board, with several exhibitions also taking place each year.

It is the Singapore Tourist Board however, through The Singapore Convention Bureau, a non-profit making organisation, which arranges the participation by foreign concerns in Singapore's exhibitions and trade shows. The Singapore Trade Development Board exists primarily to work the other way round, that is, helping Singaporean companies with their overseas exhibitions. For foreign companies, however, they can also help with enquiries from non-Singaporeans who wish to develop business in Singapore. Help is also available in assisting with representation by overseas companies in some of the fairs held in Singapore.

Useful publications include the Convention Facilities Guide, the Convention Calendar and a regular newsletter. More than 60 trade shows are held every year in the World Trade Centre's huge exhibition hall. The Singapore Convention Bureau may be contacted at the Singapore Tourist Promotion Board, Raffles City Tower 36-04, 250 North Bridge Road, Singapore 0617; tel 339-6633, fax 339-9423 (see Appendix for other offices).

Taxation

Singapore has no exchange controls or rules about the repatriation of a company's funds to the parent country. Companies based in Singapore most often pay tax at the standard rate of 33 per cent and have singular advantages over branches in terms of tax payable. A company is resident in Singapore for tax purposes if its control and management are exercised in Singapore. A non-resident company is generally also liable, though, to the same taxation as a resident company.

Against this, you may be able to write off some of the setting-up costs of the operation or you may even be able to take advantage of some of the tax incentives available to new businesses. Double-tax treaties with a number of countries also release you from what would otherwise be punitively high penalties.

Singapore is basically a duty-free port but there are a few import duties levied on a few items from birds' eggs to imitation jewellery and petroleum products, so be sure to check with the commercial counsellor the status of your item for export.

Exchange rates and currency positioning relative to US$

The unit of currency is the Singapore dollar of which there are about three to the pound sterling. The dollar (100 cents) bank notes come in 1,

5, 10, 20, 50, 100, 500, 1,000 and 10,000 unit notes. Coins are 1, 5, 10, 20 and 50 cents and 1 dollar. Unlimited amounts of foreign currency notes, cash and cheques may be brought in and taken out of Singapore. Gold, however, must be declared.

The people, their languages, and religion

Singapore is a multi-racial society (most people are tri-lingual, an ability greatly encouraged by the government) with 78 per cent Chinese population, 14 per cent Malay (the original residents of Singapore), seven per cent Indians and one per cent made up of people of other races including Eurasians and expatriates living in Singapore. The city-state also has one of the world's highest population densities at nearly 4,300 people per square kilometre although a crush is rarely obvious in daily business life.

The Malay influence is still clearly visible, despite the demographic weakness of their number in the population, through a gently creeping Islamicisation into parts of Singapore's modern sociological structure, especially in relation to the family and attachment to tradition. The Indian population which plays such a vital role, in synergy with the Chinese, in the local economy and market-place, has been present for centuries since historically the Indians, Thais and Javanese all fought each other to wrest Singapore from the Malays. Indians, who are also now pre-eminent in academic and journalistic circles, also came in in large numbers as debentured labourers in the early part of the nineteenth century. Singapore has Indians from all over the sub-continent, including Hindus and Muslims, Bengalis, Gujeratis, Parsis, Punjabis, Sikhs, Sindhis, and Tamils, The backbone of the police force and security services is staffed by magnificent turban-wearing Sikhs.

While the official government administration language is English, others spoken are a number of Chinese dialects (including Hokkien, Cantonese and Mandarin), Malay, and Tamil. The 'Use Mandarin' campaign was an official attempt both to give the Chinese peoples a common majority tongue, but also to encourage Singapore's attitude positioning towards the People's Republic of China.

It is a fact that most of the Chinese who came to Singapore from the mainland were aspiring get-rich-quick merchants. The Hakkas from Guangdong (Canton) and others peoples from Hainan, Guangxi (Kwangsi) and Fuzhou (Foochow) came hoping to earn a great deal of money and then return home richer. Of all the Chinese, it is those from Hokkien who dominated business life in the upper echelons of trade and industry. If there is linguistic confusion for the 'gweilo' in Singapore, it is mainly caused by the different Romanisation of Chinese names according to whether or not the 'pinyin' system is used, ie

Guangdong or Canton. Familiarity breeds ease, though, and such minor details become entirely irrelevant to your success in doing business.

What Singapore may lack in democratic opportunity, it more than makes up for in terms of religious options. There is a vast array of forms of worship and philosophies to choose from in Singapore including Buddhism, Christianity, Hinduism, Islam, Sikhism and Taoism as well as a few more very exotic '-isms' for good measure. Racial tolerance is stressed by the government, as is racial freedom, both key factors in making highly cosmopolitan Singapore a safe and interesting place to live and work.

Publications of note

Singapore's tough stance on what it considers unfriendly foreign publications is well-known. Tow the line, or else get thrown out. The circulation of *The Far Eastern Economic Review* was forcibly curtailed three years ago for its apparent 'interference in domestic politics'. Other international and highly respected publications have also been affected including *The Asian Wall Street Journal*, *Asiaweek* and even *Time* magazine.

On the ground though, the standard of locally produced publications which are produced under government licence is very high (one of the main reasons often cited for the re-siting of production offices of regional publications to Singapore from Hong Kong and elsewhere in the Asian-Pacific Rim) if you are not bothered by the fairly obvious 'censorship' of the media.

The newspapers are comprehensively stacked with good reporting and interesting features and the two English-language newspapers make vital daily reading for the businessman. These are *The Straits Times* and *The Business Times*. Of the domestic, non-English publications, there are two Chinese dailies, *The United Morning News* (Lian He Zao Bao) and *The United Evening News* (Lian He Wan Bao). For Malay readers there is the *Berita Harian* and Tamil readers have the *Tamul Murasu*. Most foreign newspapers with international editions, eg, *The International Herald Tribune*, are widely available.

Specialist publications of interest to businessmen include *The Economic Bulletin* (from the Singapore International Chamber of Commerce), *Singapore Business, Building Materials and Equipment SE Asia, The Manufacturer, Petroleum News* and *Shipping 'N Shipbuilder*. Many publishers of note from Europe and the US are to be found with a base in Singapore including Macmillan, Simon & Schuster and Oxford University Press to name but a few.

English television programmes are available sporadically on channels 5, 8, and 12, intermingled with programming in Mandarin, Malay and

Tamil (the papers publish the schedules). Cable television (CNN) is widely available in good hotels and many have teletext through Singapore Broadcasting from 6.00am to midnight.

Visa and health requirements

Visitors to Singapore who plan to stay for less than 14 days need valid passports, but Commonwealth citizens (as well as those from the Republic of Ireland, Switzerland, Monaco, the Netherlands and Liechtenstein) do not need visas. The Cliff Richard-haircut rule still stands: if yours is too long, you could be refused entry regardless of the importance of the reason for your visit to the country. If you are coming in from an area infected by either yellow fever or cholera, you will need a valid vaccination certificate.

There are a number of possible work permits available to non-Singaporeans who wish to work there. These include Professional Visit Passes (for conference speakers and others in Singapore for business purposes for a short time only), and Employment Passes (for those with professional, high-salaried occupations and work permits). The precise documentation you will need and help with filing and application may be obtained from the Singapore High Commission or Embassy.

High-flying entrepreneurs who wish to re-locate both themselves and an enterprise to Singapore may wish to take advantage of the 'Singapore Million Dollar Deposit Scheme' which is exactly what it says. You put one million dollars in bond with the government against future investment in a corporation or business entity approved by the government. 'Approved Industrial Experts' in fields which are in high demand by the Government of Singapore should have no difficulty gaining either employment or a temporary pass or permit.

Bullish but concerned

Tougher competition and the lack of human resources are the preoccupation of businessmen in Singapore. Although 43% of the respondents are more optimistic about the economy, compared with 38% in 1990, Singapore's Confidence Index for 1991 fell by eight points to 69.

Despite the change in leadership and the general election, political factors rank low in the minds of business leaders. Some 61% of respondents say the political succession has not altered their confidence in the government's policies towards the business sector.

By contrast an overwhelming 98% of respondents say there is a serious labour shortage or consider the labour market to be tight. Few of them expect an improvement in the foreseeable future. Some 83% feel that the government's policy on the import of foreign workers is restrictive.

Nonetheless Singaporean businessmen are bullish about the future. Some 50% of them are more optimistic about their company's prospects than they were six months ago.

In recent years Singapore has made big efforts to attract Hong Kong business migrants and persuade multinationals to transfer their regional offices from Hong Kong to Singapore. Our survey shows that Singapore's political stability, quality of life and English-speaking environment rate highly when businessmen compare the two cities.

Singapore confidence index: 69

Asian Business provides readers with a Confidence Index for each country surveyed. To compare the results of confidence surveys conducted around the region, we process the data from each survey and (in conjunction with Frank Small & Associates) arrive at a numerical rating for each country. This Confidence Index measures the following six criteria used in the survey: Local market, export market, turnover, profits, company prospects and economy.

ECONOMIC/POLITICAL

National economy: Are you more optimistic about the national economy than you were six months ago? Less? About the same?

Local market: During the last six months, has your company been operating in an expanding, a static, or a contracting local market?

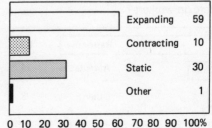

More	43	
Less	29	
Same	25	
Other	3	

0 10 20 30 40 50 60 70 80 90 100%

Expanding	59	
Contracting	10	
Static	30	
Other	1	

0 10 20 30 40 50 60 70 80 90 100%

Hunting with the Tigers

Export market: During the last six months, has your company been operating in an expanding, a contracting, or a static market?

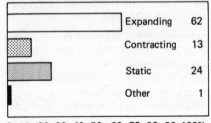

Expanding	62
Contracting	13
Static	24
Other	1

0 10 20 30 40 50 60 70 80 90 100%

Government policies: Following Goh Chok Tong's first year in office, has your confidence in the government's policy towards business increased or decreased?

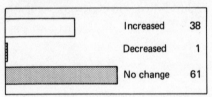

Increased	38
Decreased	1
No change	61

0 10 20 30 40 50 60 70 80 90 100%

Labour market: How would you rate the state of Singapore's labour market?

Bad shortage	47
Tight market	51
Ready supply	2

0 10 20 30 40 50 60 70 80 90 100%

Foreign workers: How do you rate the government's policy on the import of foreign workers?

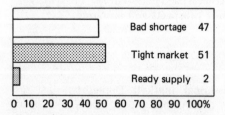

Restrictive	83
Acceptable	14
Other	3

0 10 20 30 40 50 60 70 80 90 100%

Singapore vs Hong Kong: Which of the following advantages do you believe Singapore has over Hong Kong as a base for regional offices?

Political stability	98
Better quality of life	84
English-speaking environment	80
Labour stability	73
Geographical location	66
Better infrastructure	65
Better communications	65
Availability of support industries	52
Government flexibility	52
Availability of skilled labour	51
Pro-business attitude	48
None	1

Economic prospects: On a scale of one, for very poor, to 10, for very good, how would you rate the likely economic performance of the following economies in the next 12 months?

	Average Rating	Proportion who gave a rating
Singapore	6.7	95%
Malaysia	6.5	97%
Japan	6.4	95%
Hong Kong	6.2	94%
Taiwan	6.1	94%
Thailand	6.1	94%
South Korea	6.0	96%
Indonesia	5.8	95%
US	5.7	95%
China	5.0	91%
New Zealand	4.4	93%
Vietnam	4.4	92%
Australia	4.0	93%
Sri Lanka	3.9	89%
India	3.8	93%
Philippines	3.7	95%

CORPORATE

Company prospects: Would you say you are more optimistic, about the same, or less optimistic about your company's prospects than you were six months ago?

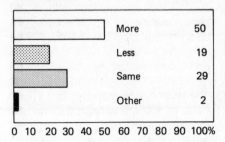

More	50
Less	19
Same	29
Other	2

0 10 20 30 40 50 60 70 80 90 100%

Company performance: Overall, would you say your company is doing:

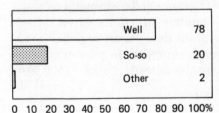

Well	78
So-so	20
Other	2

0 10 20 30 40 50 60 70 80 90 100%

Profits: During the last six months, has the trend of your gross profits been up, down, or the same, compared with the same period last year?

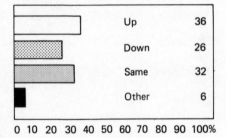

Up	36
Down	26
Same	32
Other	6

0 10 20 30 40 50 60 70 80 90 100%

Turnover: During the last six months, have your company's turnover/billings, compared with the same period last year gone up, stayed the same or gone down (ie, in real terms excluding the effects of inflation)?

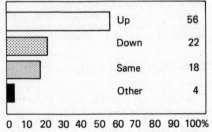

Up	56
Down	22
Same	18
Other	4

0 10 20 30 40 50 60 70 80 90 100%

Staffing levels: Do you expect employment levels in your company over the next six months to rise, fall or remain the same?

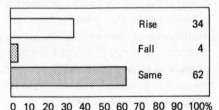

Rise	34
Fall	4
Same	62

0 10 20 30 40 50 60 70 80 90 100%

Concern for company future: Which of the following areas do you expect to be your main business concern during the next six months? (Multiple answers possible)

Tight competition	34
Labour supply	25
Insufficient demand	22
Speed of service or deliveries	5
Availability or cost of materials	4
High interest rates	3
Cashflow	2
Political instability	1
Industrial unrest	1
Other	1
None	2

The survey was compiled by Frank Small & Associates in Singapore from telephone interviews with a quota sample of businessmen. Business directories were used to construct a sampling frame. Eligibility criteria were set for number of employees in the company and for the respondent's seniority, and company quotas were set for different company types. Interviewing took place between August 5 and August 19. A response rate of 41% among eligible companies was achieved.

Respondents had the following company titles: manager 44; director 24; general manager 17; vice president 4; executive 3; controller 3; officer 2; president 1; accountant 1; company secretary 1. In terms of their companies' activities, 25% are in manufacturing, 25% in banking, insurance or finance; 24% in imports, exports or trading; and 26% in other sectors. Of the companies taking part, 35 had work forces of less than 100; 30 were between 101 and 249; 21 were between 250 and 499; nine were between 500 and 999; four were between 1,000 and 2,499; and one was between 2,500 and 4,999.

Note: 'Other' category in charts includes those who answered 'Don't know' or declined to answer.

Investment risk: Singapore: 75

The days of double-digit growth may be over for Singapore, but GDP growth for this year is expected to be 6% to 8% – a respectable result given the slowdown in the world economy over the past 12 months.

The economy in any case needs room to breathe. Since the mid-1980s Singapore has been transformed from a manufacturing-based economy to one based on hi-tech industry and services. This has put pressure on Singapore's limited labour force, keeping wage rates high.

The rate of inflation, however, has remained low, thanks to tight monetary and fiscal policies. It is expected to fall during 1992, as domestic demand eases off and the Singapore dollar strengthens.

Meanwhile the government will continue its efforts to encourage multinational service companies to locate their Asian regional headquarters in Singapore and further improvemnents in telecommunications and transportation systems are in the pipeline.

Singapore scored as follows:

1	Inflation	9
2	Interest rate	6
3	GDP Growth	7
4	Infrastructure	10
5	Labour: strife and shortages	5
6	Bureaucratic impediments	8
7	Government intervention in business	5
8	Threat of armed aggression (internal and external)	9
9	Political volatility	8
10	Business confidence level	7

Investment risk: 74
Last year's score: 75

Reproduced by courtesy of *Asian Business*

TAIWAN
(Republic of China)

Nominal GDP: US$ 161.7bn/NT$4,384bn
GDP real growth: 5.3 per cent
Exports: US$67.2bn (+ 1.5 per cent)
Imports: US$54.7bn (+ 4.7 per cent)
Net foreign debt: 0
Trade surplus: US$12.5bn
Population: 20.3m
Work-force: 8.46m (1989)
Unemployment: 1.7 per cent
Inflation (annual CPI): 3.8 per cent
Savings rate: 29.5 per cent
Overseas visitor numbers: 2.044m (1989)
Head of State: President Lee Teng-hui
Head of Government: Premier Hau Pei-tsun
Ruling party: Nationalist Party (Kuomintang)
Other political party: Democratic Progressive Party
Capital city: Taipei (GMT+8 hours)

(Figures for year ending 1990, except where stated)

Membership of international organisations: Asian Development Bank, ICAO, INTELSAT, Interpol, ITU, WMO.

Goals

Taiwan's chief concern must lie in making every attempt possible to encourage and maintain real political stability. Only then may the relationship with the mainland be turned to real commercial and economic advantages, allowing Taiwan to make the very best use of its skills where there is an abundance of willing labour.

Brief history

Situated in the western Pacific Ocean, Taiwan is shaped like a leaf, is about 394 kilometres long and 144 kilometres wide and covers a land

183

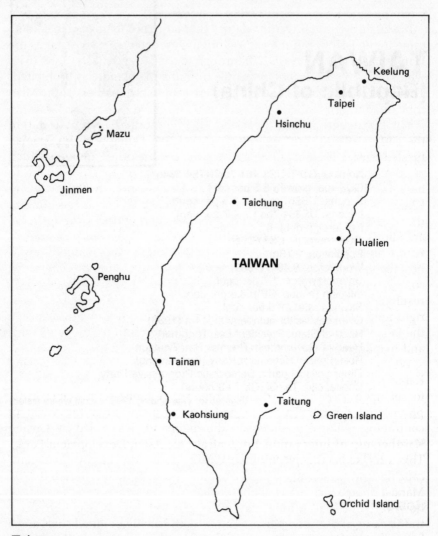

Taiwan

area of 35,742 square kilometres, only slightly smaller than the Netherlands. The spectacular mountain ranges which traverse this typhoon-
prone island run from north to south and have meant that 20 million
people have found themselves able to live on only one quarter of the
land that is habitable, mostly the plains on the western side of the
island. There are also nearly 80 smaller islands which have a link of
some kind with Taiwan, geographic, economic or administrative,
including Penghu (the Pescadores) (midway between the Chinese

mainland and Taiwan), Jinmen, Mazu (both off the coast of Fukien) and Orchid Island (74km south-east of Taiwan).

It was during the fifteenth century that large numbers of Han settlers came to the island, but the earliest origins probably go back as far as the Han dynasty (206BC to AD220) through to the Ming dynasty (1368-1644) when overseas settlement by people from the mainland was prohibited. The original inhabitants of the island are said to be members of the Miao tribe of southern China.

The Portuguese named the island 'Ilha Formosa' (Beautiful Island) in the early sixteenth century and then both the Dutch and the Spanish tussled over it, each invading and driving out the other, until the Dutch got the upper hand at the end of the seventeenth century. Theirs was to be a Pyrrhic victory because the legendary Koxinga (Cheng Ch'eng-Kung) of the Ming resistance routed the Dutch, only for the Ming to then see the Manchus subsume the island as part of their own territorial ambitions in 1683 into Fukien province. When the French quarrelled with China, Taiwan was once again kicked around like a highly-prized hostage, so much so that French troops actively occupied Formosa for some time in 1894. The island was then occupied by the Japanese as a result of the Treaty of Shimonoseki in 1895 after the Sino–Japanese war, right up to the end of the Second World War. The profound influence of the Japanese is even now clearly palpable in the culture, the work ethic and management style of the country and its people.

When the Nationalist Chinese (the 'Kuomintang') led by Chiang Kai-shek were routed by Communist forces in 1949, they fled to Taiwan to set up a *de facto* 'alternative China', a republic with Taipei as its provisional capital. This intended haven, away from the years of continuing political madness on the mainland, was ruled by Chiang Kai-shek as president until his death in 1975 when his son took over. This was to be the place where the undoubtedly highly intelligent, capable and dexterous Chinese would truly flourish, unfettered by Marxist dogma, achieving all their wildest dreams of success. That ideal, however, does fall a long way short of what Taiwan has become, a traffic-clogged but productive country, with heavily polluted cities and a history of producing cheap toys, textiles and electronics.

One of the greatest problems for the Taiwanese today seems to be just how to dispose of all the wealth they have been accumulating through their sheer industry and energy. They are also now looking rather more seriously at less materialistic concerns such as how they can cope with the vast ecological damage they have caused themselves, or with their lack of genuine political freedom and expression.

Few people realise that Taiwan, with a population of 20.3 million ranks as the country with the second highest population density in the world (560 per square kilometre) spread throughout the cities of Taipei, the port city of Kaohsiung, Taichung, Tainan and Keelung and through

rural settlements in between. Taipei's population is around 2.6 million.
The high-tech centre of Taiwan is considered to be Hsinchu in the south.

The country's strengths

● Tariff reductions and improved market access for foreign goods.
● Gradual relaxation of foreign exchange controls and investment
restrictions.
● Improved protection of intellectual property rights.
● Improving efficiency in national resource allocation.

The country's weaknesses

● Soaring wages.
● An acute labour shortage.
● A capital crunch.
● The rising tide of protectionism and stiff competition in the global
marketplace.
● Prohibitive land prices for commercial/industrial development.

Politics

Technically speaking, Taiwan is a constitutional democracy, based on Dr
Sun Yat-Sen's borrowed Three Principles of The People, 'a government
of the people, by the people and for the people'. The main problem has
always been that, until Chiang Ching-kuo's death in 1988, these 'people'
were those who originated from the mainland and it was not until the
present incumbent, Lee Teng-hui that the country has had a ruler whose
real roots lie in Taiwan itself.

As a result, there has been very little grassroots support for, or
interest in, the politics of outsiders who had come to Taiwan and
established a government over a native people who really did not want
to see themselves as part of a greater argument. That is now changing,
most likely because increasing prosperity has made politics less of the
geriatrically dominated nightmare than it used to be. It is becoming the
pastime of better-off and better-educated idealistic youngsters, but it still
has a very long way to go.

The basic system allows for a President, a National Assembly and five
'Yuan' or ministries who carry out executive (the Cabinet), legislative,
judicial, examination and control functions. The National Assembly has
the power to elect the President (for a six-year term) and the vice-

president and to revise the constitution. The President is also the commander-in-chief of the armed forces. He represents the country in foreign affairs and makes other key appointments (such as the Premier and the Auditor-General).

Taiwan is not a country used to abrupt political change but back in 1987, during the presidency of Chiang Ching-kuo, son of Chiang Kai-shek, martial law was finally lifted. Chiang Ching-kuo himself died on 13th January 1988 signalling the end of a dynasty but the potential beginnings of new freedom. For the first time, opposition parties were allowed by the National Security Law of 15th July 1987, the bureaucracy was somewhat liberalised and a measure of greater freedom of the Press was permitted. Then the Taiwanese were given the chance to visit their relatives on the mainland from whom they had been unjustly separated for so very long.

Chiang Ching-kuo's reforms have been continued by Lee Teng-hui, the first Taiwanese-born president. Most significant of all was the repeal of the Sedition Law which has long been used to suppress all measures of dissent. The outcry from the people at the arrest for sedition of four dissidents for supporting a more radical arm of the Taiwan independence movement so worried the government that they realised profound reform was required to keep the people calm and working for yet more prosperity.

In May of 1991, Lee declared an end to the war with the Communists on the mainland and laid the groundwork for a more genuinely representative government on the island, a move which has not as yet provoked a response from Beijing. There are now possibly as many as 14 opposition parties in Taiwan, but the main one, the Democratic Progressive Party has been able to win seats in the Legislative Yuan and is gradually democratically booting out the 300 or so fusty octogenarians who have run the country for so long. They have, however, suffered at least two defections by key politicians over the party's radical stance in support of complete independence from the mainland. The question over the degrees of putative independence of Taiwan from the mainland is the real thorn that still festers now in the country's political side.

Taiwan's trade and investment on the mainland, just across the one hundred mile-wide Taiwan Strait, are growing and more and more people from Taiwan are getting involved in the PRC in one way or another. The area that lies directly across in Fukien is a 'little Taiwan' fuelled by still 'illegal' direct investment from the ROC. The whole process may well take another decade or so of smooth transition but it is fairly likely, sooner or later that a reconciliation will have to take place. The move to keep Taiwan and the PRC as two separate entities will ultimately break down as the two countries increasingly recognise their interdependence and genuine need for each other's capabilities and resources.

Domestic economy, current economic policy and forecasts

Taiwan's wealth is prodigious. The country is said to have about US$70bn in yen, dollars and other foreign currencies sloshing around in bank accounts around the world (Japan has US$84bn, and that is with six times as many people) and also has the benefit of around US$3,500 per head of population of foreign cash. The trouble is that the Taiwanese, who for so long never touched their savings, are now learning to spend with a vengeance having hoarded every penny for over 30 years. Comparatively freed up from the Kuomintang's obsessions with security, and with export-led wealth as a way to maintain that security, vast amounts of money have started to flow out of the country in the last three to four years into foreign stocks and bonds, as well as into real estate, acquired companies and investment in new overseas plants. Thailand is one of the hot spots for Taiwanese money, with some one billion dollars pouring in since 1988. The frugal Taiwanese, though, still save roughly one third of their earnings but buying more consumer goods with spending of nearly $40bn per annum on imported goods. The equation is beginning to change, calling the very fundaments of this export-led economy into question.

Taiwan's economic policy is still essentially linked to national security and will continue to be so as long as the relationship with the PRC remains stagnant. Regardless of what both sides may say, the ties between Taiwan and China are growing, so much so that just a couple of years ago, Taiwan offered the PRC nearly ten billion dollars to rev up the mainland economy. The farsighted proposal, put by a delegation of leading Kuomintang officials, merely asked in return that the mainland throw off all Communist policies and ideology. Not much has happened since then. Direct investment in the PRC is not allowed as yet but there is increasing pressure from Taiwan manufacturers to allow direct communications, trade agreements, legal agreements, and so on. Xiamen, is an economic zone in the mainland just across the Taiwan Strait and there are a couple of dozen or more small textile firms there, some of which are joint ventures between Taiwan and the PRC. The control of inflation continues to be one of the highest priorities in economic policy and tight banking controls will continue to be necessary for some time.

The economy has also been quite seriously in the doldrums for some time, even though more than one third of Taiwan's export-orientated manufacturers, the backbone of the island's once fast-growing economy, say they are optimistic enough to expect an economic upturn in the not-too-distant future. This does not, however, mean that they are rushing to make new investments domestically. A recent Government-sponsored survey of 8,000 manufacturing firms showed that as many as 38 per cent of the respondents painted a rosy picture of the economy, with those in chemicals, textiles, electronics and electric machinery being especially optimistic. Those in small-sized labour-intensive enterprises, however, around one fifth of the respondents, said that they were just waiting to see, neither pessimistic nor optimistic, but 39 per cent expected the economic conditions to remain the same, that is at best unexceptional.

The truth is now that soaring wages, and acute labour shortage, a capital crunch and prohibitive land prices have stopped many manufacturers from making new investments. Growing labour costs are usually considered to be the most serious problem by the manufacturers themselves, followed by the increasingly cut-throat competition and the manpower shortage. The Taipei authorities have been lowering economic growth targets because of the increasingly weak state of domestic investment.

In order to ensure the continued expansion of the economy of Taiwan and, they hope, to make it the ideal Asian-Pacific Rim capital for the year 2000, the government has undertaken an ambitious Six-Year National Development Plan which will involve a total expenditure of US$303bn and, they hope, fuel further industrial development and balanced regional development. A number of these present significant opportunities for involvement for foreign firms. It is hoped also that per capita income will be increased from its already high present level of US$7,347, as a result of investment and development efforts.

Taiwan's greatest *bête noire* in recent years has been South Korea but now the two are beginning to try and ally themselves economically more and more to each other's advantage. Trying desperately to reduce their trade deficits with Japan, both countries are now looking to double their bilateral trade to cut loose from the binds that tie them to financial indebtedness to Japan. However, the only two areas in which they do not directly compete are in cars and shipping so the 'difficult brothers' may find that the antipathy between them that always lies only just below the surface may prove to be victor in the end. The Taiwanese are also becoming increasingly involved in Indonesia and Vietnam, and further afield even in New Zealand and Australia, seeking to take advantage of vastly cheaper land prices and in the case of Indonesia, pools of inexpensive labour.

Banking and finance, equity market outlook, stockmarkets

The Ministry of Finance and the Central Bank of China between them decide on and implement banking and finance policies, and manage foreign exchange, the issue of currency and the regulation of the money supply and credit. Exchange controls have been relaxed somewhat in recent years, especially since July 1987 when the government decided it had to free up capital inflows and outflows in order to stimulate the economy. At the same time, there was a sharp appreciation in the NT dollar, making Taiwanese goods not quite as inexpensive as they had been previously. The boot was suddenly on the other foot, since it now made sense for the first time in years for Taiwan to make a concerted positive effort to import more from abroad. Not only that but the powers that be realised that there was a lot to be gained from encouraging overseas investors who would allow more Taiwanese companies to hook up with foreign interests and therefore ultimately expand their own interests. Far from being an interfering nuisance, the new presence of these foreigners would increase Taiwan's avenues out into the world. An almost complete volte-face.

Taiwan has already achieved a good deal of success in liberalising its financial markets and is trying, like nearly every other country in the Asian-Pacific Rim, to secure its position as the financial centre of the region. In fact, it is unlikely to do so since because so many investors are still wary of Taiwan's history of truculence and inflexibility, whatever the present situation may be. In 1988, a 15-year ban on new brokerage licences was lifted and now a campaign is seriously underway to lure in more foreign brokerage houses. It is unlikely – unless Hong Kong falls into the sea tomorrow or the Red Army walks in – that people will be tempted away from the *laissez-faire* environment where they currently find themselves operating into a place where bureaucracy and political machinations are still the order of the day. Recently the Taiwan Government allowed the creation of private banks, which some are worried may create a banking free-for-all that could, as the government knows, swamp the government-owned banks. As in Korea, a vast growth in convertible bonds is predicted.

Nevertheless, since 1987, the Taiwan stockmarket has seen tens of thousands of fledgling investors pour money into the market, so much so that price/earnings ratios hit a staggering 100 times in a previously comatose market that had previously been the domain of only the very speculative investors. Putting paid to this somewhat though has been a major stockmarket fraud which was exposed not long ago when a ring swindled $115m from ten Taiwanese stockbroking houses, using stock certificates to raise capital and then selling the stock elsewhere. A government plan intends to privatise nearly half of the country's 45 state-run companies and will give the stockmarket plenty of meat to play with.

Foreign earnings may now be sent out up to an annual limit of $3m each year and the days are also long gone, thankfully, when a foreign exchange license was necessary to engage in trade to or from Taiwan. Instead dealings now merely have to be officially reported. Stockmarket capitalisation has in recent times achieved the position of the third largest in the world after Tokyo and New York and foreign reserves have been up in the $70bn arena. Of all countries in the Asian-Pacific

Rim only two are generally considered to be low-risk in terms of creditworthiness – Taiwan and Singapore.

The insurance industry, also since 1987, has started to open up with seven US companies gaining a foothold, Life Insurance Co of Georgia, Aetna International, American Family Life, Metropolitan Insurance & Annuity Co, Chubb Corp, Cigna Corp, and American International Underwriters.

Trade and Industry

The Taiwanese always accuse us, foreign business concerns that is, of not being aggressive enough in taking advantage of the Taiwanese favouritism towards non-Japanese products. The country is literally urging all its folk to go out and buy foreign, and in nothing like the same half-hearted and lip service vein that was seen when prime minister Nakasone of Japan ostensibly urged his people to do the same. Taiwan really does mean it, if only because it is somewhat desperate to get itself out of hock with Japan after so many years of buying Japanese products. Now that the Taiwanese are clearly interested in spending their money, we should definitely get in there and help them spend it.

Taiwan's economy has, in recent years, been somewhat liberalised, with the removal of thousands of fiddly and sometimes incomprehensible tariffs and non-tariff barriers to business and trade. A staggering 3,500 items had their tariffs cut by as much as 50 per cent and the government allowed the New Taiwan dollar to rise against the US dollar, making foreign goods even more competitive. This, together with some relaxation in exchange controls, has given a major shot in the arm to Taiwan's international trade.

Taiwan is not rich in natural resources but there are sizeable deposits of marble and dolomite, and small amounts of copper, gold, petroleum, natural gas and coal, none of which are large enough to begin to satisfy the domestic demand. The abundance of forests on the island is largely inaccessible and often of poor quality or protected by the new strict conservation policies. Nearly all raw material needs for Taiwan's hungry industries are met from abroad.

The total work-force is made up of 8.46 million people of whom 44.87 per cent are white collar, 42.24 per cent are industrially employed and 12.9 per cent work in agriculture and fishing. The labour force in Taiwan has roughly 300,000 new workers every year and constitutes approximately 40 per cent of the total population and unemployment is only around two per cent. There is a continuing wage spiral as workers move on to other jobs for increased pay and it is important to remember that the wages you will pay here are already substantially higher than in some of the possible alternative markets for your business. As in many other Asian-Pacific Rim countries, agriculture's share of the labour market is falling off, from 19.5 per cent in 1980 to 12.7 per cent in 1989 and, not surprisingly, the industrial share is growing. The government's focus is increasingly on the service sector and the Council for Economic Planning and Development would like as many as 50.6 per cent to be employed in services by the year 2000. At the moment, industry in Taiwan is undergoing a transition from labour-intensive to capital-intensive production and the industrial structure is being upgraded and streamlined. There is a huge demand consequently for modern capital equipment and advanced technology, as well as scientific and technological know-how.

The Government of Taiwan is also singularly determined to reinforce Taiwan's bid to become the centre of the Asian-Pacific's high-tech industry. The entrepreneurial zeal on the island should be one of the seven wonders of the world in that Taiwan is now possibly the world's ultimate silicon island. Information industry exports are now projected to reach $10bn this year, outranking the three leading NIEs. South Korea's output this year will be around $6bn, Singapore's $5.7bn, and Hong Kong's just $1.7bn. Taiwan is also home to one of the top ten computer companies in the world, Acer. The company's chairman, Stan Shih, is personally ambitious for the company to become one of the top five IBM compatible producers in the world and is working towards this with both laptops and workstations for the next generation of computers.

The government is also extremely keen to encourage Taiwan's potential as a marketing centre for foreign products throughout the Asian-Pacific Rim. The spirit is undoubtedly extremely willing although the bureaucratic flesh is still primarily weak and yet complex. Persistence and a network of local contacts, plus a good measure of commercial endurance, are certainly needed to achieve in Taiwan a very good Asian-Pacific base. After Tokyo, and in the present political scenario *vis à vis* Hong Kong, Taiwan nevertheless remains one of the best choices for future development potential for Western companies seeking an Asian-Pacific base.

The government has a programme of incentives to attract new business, particularly in technology and capital-intensive areas, namely, information technology, consumer electronics, telecommunications, automation systems and advanced materials. Special tax incentives are also given in 100 priority industrial projects. These include tax concessions and allowances, new industrial estates with port facilities, and accelerated depreciation of fixed assets for new product development or energy conservation. To date, however, the spinoff for foreign companies seeking to break in is slight. There are still less than 20 representative offices of European firms trading in Taiwan but approaches are being made from many others seeking to become involved in helping with the country's new Six-Year National Development Plan which covers a number of sectors from telecommunications and pollution control (eg, for products such as the Tamsui river which had a total spending budget on clean-up of $2.17bn in 1988), the high-speed railway, aircraft manufacture and the nuclear industry.

There are, however, real and increasing opportunities for the marketing of European goods in Taiwan from high-fashion garments and cosmetics to consumer appliances and high-end manufacturing machinery. The demand for these goods is growing in part because of Taiwan's continued negotiations for a better stance in relations with the EEC and also because better marketing efforts are being made by Western firms who are increasingly aware of Taiwan's prosperity and lucrative market.

Taiwan also has increasingly good trading opportunities with other Asian-Pacific Rim countries, exporting goods to Thailand, Malaysia, the Philippines and Indonesia amongst others, and in return purchasing consumer goods and raw materials for use in manufacture.

The trade promotion organisation of Taiwan is the China External Trade Development Council (CETRA) which used to be a fairly single-minded one-way street intent on maximising Taiwan's outbound trade. Things have changed. CETRA has now become a useful starting place for businessmen seeking to obtain as much helpful information as possible about the market and the kinds of products and services that are genuinely in demand and would therefore have a good chance of success.

Headquartered in Taipei, the organisation has some 600 staff who are able to give comprehensive information (on 16mm microfilm, not electronic database) on domestic importers and 11,500 suppliers and access to foreign-language trade journals that may be relevant to your chosen area. These provide the latest published information on Taiwan's products and market conditions. The Traders' Express Service (see, Taipei World Trade Centre in the 'Conferences' Section) will help overseas buyers, and sometimes sellers, with introductions to possible business partners. There is no doubt that overseas buyers have the better deal with several highly efficient services including a Taiwan Industrial Products Services bureau, and the Trade Opportunities Project both of which are designed to make large volume buying of hot Taiwanese products as effortless as possible.

The companion organisation to CETRA is the Far East Trade Service which is only a suitable resource for those seeking to export products, such as sporting goods or other items, out of Taiwan to home markets.

Foreign investment has been steadily growing to around $1.5bn per annum. Contributing factors have been the growing uncertainty over the future of Hong Kong, the lifting of martial law, stringent foreign exchange controls, and much simpler investment procedures. Although the Taiwanese dollar is on the upward rise, one attractive feature is the ample if not always appropriate labour. Unemployment has dropped as low as 1.5 per cent. Encouraged by these factors, ten American states have so far set up commercial offices in the Taipei World Trade Center.

Apart from banking, investment, insurance, car rentals, advertising, marketing and fast food, there are said to be a number of opportunities in Taiwan for foreign investment. Nearly 40 per cent of the GDP is based in the manufacturing sector, followed by 19 per cent for finance, insurance and real estate, and 16 per cent for the wholesale and retail trade. Construction constitutes approximately five per cent of the GDP, agriculture, hunting, fishing and forestry five per cent and transport, storage and communications seven per cent.

Taiwan is a major offshore production base for the Japanese automotive industry and is expected to manufacture one million cars a year by 1995 with a minimum of 70 per cent domestic content. Apart from finished cars, Taiwan would like to become a major supplier of car components and spare parts in an industry that could be worth nearly one billion dollars a year in trade. The domestic market is also fairly insatiable considering the widely held prediction that there will be 175 vehicles per 1,000 people within the next five years.

A manufacturing plant to produce aircraft, Air Asia Co, was started recently by Taichung Machinery Works, and Yue Loong Motor Co, in conjunction with components made by Boeing and McDonnell Douglas Corporation.

In 1989 there was a partial deregulation of the telecom network with the start of value added networks from the private sector offering information processing services, home banking, e-mail, voice mail, etc. The government controls telephone, telegraph, telex and packet switching. Foreign companies are not eligible to become involved as yet.

Companies of note

Chia Hsin Flour Feed &
  Vegetable Oil Corp
China Steel Corp
Evergreen Marine Corp
Far Eastern Textile Ltd
Formosa Chemicals & Fibre Corp
  (textiles)
Formosa Plastic Corp
Hualon Teijin Co (textiles)

Nan Ya Plastics Corp
President Enterprises Corp (food)
Sanpo Corporation
Tang Eng Iron Works
Tatung Co (machinery)
Yue Loong Motor Co Ltd
Yuen Foong Yu Paper
  Manufacturing Co

A thorough study of the history, as well as of both the annual and stockbrokers' reports (where available), of the companies of note will give you a good idea of the commercial 'inner game' psychology of the countries in which you plan to do business.

Agriculture

Taiwan is blessed with a mixed climate and varied topography because of the large number of mountain ranges and despite the fact that there is only very limited arable land available, there is quite a prosperous agriculture in the country largely in the form of multicropping. The country is self-sufficient in rice and grows at least 50 different kinds of fruit, an abundance of vegetables and a number of varieties of tea. Pork, poultry and sugar are also important export items. White chrysanthemums and a number of other flowers are also increasingly cultivated for the Japanese market.

Fishing and aquaculture have enjoyed considerable growth and development over the years but are tending to fall off as hi-tech in Taiwan, just as in Japan before her, is stealing labour from the land. The lure of high wages in component and other factories is increasingly drawing people into towns and leaving a shortage of agricultural labour in the countryside. Currently the average rice yield at one hectare per 2.47 acres, according to the Institute for Food and Development Policy, is the lowest in the Asian-Pacific after the Philippines and Vietnam.

The tenth four-year economic development plan has reorganised farm land into rectangular fields in order to allow the greater use of machinery and automation. The sector will however decrease in importance as a result of government plans to change the use of agricultural land to housing, industrial sites and public works, at the rate of 2,500 hectares per annum over the next few years.

Tourism

It was only as recently as November 1987 that the Taiwanese were allowed to go to visit their relatives in the mainland from whom most have been separated since 1948. Since that time, well over one million tourists have hopped across the Strait, creating a whole new destination for the Taiwanese market. In general though, the government is now actively encouraging the people to get out and about and to adopt a more international attitude. A major tourism festival was held last year to open local eyes to the wonders of foreign travel and a congress of the American Society of Travel Agents also whet the appetites of the people. With so much disposable income, the Taiwanese need little encouragement to go abroad and see what the world has to offer and the conditions present ripe opportunities for foreign interests to get in and help develop the market.

Infrastructure

Of the total budget, 18 per cent is allocated to further infrastructural development on modernisation of transport, energy and telecommunications. Among the many projects on the drawing board are a high-speed railway and the introduction of rapid transit systems (along the lines of Hong Kong's MTR) in many major cities, to cost US$16bn or more. A major French company has supplied nearly $300m worth of equipment and know-how for the new route between the internal airport in Sungshan and a Taipei zoo in the suburbs. The highways are being expanded and improved.

In terms of power generation and capability, a new, fourth nuclear power plant will come on line and new petrochemical plants will come into operation. Other areas being tackled are those relating to pollution control, additional mass housing, and a number of research and development facilities to aid industry and technology.

Communications

The recent growth in telecommunications has been rapid in urban areas, with some 8.4 million subscribers in towns and cities at the end of 1990. Nineteen-seventy saw the launch of two Asian and trans-Pacific satellites which has led to direct-dial services from Taiwan to over 100 countries and direct-fax services to 40. Fax and telex are widely available.

Transportation

There are two international airports in Taiwan, the Chiang Kai-shek International airport 40 kilometres or one hour from Taipei and Kaohsiung International. There are half a dozen other domestic airports for both freight and passenger traffic which are served by domestic carriers. The main national and international airline of Taiwan is China Airlines and there are seven other domestic airlines including Far Eastern Air Transport.

Taiwan is now the fourth largest cargo handler in the world after the United States, Japan and the UK with some 237,336.3 tonnes of inbound freight by air in 1990 and 357,306.5 tonnes outward bound and 117,857,897 tonnes moving through the island's ports. Kaohsiung is in fact the world's third busiest port in terms of overall container volume, and is expected to overtake Hong Kong by the year 2000. Almost all of the major international air and ocean freight carriers are represented in Taiwan.

The Taiwan Railway Administration runs an extensive 1000 kilometre rail network for both freight and passenger traffic. Special business class cars equipped with mobile phones, and comparable to the 'Green-sha' (Green Car) compartments on the Shinkansen in Japan, are being added to the 'Tzuchiang' high-speed trains on the Taipei-Kaohsiung route.

There is a main highway from Keelung and Kaohsiung currently undergoing expansion work. Good bus services go right round the island and also thoroughly cover the inland areas. Ferry services run from Kaohsiung, Twinan and Chiayi to Penghu, and from Taitung to the Lanyu and Green Island and from Keelung to Okinawa, Japan. There is a car ferry service between Keelung and Hualien.

Conferences, conventions and trade fairs

Taipei's World Trade Center (5 Hsinyi Road, Section 5, Taipei; tel 725-1111, fax 351-3603) provides a very useful focal point in a fairly chaotic and busy city for overseas businessmen and offers first-class facilities. Now just five years old, the building has nearly 100,000 square metres of exhibition space with the latest facilities available. The Trade Center has an average of one new trade show every two weeks giving comprehensive cover and exposure to all facets of Taiwanese trade. There is also a large area dedicated to permanent trade exhibitions and a show case for products ... the perfect starting point in Taiwan to begin exploring the market for ideas.

Taxation

In Taiwan it is the local government, not the central administration, which is responsible for all tax collection but the Ministry of Finance obviously has the ultimate responsibility. Income tax is payable by residents and non-residents alike who are in the country for more than 90 days in any one calendar year. If you are in Taiwan for between 90 and 183 days a year, tax on income is levied at a flat rate of 20 per cent and no deductions are allowable. Residents who are in the country for more that 183 days in one year pay rates, after various deductible allowances of around between 10-20 per cent, starting at six per cent from income of less than NT$79,999, right up to 50 per cent for income of NT$3.4m and over. However, an expatriate businessman who is in Taiwan for more than 183 days in one year, starts to pay tax from the ninetieth day at a flat rate of 20 per cent but there is a claimable allowance of 20 per cent of gross or NT$36,000 whichever is the lower. You may also deduct a standard ten per cent (15 per cent for married couples) for such items as insurance payments, medical expenses, charitable donations and, believe it or not, property losses. This is intended only as a very rough guide in order to allow you comparison with other Asian-Pacific Rim countries, but it is essential you get expert advice from reputable firms on your personal case.

The fiscal year runs from 1st January to 31st December but arrangements may be made to change this to suit your company's usual financial practises if needed. Corporate tax rates, levied on all non-resident companies on income produced in Taiwan, basically vary from nil to 25 per cent after allowable expenses from gross income but are as high as 35 per cent on dividends to non-resident companies.

VAT of between five and ten per cent is payable on most goods bought.

Exchange rates and currency positioning relative to US$

The Taiwanese dollar, or NT (New Taiwan) dollar is more freely exchanged now than since before 1987 and the relaxation of foreign currency controls. A foreign visitor, whether businessman or tourist, may bring in up to US$5,000 or NT$40,000 which must be declared upon entry to the custom's official. Officially, only authorised banks and dealers may change foreign currency, as in designated banks, hotels and at the airport. The dollar is denominated in one, five, and ten-dollar coins and 50, 100, 500, and 1,000 dollar notes.

The relaxation of foreign exchange controls led to a marked appreciation of the NT dollar in recent years. It surged about 30 per cent against the US dollar, nearly matching that of the Japanese yen during the 1986-87 period. It stabilised thereafter but not before the NT dollar became so high that exports were for some time priced out of European and North American markets.

The people, their languages, education and religion

The official language of Taiwan's 20 million people, and the one taught throughout the school system, is Mandarin. However a Fukien dialect, that is referred to as 'Taiwanese', is the spoken language most commonly used by people in rural areas in daily conversations. There were large numbers of economic immigrants to Taiwan from mainland China around 100 years ago, mostly from Fukien and Kwangtung provinces but in 1949 there was a mass wave of immigration after the political schism opened up in China causing people to flee from the Maoist regime to set up the Republic of China. Most Taiwanese people are either Buddhist or Taoist but there are some Muslims and a few Roman Catholics and Protestants.

In business use, a working knowledge of Mandarin would be the most useful although you will most certainly get by without any knowledge of the local languages at all. Japanese is widely spoken or at least understood, especially by the older generation because of Japan's historical connections as a former occupier of Taiwan for 50 years. This ended with the cessation of hostilities in the Second World War. (Many Pacific Rim pioneers coming to do business in Taiwan for the first time, do so because they have been 'introduced' through connections in business with Japan. It is not unlikely, therefore that since spoken Japanese is one of the most easily acquired of the Asian languages, some readers will be able to make use of Japanese in Taiwan.) While out on the streets English may not be as widely used as the businessman might wish, most hotels and companies have several dozen fluent English-speakers to help out in case of difficulty. Remember that, on the whole, taxi drivers speak no English whatsoever so it is imperative that you carry written Chinese instructions of your intended destination with directions given to you by hotel staff before you start your journey.

Education is given a very high priority by the ROC government who are anxious to ensure that they have a quality work-force equal to none. A special emphasis is placed throughout on technological and scientific training. For expatriates, there are also a number of international schools in Taipei for children from the United States and Britain, Japan and Germany and French and Dutch elementary schools are shortly about to open. The four main Chinese-language schools are the Mandarin Training Centre, the Mandarin Daily News Language Centre, the Stanford Mandarin Centre, and the Taipei Language Institute.

Visa and health requirements

Visas are required for visitors to Taiwan and are usually valid for three months from the day they are issued. A maximum of 120 days of extension is allowed with two further endorsements from the government immigration office. The status of your visa is entirely dependent on your nationality and whether or not that country has a reciprocal relationship with Taiwan. Expatriates who plan to live and work in Taiwan must have a resident's visa which allows you to live there for up to one year, or in the case of multiple entry, for 36 months. As in Japan, it is necessary to apply for an Alien Resident's Certificate at your nearest city police headquarters within 20 days of arriving in the country. If you are arriving from an area infected by cholera, it is essential that you have proof of inoculation administered more than seven days, and less than six months, before your date of arrival.

Publications of note

There are two English-language daily newspapers published in Taiwan out of the total of 59 with a combined circulation of around 5.7 million. These two, *The China Post*, and *China News*, are the best source of information about domestic events and business. They also draw widely from all the wire services giving fairly comprehensive coverage of world-wide events. Press freedom is considerably greater now than it has been in past years. Also worth noting is, *Industry of Free China*, a bilingual monthly publication from the Executive Yuan's Council for Economic Planning and Development.

The 24-hour English-language radio station, International Community Radio Taipei, has items of interest to business visitors including economic and political features, as well as music. Apart from these, there are also a few English-language films, both American and English on one of the three television stations in Taiwan but there are very few other Western programmes at all. Please note that the video standard used in Taiwan is the American standard, NTSC.

Of particular help to foreign businessmen when dealing with Taiwan are publications from the China External Trade Development Council, especially *What You Can Sell To Taiwan* and *What You Can Buy From Taiwan*. Although you may be snarled up reading the intricacies of import requirements, there is a fair bit of useful information about the kinds of products that are being imported and how to get your products into the retail network.

Scores reflect business worry

The tide of anxiety running through Taiwan's business community is reflected in the *Asian Business* confidence index score of 58 – a fall of 13 points from last year.

Nearly two-thirds of respondents are pessimistic about the chances of an upturn in the economy. Profit declines were recorded by 46% in the past six months, and 59% expect the oil crisis to damage their businesses.

More worrying than high oil prices, the survey shows, are tight competition, insufficient demand and labour shortages. Respondents also fear that the collapse of the local stock market, coupled with strict monetary controls, will restrict their access to capital.

Economic rather than political considerations predominate. Only 7% are worried about political instability.

The survey isn't entirely negative. Only 14% of respondents claim their companies are performing badly, compared with 51% who say they are doing well.

Taiwan confidence index: 58

Asian Business provides readers with a Confidence Index for each country surveyed. To compare the results of confidence surveys conducted around the region, we process the data from each survey and (in conjunction with Frank Small & Associates) arrive at a numerical rating for each country. This Index measures the following six criteria used in the survey: Local market, export market, turnover, profits, company prospects and economy.

ECONOMIC/POLITICAL

National economy: Are you more optimistic about the direction of the national economy than you were six months ago? Less? About the same?

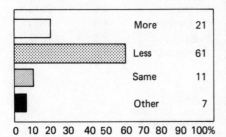

More	21
Less	61
Same	11
Other	7

0 10 20 30 40 50 60 70 80 90 100%

Local market: During the last six months, has your company been operating in an expanding, a static, or a contracting local market?

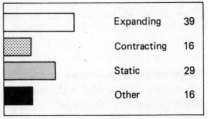

Expanding	39
Contracting	16
Static	29
Other	16

0 10 20 30 40 50 60 70 80 90 100%

Export market: During the last six months, has your company been operating in an expanding, a static, or a contracting export market?

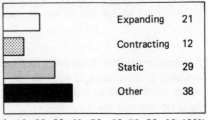

Expanding	21
Contracting	12
Static	29
Other	38

0 10 20 30 40 50 60 70 80 90 100%

201

Labour market: What effect will the increased labour supply, caused by the stock market collapse, have on the national economy?

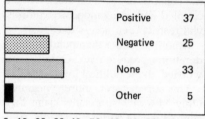

Positive	37
Negative	25
None	33
Other	5

0 10 20 30 40 50 60 70 80 90 100%

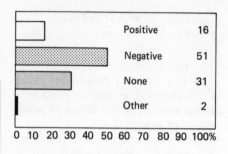

Positive	16
Negative	51
None	31
Other	2

0 10 20 30 40 50 60 70 80 90 100%

Oil prices: What impact will the current oil crisis have on your company's operations?

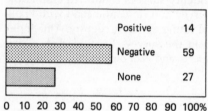

Positive	14
Negative	59
None	27

0 10 20 30 40 50 60 70 80 90 100%

Economic prospects: On a scale of one, for very poor, to 10, for very good, how would you rate the likely performance of the following economies in the next 12 months?

	Average Rating	Proportion who gave a rating
Japan	7.2	97%
Singapore	6.2	97%
Malaysia	6.0	94%
US	6.0	95%
South Korea	5.9	96%
Thailand	5.8	95%
Taiwan	5.7	96%
New Zealand	5.6	84%
Australia	5.6	88%
China	5.2	96%
Indonesia	5.1	94%
Vietnam	4.6	85%
Sri Lanka	4.3	73%
India	3.9	79%
Philippines	3.8	95%

Trade with the mainland: In the next 12 months, will trade with mainland China increase or decrease?

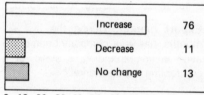

Increase	76
Decrease	11
No change	13

0 10 20 30 40 50 60 70 80 90 100%

CORPORATE

Company prospects: Would you say you are in general more optimistic, about the same, or less optimistic about your company's prospects than you were six months ago?

Access to capital: What effect will the limitations on access to capital, as a result of the stock market collapse, have on the national economy?

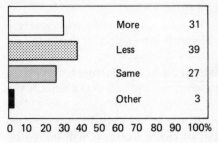

More	31
Less	39
Same	27
Other	3

0 10 20 30 40 50 60 70 80 90 100%

Company performance: Overall, would you say that your company is doing:

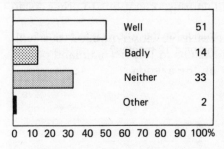

Well	51
Badly	14
Neither	33
Other	2

0 10 20 30 40 50 60 70 80 90 100%

Gross profits: During the past six months, has the trend of your gross profits been up, down, or the same compared with the same period last year?

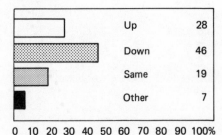

Up	28
Down	46
Same	19
Other	7

0 10 20 30 40 50 60 70 80 90 100%

Turnover: During the last six months, have your company's turnover/billings, compared with the same period last year, gone up, stayed the same or gone

down (i.e. in real terms excluding the effects of inflation)?

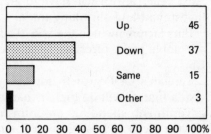

Up	45
Down	37
Same	15
Other	3

0 10 20 30 40 50 60 70 80 90 100%

Staffing levels: Do you expect employment levels in your company over the next six months to:

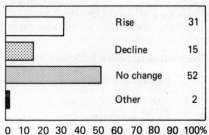

Rise	31
Decline	15
No change	52
Other	2

0 10 20 30 40 50 60 70 80 90 100%

Concern for company future: Which of the following areas do you expect to be your main business concerns over the next six months? (Multiple responses possible)

Tight competition	18
Insufficient demand	14
Labour supply	14
Strong currency	9
Availability or cost of materials	9
Political instability	7
Industrial unrest	6
High interest rates	5
Devaluation	4
Cash flow	3
Speed of service or deliveries	2
Oil prices	2
Other	7

Investment risk: Taiwan 65

Next year Taiwan will have to grapple with lower productivity, falling investment and shrinking trade.

Plus factors include the US$70 billion in foreign exchange reserves, an adaptable work force, and the decreasing reliance of exporters on the US.

Taiwan's GDP growth for this year, while unlikely to surpass this year's figure, will be higher than that of Hong Kong. It will be led by government spending on infrastructure plus the expansion of the service sector, whose growth has now outstripped manufacturing.

Rising unemployment hasn't eased Taiwan's labour shortage significantly. A tight labour market plus rising wage costs will encourage the continued exodus of low-end manufacturing operations to other Asian countries.

As Taiwan's Asian trading partners forge closer political ties with Beijing, there will be more calls for revisions to Taipei's mainland policy. Political liberalisation is now firmly on the agenda.

Taiwan scored as follows:

1	Inflation	8
2	Interest rate	5
3	GDP growth	5
4	Infrastructure	8
5	Labour: Strife and shortages	5
6	Bureaucratic impediments	7
7	Government intervention in business	8
8	Threat of armed aggression (internal and external)	6
9	Political volatility	7
10	Business confidence level	6

Total investment risk: 65
Last year's (1989) score: 70

Reproduced by courtesy of *Asian Business*

KINGDOM OF THAILAND

Nominal GDP: US$81.1bn/Bt2,051.2bn
GDP real growth: 8.5 per cent
Exports: US$23.2bn (+ 20 per cent)
Imports: US$33.3bn (+ 24 per cent)
Foreign debt: US$22.0bn (26.7 per cent of GDP)
Trade deficit: US$10.1bn
Population: 57.6m
Overseas visitor numbers: 5.3m
Work-force: 32.6m
Head of State: The King of Thailand, Rama IX, in the Chakri
    Dynasty (King Bhumibol Adulyadej)
Head of Interim Government: (Caretaker) Prime Minister
    Anand Panyarachun
Ruling party: Chart Thai Party
Other political parties: Democrats, New Aspiration Party, Samakki
    Tham (United in Virtue) Party, Social Action Party, Citizen Party
    ('Rassadorn'), United Democratic Party, Mass Party.
Capital city: Bangkok (GMT+7 hours)

(Figures for year ending 1990)

Membership of international organisations: ANRPC, ASEAN, ASPAC, Asian Development Bank, Association of Tin Producing Countries, CCC, Colombo Plan, EC and Trade Co-operation Agreement, ESCAP, FAO, GATT, G-77, IAEA, IBRD, ICAO, ICO, IDA, IFAD, IFC, IHO, ILO, IMF, IMO, INRO, INTELSAT, Interpol, IPU, IRC, ITC, ITU, UN, UNESCO, UNIDO, UPU, WFC, WHO, WMO, World Bank, WTO.

Brief history

The concept of 'nation, religion and monarchy' is the bedrock of Thai society and of the Thai cultural heritage. The people are thought to have come in waves of migration from south-west China as early as the seventh century. Countless wars with the Burmese, Khmers, and Vietnamese were fought along the way. The country has one of the

205

Thailand

oldest monarchies in the world, existing as an independent sovereign state for over 700 years.

Thai history falls into four distinct periods, the Dvaravaty period (seventh–eleventh centuries), the Sukhothai period (thirteenth–fourteenth centuries), the Ayuthaya period (fourteenth–eighteenth centuries) and the Rattanakosin period (mid-eighteenth century to the present day). Over the centuries, from the sixteenth century onwards battles were also fought with Portuguese, Dutch, English and French seafaring traders who had stumbled across Siam, as it then was. The monarchy ruled the country until 1932. Since then it has been dominated by military-led governments, partially explainable if only because the national traditions to go into the army and to spend time as a buddhist monk have always been so strong that the elite could always be found amongst their ranks.

Bangkok was founded in 1798 by Cho Phraya Chakri, King Rama I and antecedent of the present dynasty. It was Rama III, or King Mongkut, an internationalist along the lines of Japan's emperor Meiji, who introduced Western ideas at the end of the nineteenth century.

The country's strengths

- Thailand has enjoyed the highest GDP growth rate in the Asian-Pacific Rim at an average of nearly ten per cent per annum for three out of the last four years.
- A consumer-spending boom continues as evidenced, for example, by the purchase of household furnishings which have risen by some two-thirds in the last two years.
- Becoming a capital-exporting country. Last year Thai corporations invested more in the US than US corporations invested in Thailand.
- The country has a broadened manufacturing base with an upgraded technological level of exports and with increased local sourcing of components.
- The private sector is both strong and increasingly internationally orientated.
- It provides the perfect business conduit for 'The Golden Pentagon', Indo-China and Myanmar (Burma) a potential market of over 120 million people with substantial human and natural resources after 15 years of near isolation.
- Government intervention in the economy is low, except where liberalisation reforms are required, and is diminishing.
- There is an inherent resilience to the transition of political power so that it has little effect on business confidence in the country.
- Thailand is resource-rich in both agriculture and labour.
- Many believe that Thailand is poised to become the super newly industrialised economy of the 1990s.

The country's weaknesses

- Enforcement of protection over intellectual property rights remains poor.
- The narrow and shallow domestic capital market has a limiting effect on the liquidity of short-term financing.
- The poverty gap is widening with increasing income inequalities.
- The infrastructure is insufficient in terms of physical structures and managerial and technical capabilities to maintain the rate of growth.

Goals

Thailand's main national goal must be to avoid the overheating of the economy with too fast a pace of growth against its weak infrastructural background. All measures must be taken to augment both political and financial stability as well as constancy and to liberalise the financial markets.

Politics

Thailand, one of the six ASEAN nations, is something of a political and economic miracle. It is basically stable, especially when compared with its neighbours Cambodia, Myanmar (Burma) and Laos. There is no doubt that when it comes to her neighbours, the Thai Government would be extremely happy to turn them all collectively into a lucrative market-place for its services and goods. Politics in Thailand is generally regarded as something of a spectator sport and is now very unlikely to derail the juggernaut of economic expansion.

The constitution, which has recently been reviewed, provides for a reigning monarch as head of state, protector of religion and head of the armed forces. There is a bicameral National Assembly, with a 347-member House of Representatives elected by universal adult suffrage for a four-year term, as well as a 268-member senate, appointed for six years by the king on the recommendation of the Prime Minister. The Prime Minister is appointed by the King at the behest of the National Assembly and he in turn appoints a Council of Ministers or Cabinet. There are 73 provinces, each with a governor and there is an independent judiciary.

The country, domestically speaking, is currently ruled by a military junta, headed by businessman and ex-diplomat Anand Panyarachun as Prime Minister. This follows a bloodless but nevertheless fairly dramatic and unsettling coup on 23rd March 1991 which ousted the incumbent

General Chatichai Choonhavan of the then ruling Chart Thai party from his premiership to voluntary exile in London and Switzerland despite the fact that he had a safe parliamentary majority.

It also saw off Major General Manoon Roopkachom who fled to Germany, amidst accusations that he had been involved with an assassination attempt against Queen Sirikit in 1982. Also out was the deputy prime minister, Arthit Kamlang-ek who had only just become Deputy Defence Minister at the time. They were all accused of having used their positions for their own material gain and of supposedly subverting the bureaucracy and the police force, hence the coup.

Thailand seems to have coups as often as other countries have local council meetings and by now they merely leave everyone with a feeling of having seen it all before. What was very strange, though, was that Chatichai had been heralded as the country's first elected prime minister in a decade and all proclaimed that democracy had at last come to Thailand. Maybe they were just tempting fate.

The main reason for the coup, it was widely agreed, was the apparently unprecedented corruption and rampant greed within the Cabinet itself, which the military would no longer tolerate. It has since been established by the Assets Examination Committee that both Chatichai and his chief aide were both 'unusually wealthy'. Chatichai was so annoyed by this pronouncement that he even threatened to come out of political retirement to salvage his reputation by standing for election one more time as leader of the Chart Thai party. While it is undoubtedly true that the organised-crime syndicates in the country are now feeling the heavy hand of the law coming down to suppress them, the level of corruption which runs the flourishing businesses of drug dealing, prostitution, arms and narcotics does not seem to have been diminished whatsoever.

So far the junta has kept one promise, to end martial law, which it did quite quickly in early May 1991. The problem with the original revision of the constitution lay in the putative power of the senate to help choose the country's next prime minister. This clause was correspondingly eliminated from the draft as a result of pressure from both stockmarket reaction and public criticism. The interim government did, however, stick to its word on holding free elections so that power might be turned over to a civilian government. For the first time, a taste of plurality and real democracy has been tempting the electorate and the growing middle classes and they are now beginning to feel they would like a lot more. Since the overthrow of the absolute monarchy in 1932, there has been a steady erosion of military might in Thailand in favour of big business as represented by the politicians. Thai politics is dominated by many different political power groups which are in a constant state of friction. The major groupings are generally considered to be the bureaucracy/technocracy, the politicians, the military and big business.

The Chatichai government was replaced by the National Peace Keeping (*sic*) Council (NPKC) but, ever since, the rumour mill has not wasted an idle moment in stirring up ever more lurid and far-fetched stories of yet more coups just around the corner. There are constant worries about the stability of interim Premier Anand's government and about the question of his succession, even though Anand, by all accounts, is doing a stirling job. He has renegotiated the telephone expansion project with CP Telecom (so long held up by internal wrangling), liberalised the motor vehicle industry, passed the long-awaited VAT bill (seven per cent plus one per cent municipal tax) and successfully hosted the recent World Bank/IMF meeting in October 1991. Both the rule and practice in Thailand is that of government by consensus, not by confrontation, regardless of the military element.

The choice of successors at the moment, if Anand were not to be allowed or indeed want to continue, comes inevitably from the Thai military and possible contenders include the deputy chairman of the NPKC, General Suchinda Kraprayoon, Supreme Commander and Army Commander-in-Chief who masterminded the February coup and who possibly protests a tad too much that he does not want to be prime minister. If he were to have his arm twisted, and it is taken for granted in Thailand that generals are necessarily politically ambitious, he would naturally be the armed forces number one choice. It would allow what few people really want which is the extension of the NKPC's power for another term, even after the elections. Suchinda is also the choice of the ousted Chatichai and of General Sunthorn Kongsompong, the present NPKC chairman.

Opposition to Anand which is largely split comes primarily in the shape of Chaovalit Yongchaiyut, Suchinda's predecessor as army chief who now leads the New Aspiration Party (NAP). Also opposing is the new Samakki Tham (United in Virtue) party which is said to be touting for Suchinda as prime minister although he emphatically denies all such claims. The party which used to be the country's second largest, the Solidarity Party, has now fragmented, with its former members largely dissolving into either the NAP or the Samakki Tham. The Democrat Party, the doyen of all Thai political parties, seems to have come through unscathed, perhaps benefiting from its very long years in the Thai political game.

Anand's government is generally believed to be one of the most competent and cleanest governments that the country has had in recent years. Together with his merry band of technocrats, he is widely lauded for his successful efforts in luring back overseas investors who had their confidence shaken by yet another coup. The same group have also worked hard on the necessary programmes to liberalise economic, monetary and fiscal policies and to revise the tax laws, as well as the companies act, the civil and commercial code and financial and banking regulations. Foreign policy has not changed much in that the country still works towards its stated aim of forging closer business ties with Vietnam and Cambodia, and more quietly with Laos and Myanmar, for its own sound economic ends. They call it their 'battlefields into markets' policy. Indeed, Thailand is better able to play a more important role in finding peace in Cambodia now that Chatichai, with his heavy inclination towards Vietnam and Hun Sen, is gone. Regardless of the make-up or political disposition of the government, the army in Thailand always has ultimate control in the most important areas of the country's foreign policy. In particular, only the military command can influence relations with Cambodia, Laos and Myanmar. The motivation now, even for them, is serious business rather than the paying of lip-service to ASEAN leaders for impression's sake.

The truth is that in the first days of the present government, the military leaders of Thailand were antagonised on a number of counts by Anand and his men by causing them, it would appear, to 'lose face'. They would not allow the military a bigger chunk of the national budget for defence spending. Furthermore, no key positions in the government were given to these military men, a situation guaranteed to inflame their sensitive egos. Anand has also shown that his political and economic performance as a government has been vastly superior to that of the NPKC. They nevertheless consider that they risked their lives in organising the coup and should now therefore be rewarded with government of the country. A compromise will more than likely be reached before push comes to shove.

As a Newly Industrialised Country, Thailand no longer receives substantial aid from Britain: the figure is currently around £3m for technical co-operation and scholarships. US aid was suspended at the time of the coup but Japan continues to grant large amounts of aid, both official and unofficial.

Domestic economy, current economic policy and forecasts

Thailand, with a growth figure in 1991 of around 8.5 per cent (down from the double digits of the past few years, but still high) continues to vie with neighbouring Malaysia and Singapore as the ASEAN economic pacesetter. Thailand has perhaps been the most surprising of countries to enjoy economic success in the Asian-Pacific Rim given the parlous state of its fragile democracy and the political shenanigans in the background. Nevertheless the country has gone from a GDP of US$775 to one of US$1420 in just the period 1986-90. Now finally the economy is coming off the boil just as it appeared to be heading towards a

211

boom-and-bust cycle as a result of property and stockmarket speculation, but our worst fears have been allayed by Prime Minister Anand's
careful economic direction.

The generals in the junta, Anand's bosses at the NKPC, have
themselves benefited enormously, it is said, from gains in both property
and stockmarket speculation and will now take great pains to make sure
that a sound footing is established for long-term growth if only for the
benefit of their own pockets. Shrewdly, they have protected their
investment, both politically and in terms of hard cash, with the Anand
cabinet's liberal policies of deregulation and new investment codes to
stimulate foreign investment. Many of the monopolies and oligopolies
which have stopped progress being made in the past have now been
broken up and a number of import tariffs have been reduced. Other
notable achievements to date include the re-negotiation of the telephone
expansion project with CP Telecom, the liberalisation of the motor
vehicle industry, the passing of the long-awaited VAT bill (at seven per
cent plus one per cent municipal tax) and the successful hosting of the
World Bank/IMF meeting in October 1991.

Inflation is a continuing problem even though government measures
to tighten monetary policy seem to now be making some progress in
tackling it. Increased minimum wage rates, income tax reductions,
higher public sector salaries and strong inflows of overseas capital are
still pushing upwards. So, too, are production costs with the increased
costs of imported raw materials.

The most pressing problem remains the current account deficit. Both
in terms of scale and likely duration, it is a major headache for the
central bank. Recent estimates suggest a figure of 200 billion baht, or 9.3
per cent of the GDP for 1991, and 220bn baht in 1992. Apologists have
pointed out that the large capital goods element of this figure (some 47
per cent of total Thai imports) are tied to the creation of larger, improved
manufacturing capacity for Thailand. This is probably true and will
continue to be a major contributory factor to the high levels of economic
growth in the next few years. The domestic savings that are needed for a
balance are still insufficient. Even though the national balance of
payments for Thailand is in surplus, Thailand has had to push up
interest rates in order to attract the foreign funds it needs.

The fact remains, though, that the rewards from the country's success
have yet to reach those still living in rural poverty or in areas where the
mercurial development has taken a heavy toll on the environment and
resources. Air pollution and toxic waste are already urgent issues. There
are now a great many opportunities for overseas concerns to take part in
the 'greening of Thailand' and the rapidly growing industrial and
service sectors need large investment in both waste treatment and
pollution control facilities. Competition between farmers, and both
private and industrial users, is fierce because the country also has
serious water shortage problems.

Banking and finance, equity market outlook, stockmarkets

Recently the financial market of Thailand has seen some much-needed and significant reforms including an end to foreign exchange control and an important increase in the upper limit of money allowed out of the country without the Bank of Thailand's formal permission. In 1992, any last remnant of financial restriction will be swept away as the last part of the liberalisation programme comes into force. These reforms are in line with Article 8 of the International Monetary Fund Agreement.

The commercial banks rule the roost in the Thai money market, with finance and security companies following on behind. This group, made up of 14 branches of foreign banks (eg, Bank of Tokyo, Mitsui Bank, Hongkong & Shanghai, Chase Manhattan and Citibank, etc) together accounts for around 76 per cent of the country's aggregate savings. There are also 31 representative offices of foreign banks. All have been restricted from going for more than their formerly held two per cent share of total bank deposits. This should now change given the programme of liberalisation that the government has been pushing through. The new capitalisation adequacy guidelines from the Bank of Thailand will revise the valuation rules for banks and finance companies will face increasing and much-needed regulation.

An attempt is being made to inject some lifeblood into the savings arena with the encouragement being given to banks to broaden the scope of their activities, in particular to increase the availability of long-term funds. The Foreign Ministry also held a series of talks with foreign banks based in Thailand to make sure that the conditions are such as to attract the optimum amount of foreign investment.

The huge returns on Thai securities and the high world profile that Thailand has received as a Newly Industrialised Country in recent years has brought a lot of attention and foreign investment to the stockmarket. Foreigners now account for around 15 per cent of the total holdings. The Securities Exchange of Thailand (SET) was a major casualty of the Gulf crisis, but it has since recovered somewhat despite the major hiccup of the coup. Under Anand's premiership it is staying on a stable if less interesting course. The SET in Bangkok has seen real growth in recent years from 175 listed companies in 1988 with a market capitalisation of US$28bn to a total capitalisation of US$29.927bn at the end of 1991.

Computerised trading has been introduced and will soon be followed by computerised settlement and scripless trading. Procedures for new listing applications which had formerly been widely criticised, have also been reformed to provide more protection for investors and to prevent interfering politicians from stopping new listings. A second board with a lower listing requirement for stocks was also set up to encourage new and smaller companies to list. The flotation of state air carrier Thai Airways International is also planned. Since the new reforms, securities companies are also allowed to open branches around the country.

There is a ceiling of between 25 and 49 per cent on the amount of stock that may be held by foreign interests in a company. There are, however, an increasing number of offshore investment funds, both dedicated to the market specifically or part of an 'emerging markets' fund. Investment capital in these is estimated to be around US$600m or 15,000 baht. The mutual fund industry has four new licences to offer to financial institutions. These must have have a minimum paid-up capital of 100m baht of which Thai financial institutions can hold up to 100 per cent. Equity finance will become increasingly important in the near future as more and more companies seek new funding for more capital intensive production.

Thailand's problems of excessive imports and rising inflation are a regional phenomenon in the Asian-Pacific Rim. This is bad news for both the economy and the stockmarket over the medium term as harsh measures are introduced to slow down growth and to redress the imbalances. To the Thai policy makers credit, however, they were amongst the first to recognise the problems. The government has taken well-documented measures to curb excessive money growth and to attract foreign savings. The momentum of overspending will take some time to arrest but some progress has been made. The higher rates have probably already worked their magic and consumption spending looks as though it has started to moderate.

Rates should fall as low as 13 per cent and fixed deposit rates should fall even faster as banks no longer need to attract funds to finance a rapidly expanding loan portfolio. Even if the Bank of Thailand wants interest rates to stay high so that it can keep a handle on inflation, it may not be able to convince the banks to keep them up artificially if the market will not sustain them. A problem is arising in view of the fact that these foreign funds are increasingly placed only short-term, exposing them to the greater sensitivity of international interest rates.

The country's economic balance has nevertheless seen certain areas of improvement in the recent past. Credit growth has levelled off gradually from a high of 30 per cent slowly towards the government target of 25 per cent. The national inflation rate is high but stabilising at this level, with cheaper oil and food prices being the major factors.

The gap in corporate savings and investment is now an important factor which has to be given remedial attention either by an increase in national savings or a cut back in levels of investment in order to finance the ten per cent gap. This stockmarket is not yet cheap, and it looks as though interest rates are unlikely to come down significantly in the near future.

Back in 1984, the Thai baht was delinked from the US dollar and pegged to a weighted basket of currencies including the US dollar, pound sterling, Deutschmark, French franc, Japanese yen and both the Singapore and Hong Kong dollars. The switch to the managed float

214

system contributed significantly to the improvement in the trade deficit, the current account and the balance of payments. It also made the baht more readily adjustable and resilient.

Increasingly Thailand is beginning to realise that it could have a very big regional role to play in the Asian-Pacific Rim even if it were only to concentrate on the prospects that Cambodia and Vietnam, and possibly Laos and Myanmar, are offering. Stocks reflecting this are beginning to do very well. The Bank of Thailand is acting as a friendly brother and adviser in setting up banks in various parts of Indo-China and is being allowed to set up branches in Vietnam, Laos and Cambodia in return. Every little bit helps on the road to making the baht more freely convertible.

Trade and industry

Thailand is becoming increasingly exposed to the international economy. It has started to become a major export platform for a large number of companies who have relocated large-scale manufacturing facilities there, but is getting to the stage where exports have got to be kept competitive. Wages and property prices are on the rise and shrinking margins mean that companies may increasingly start to look to cheaper countries like Indonesia and the Philippines for their manufacturing sites. Several overseas organisations and companies have also already selected Bangkok as their regional hub in anticipation of the future development of the rest of Indo-China and in the anticipation of a Hong Kong fallout.

The importance of the immediate area of the Asian-Pacific Rim that surrounds Thailand, specifically Vietnam, Laos, Myanmar and Cambodia, cannot be stressed enough. It is in conjunction with these countries that the great opportunities lie. For example, Thailand has granted Laos a 200 million baht (US$7.7m) a year aid grant to help with technology transfer to that country and to fund scholarships for the education of her people in industry and services. Thailand could be forgiven for regarding Laos as its economic hinterland because the connections between them, in terms of both linguistics and culture, are very strong even though they run in to problems of envy on one hand and greed on the other.

The UN and the World Bank function here very effectively and the IMF summit of 1991 served as a prestigious example of what can be achieved even in a city that is as seemingly chaotic as Bangkok. In terms of markets, the United States and Japan account for a large proportion of Thai exports (22.7 and 17.2 per cent respectively) with 20 per cent to the EC, and 11.4 per cent to ASEAN markets but new opportunities in countries such as Saudi Arabia, China, eastern Europe, South America and of course, Indo-China, are becoming increasingly important.

In the year ending 1990, UK exports to Thailand remained stable at about £420m, whilst UK imports grew by ten per cent to £480m. Britain's top five exports to Thailand are beverages (15 per cent), specialised machinery (12), road vehicles (7), electrical machinery (6) and non-metallic mineral manufactures (6). The top five Thai imports to the UK are clothing (22 per cent), fish (17), manufactured goods (16), miscellaneous electrical machinery (13) and footwear (12).

The rapid industrialisation of the Thai economy has of course caused structural shifts in the breakdown of GDP. Whereas 30 years ago, she was a primary commodity producer and exporter, Thailand is now a major regional manufacturing force. Manufacturing's share of the economy rose from around 16 per cent in 1970 to almost 26 per cent in 1989, while the manufacturing share of exports increased even more from under ten to nearly 70 per cent in the same period. On average, one new factory starts operation in Thailand every day, so adding to the export-orientated manufacturing base.

Manufacturing was very mixed in 1991 with relatively poor performance compared with the previous years. Some 39.9 per cent of the total manufacturing sector is made up of non-machinery manufactured goods, food contributes 28.2 per cent and machinery is up to around 22.3 per cent. The agricultural contribution fell to around 12.4 per cent in 1991. Service industries now make up over half the GDP and other industries account for around 7.6 per cent.

Industrial production has now re-arranged itself into a number of spheres including more consumer and manufactured goods, and Thailand is now a leading exporter of canned foods, gems, textiles and garments, leather products, plastic products and sports shoes. Other sectors on the increase are electrical and electronic consumer goods, computer peripherals and components and cars and car parts. MMC Sittipol, for example, is a joint venture between a Thai company and Japan's Mitsubishi Motor Corporation exporting over 500 kinds of auto parts. Toyota Motor Thailand is one of Toyota's few world-wide production bases for dies and jigs. Peugeot, Citroën and BMW cars are assembled by the Yontrakit group and other companies produce Volvo, Mercedes Benz, Renault and Opel cars. Heavy industries are coming more into play, especially on the eastern seaboard where a very large petrochemical complex has been established.

The great potential now for those new to the market lies mostly in telecommunications and technical and managerial manpower, as well as in mineral production. Minerals have consistently represented one of the top five foreign exchange earners for Thailand. Of over 30 which are commercially produced, tin, fluorite, tungsten, baryte and antimony have been the major exports. The government would very much like to further explore and exploit its gold deposits.

There is a wealth of entrepreneurial talent in the country, from the farmers to the family firms that are rapidly metamorphosing into modern corporations. It is not that surprising therefore that ASEAN's largest bank, agro-industrial conglomerate and integrated textile and garment group are all Thai-owned and operated. The work-force is well-educated, keen for more skills and training, and has a high degree of manual dexterity which long ago identified by Japanese manufacturers searching for new sources of capable labour.

Research and development has been a key factor in the Board of Investment's programme to encourage innovation and self-reliance in the country, and to acquire, adapt and operate the latest in technology from overseas. One agency, NECTEC, the National Electronics and Computer Technology Centre, under the Ministry of Science, Technology and Energy has been developing a number of products in conjunction with the private sector and universities. These include very large scale integrated circuits (VLSIs), electric appliance motors and air-conditioners. Areas to watch with interest are in fields of biotechnology, materials, electronics and information technology.

The government agency that is responsible for encouraging investment in Thailand, and the one most foreign companies find themselves dealing with in their One Stop Service Centre as the first port of call when considering the market, is the Board of Investment (BOI). The BOI was set up over 30 years ago but was properly secured and governed by the 1977 Investment Promotion Act. It was the first of its kind to be established in south-east Asia. The board is chaired by the Prime Minister, carries out day-to-day investment promotion activities and establishes priorities. These are projects which are considered likely to strengthen the country's industrial capability, use domestic resources, create employent, develop basic and support industries, earn foreign exchange and contribute to the economic growth of regions outside Bangkok.

Particularly sought are joint venture projects where production is mainly for the domestic market (Thai nationals must own 51 per cent of the equity or more), projects in agriculture, animal husbandry, fishery and mineral exploration or services (where Thais must own 60 per cent or more), as well as in the export arena in which case foreigners may hold the majority of shares. Certain conditions are stipulated in each instance which vary from case to case, such as the amount of investment, level of technology, local employment, plant location, and social and economic benefits for the employees.

In BOI terms, the country is split up for regional development purposes into the north, the north-east, the east and the eastern seaboard, the south, and the southern seaboard. The eastern seaboard development programme is coming to a successful conclusion with the development of an integrated industrial complex along the coast of three Thai provinces to the east of Bangkok. Industrial investment has been attracted, and is continuing to come in, drawn by incentives and the growing infrastructure. The government has as a mainstay of its policies a determination to encourage decentralisation away from Bangkok and to provide work for rural people from the north and the north-east who are increasingly moving away from the land into the urban areas.

Clearly each of these six aforementioned areas has different goals and a thorough exploration of the potential of each of these by you and your company with the help of the BOI is essential to find the best environment in Thailand for your operations. Businesses may be established as sole proprietorships, different kinds of partnerships, public limited companies with a minimum of 15 promoters and 100 shareholders, or private public limited companies with seven promoters and seven shareholders. Representative offices can only engage in 'non-trading activities' such as product search or quality control and are bound by specific restrictions.

The Alien Business Law categorises business activities into three different groups, A, B, and C. Those in the A group are not open to foreigners at all, the B group is only open to foreigners if the company's sector is being specifically promoted by the BOI and C companies are only open to 'aliens' if the authorities have reason to believe that they cannot be run well without a foreigner. Further advice, again, needs to be obtained on a case-by-case basis with the BOI. The country also has strict labour and employment regulations covering medical and maternity leave, wage guidelines and overtime, severance pay and other stipulations which all investors from the US and Europe will be well acquainted with and already incorporate in the management of their home businesses anyway as a matter of course.

A comprehensive scheme of guarantees and incentives is now on offer and there are even more available for those prepared to set up enterprises in the Special Investment Promotion Zones or for setting up export enterprises. There is no problem at all with bringing in teams of staff to do feasibility studies, as well as foreign technicians and other experts to work on projects. Incentives include a maximum reduction of 90 per cent of business tax on the sales of products for a period of up to five years, a reduction of 50 per cent of corporate income tax for five years after the end of the normal income tax holiday, allowances for transportation, water and electricity supply and deduction of up to five per cent of the investment costs from the taxable corporate income for ten years from the date of the first earned income. There are a large number of additional exemptions from duties and taxes normally payable available to the overseas investor. Only restricted privileges, however, are given to businesses which are established in Bangkok, Samut Prakan, Samut Sakhon, Nakon Pathom and Pathum Thani.

You should be aware of the Thai Government service, the Department of Export Promotion, which helps visiting overseas businessmen make connections with their Thai counterparts. The DEP (22/77 Ratchadapisek Road, Bangkok 10900, Thailand; tel 662-511 5066 77; fax 662 512 1079, 513 1917) is the country's export showcase and will provide a list of major Thai manufacturers and exporters. They will also arrange appointments and factory visits, even allowing you to use their courtesy offices for the meetings.

Companies of note

Bangkok Produce (agribusiness)
Berli Jucker Co Ltd (trading company)
The Borneo Company (Thailand) Ltd (trading company)
CP Feedmill (agribusiness)
East Asiatic Co (Thailand) Ltd (trading company)
International Cosmetics Co Ltd
Saha-Patthanapibul Co Ltd (consumer)
Saha-Union Corp Ltd (commerce)
Serm Suk (food and beverages)
Siam Cement Co Ltd
Siam City Cement Co Ltd
Thai Tinplate Manufacturing (metals)
Unicord (food and beverages)

A thorough study of the history, as well as of both the annual and stockbrokers' reports (where available), of the companies of note will give you a good idea of the commercial 'inner game' psychology of the countries in which you plan to do business.

Agriculture

'The Rice Bowl of Asia', Thailand is one of the world's leading net exporters of food. Agriculture plays a very large part even now in the national economy (12.4 per cent of GDP, down from 16.3 per cent in 1986)) and employs nearly 65 per cent of the nation's work-force. However, the traditional exports of rice and tapioca are becoming less competitive and are too vulnerable to international commodity prices, so farmers are being encouraged to diversify.

There is a drain of workers to the cities so industrialisation is being brought to the countryside, as an essential means of keeping at least some members of the family on the land. New products are being developed such as frozen seafood and poultry. Thailand's major crops apart from rice are coffee, tobacco, cotton, jute, beans, tapioca, rubber, rice, sugar maize, cassava, pineapples and other fruits, and oilseeds.

Recent typhoons have been battering both the crops themselves and farmers' incomes, causing a slight slowdown in the sector's growth figures.

Agro-industry, on the other hand, is going through a dramatic growth phase geared towards expanding world demand for processed foods. Examples are the transformation of tapioca slurry into modified starch to support the paper and chemical industries, or technology to increase yields and quality

Fishery products have been increasing as Thai fishermen have gained access to more of their neigbouring waters. The production of black tiger prawns is growing very rapidly. On the other hand, the hike in the price of animal feed has had a negative effect on the livestock industry. Forestry is also in the doldrums as the government takes sound note of virulent criticism from ecologists. The forests which in the 1960s and '70s brought wealth to the country through timber exports are now providing furniture, veneer and other value-added products.

Tourism

The odd coup or two, terrorism, the Lauda Air crash and the Gulf conflict, together with Bangkok's pollution and traffic problems and the rampant criticism from ecologists and concerned citizens about over-development, have snarled this industry up in a maelstrom of both real and anticipated problems. The nail in the coffin for many has also been Thailand's widespread image as a market dominated only by sex tours. The fact that Thailand also has the 'Best Hotel in the World'. The Oriental, voted for the tenth consecutive year by the New York-based magazine, *Institutional Investor*, does not seem to get quite the same publicity.

Internally, all levels of society and the military are beginning to seriously question whether or not they want to maintain the business of tourism at the dizzy heights of the last few years. The most vociferous malcontent is none other than the Minister of Tourism himself, Mechai Viravaidhya. He believes that what he sees as chaos of tourism should have some order put into it, even if its means a 50 per cent decrease in volume. That would hit foreign earnings extremely hard. A key point on his agenda is his 'Women's Visit Thailand' (*sic*) promotion in 1992 to shake off the shabby 'men only' image the country somewhat justifiably still bears. A long delayed tourism bill to regulate the industry and to give the Tourism Authority of Thailand more power as a watchdog is expected to become law soon.

Thailand's largest number of visitors come from Malaysia, followed by Japan, Taiwan, Hong Kong, Singapore and the United States. In 1991, there were 5.4 million arrivals of which 7.5 per cent were visiting the country on business. This total was all the country seemed able to manage, even with an intensive discounting programme throughout the industry by both hotels and operators. This is a very long way short of the progress that needs to be made in order to achieve the government's goal of 12 million a year by the year 2000.

Receipts are down around 30 per cent over the last year and this in the sector that provides the country's largest single source of foreign income (around US$4.5bn in 1990). Even though Thailand has the singular fame of having more hotel rooms (around 170,000) than any other country in the Asian-Pacific Rim, construction of yet more is still in progress. Only one hotel group, the Dusit Thani has had the foresight to hold back, in their case by putting off major plans for three resort hotels.

This past year has seen hotels, resorts and tour companies close for business. Staff have been laid off or have had to accept substantial pay cuts, all because occupancies have consistently hit unusually low rates. While the staggering growth of tourism and investment led to a remarkable boom throughout the 1980s, problems are now coming home to roost. The real downside of tourism, though, is that Thailand now faces the worst AIDS crisis in the Asian-Pacific Rim.

Thailand's neighbours, Myanmar (Burma), Laos, Vietnam and Cambodia, are very important to the country's own tourism development as there is an increasing likelihood that the mantle of regional hub can only fall on Bangkok's shoulders. Thai Airways, for example, is helping Vietnam develop its airline (as is, apparently, Japan's JAL). The Tourism Authority of Thailand is taking great pains to build new relationships bearing this scenario in mind and there are possibly great openings for foreign companies to take part in the process. At the moment an important tourist agency is already booking tours to Cambodia, to Angkor Wat and Angkor Thom, and direct flights have now started from Chiang Mai to Yangon (Rangoon) which will increase further the tourist traffic on that route to Thailand's benefit.

The Asian Games will be held in Bangkok for the fourth time in 1998 and the hotel industry will hold the 13th Asian hotel meet in Bangkok in the same year. A new hotel training school has been set up, run by the Tourism Authority of Thailand and the Tourism Training Institute at Bang Saen Beach in Chon Buri Province, 50 kilometres from Pattaya. Over the next five years the number of graduates will gradually increase to around 480 annually.

Infrastructure

The main problem with Bangkok's infrastructure is quite simply, the lack of it. Plans are littering drawing boards from one end of the city's government offices to the other, all intended to put in some kind of cohesive framework to stop the place dissolving into chaos. The government will frankly admit that the unprecedented growth of recent years has put the most enormous strain on the system.

In order to try and sort out the chaos, the Sixth Plan (1987-91) budgeted for some US$3bn worth of government expenditure, in addition to funding from the private sector, and infrastructure is still at the very top of the list for the current Seventh Plan (1991-95). The struggle to break down the state enterprise monopolies and achieve privatisation in electric power, water, telecommunications, and transport is the main problem and cause of delay of progress. A large number of industrial estates have been constructed, the two key ônes being on the eastern seaboard at Laem Chabang and Map Ta Phut. More than 25 private sector industrial estates have also been finished in the last two years. The Thai Factory Development Company Ltd finances factory construction and has been involved in building standard factory facilities on these estates.

The collective brains behind the Thai economy have focused their attention on promoting the diversity of the industrial structure. They are very keen therefore to develop and vastly improve the range of basic infrastructural services available so as to make their country as competitive as it can be with other countries in the Asian-Pacific Rim. Also of key importance is the development of human resources to work in the industries, specifically with regard to the future development of science and technology. Thai economic managers also recognise the vital importance, as part of their grand plan, of distributing both income and prosperity around the country by taking the work to the people.

The previous government had a project to build a bridge over the Mekong river between the capital city of Vientiane in Laos and the Thai border town of Nong Khai and this will still probably go ahead. Future projects include the Lavalin and Hopewell mass transit systems, electricity generation projects, road, expressway and port development projects.

Communications

The contracts for the much-needed revamp of the telephone systems of Thailand were the subject of a great deal of infighting and controversy. Supposed corruption over the issue was said to be a factor contributing in no small way to the downfall of the Chatichai government in the spring of 1991.

Neverthless, telecommunications are in the process of being revitalised by the Telephone Organization of Thailand (TOT) and a large multi-billion dollar concession has been awarded to CP Telecom, a private company, for the installation of new telephone lines. Thailand's first communications satellite concession has been agreed and granted to Shinawatra Computer. The number of phones has doubled in the last three years alone. A cellular phone service is provided by TOT and the Communications Authority of Thailand. Soon ISDN and a teleport system to link Map Ta Phut with the Silom-Suriwongse area of Bangkok will also be installed. A Data Processing Zone will be established to provide a wide range of modern internal and international telecommunication services for the financial sector and for commerce.

Transportation

The transportation infrastructure in Thailand still leaves a great deal to be desired and it has been designated a priority for development with funds allocated for the work. Thai Airways is the country's excellent international and domestic carrier and won the 'Airline of the Year Award' in 1990 from *Executive Travel* magazine after a survey of 50,000 frequent business travellers. The country also has another, Bangkok Airways. Altogether 60 foreign airlines call at the five international airports and many more are negotiating to do so. These airports are Bangkok's Don Muang, Chiang Mai, Haad Yai, Phuket, and U-Tapao. Ubon Ratchathani airport is going through an upgrade to bring it up to international standard and a new one is under construction at Ban Hat Yai. There are 22 other regional airports. Bangkok handles more than 16 million passengers a year and 400,000 tons of goods.

The rail system, with a new link on the fast-rising economic centre of the eastern seaboard connecting Chachoengsao, east of Bangkok with Sattahip and Rayong, runs throughout the country tying up all major cities with the notable exception of Phuket. Trains are good, clean and cheap and some have couchettes and restaurants on board. The mass transit 'skytrain' system for Bangkok should be finished by 1993.

The main highways and roads (some 44,500 kilometres of them) are modern and usually metalled but there are well over 100,000 kilometres of back roads where conditions are at best bumpy. The long-distance coach network that runs the length of the country is adequate but bus systems in the smaller towns and outlying bandit country areas are not recommended. Getting around Bangkok is well nigh impossible in a car and the congestion is going to be tackled through the construction of a number of overpasses and tunnels. The second stage of the expressway is due for completion in 1995. The first stage of the mass transit sky train will also be finished in 1995 and there is also to be an elevated expressway from the city out to the international airport. A number of delegates at the October 1991 World Bank/IMF conference were said to have missed their flights because they had underestimated the inordinate amount of time it would take them to reach the airports from their downtown hotels. New roads are being built to link the eastern seaboard with the north-eastern region of the country.

Thailand has six international deep sea ports handling around 15.5 million tons a year, but this year (1992) that capacity is due to increase to 25.5 million tons. These are at Klong Toey in Bangkok, Sattahip on the eastern seaboard, and Songkhla and Phuket in the south, and the new Map Ta Phut and Laem Chabang ports. There are a number of inland waterways throughout the country which are well-served by both passenger and cargo vessels. Four more private ports will soon be allowed to handle computerised cargo. Maritime law is being drafted and two state lines, the Thai Maritime Navigation Co Ltd and United Thai Shipping Co Ltd will be merged and streamlined. More than 40 per cent of the current account deficit in recent years has been directly related to shipping.

Driving is on the left-hand side of the road and cars may be hired in Bangkok, Pattaya, Phuket, Chiang Mai and Hat Yai. The city's yellow cabs are plentiful in Bangkok but be sure to agree a price to your destination before setting off, and take with you the address of where you are going (plus instructions, if necessary) written out in Thai. Tipping is not necessary for cabs.

Conferences, conventions and trade fairs

Bangkok has a brand new state-of-the-art conference, trade and convention centre just minutes from downtown's central business district. Built in less than one year, the 65,000 square metres centre was the site for the World Bank and the IMF meeting and stretches over 17.5 landscaped acres. Facilities include 25,000 square metres of exhibition space, multi-purpose units, and a plenary hall with ten-metre high headroom and seating for 5,000. This is sub-divisible by electronically operated walls into three smaller venues, and is equipped with multi-lingual facilities and high-tech video projection systems telecasting the speaker's image on two walls.

Thailand's Expo, which was to have been held in 1992, has now been delayed until later in 1993 to allow more work to be done on public utilities and on construction at the site at Nakhon Ratchasima in the north-eastern province. The two month event, intended to be the biggest of its kind ever held in ASEAN, is to promote the development of agriculture, agro-industry, and industrial technology in the region as Thailand moves closer to becoming an NIC (newly industrialised country.)

Taxation

If you are living and working in Thailand on a business visa, you must get a tax clearance certificate from the relevant department to produce upon departure.

Thailand's tax laws are involved and complicated and expert advice must be sought, but generally speaking business tax is levied on gross receipts and is calculated monthly with the rate depending on the nature of the business. Municipal tax at the rate of ten per cent of the business tax is also levied. Depreciation is allowed at a rate between five and 20 per cent when computing net profits and net losses may be carried over for five years. Corporate income tax is payable on profits and is assessed twice a year. The fiscal year in Thailand is the calendar year ending 31st December, but other arrangements are permitted for foreign companies.

Exchange rates and currency positioning relative to US$

The unit of currency is the baht (100 satang). Notes are denominated in 500, 100, 50, 20 and 10 baht, while coins are 5, 2, and 1, as well as 50 and 25 satang. The baht is linked to a basket of currencies dominated by the US dollar.

There are no restrictions on the amount of foreign currency which you may take in to Thailand but it must be declared upon arrival. There is an upper limit of US$10,000 which can be taken out without a declaration. You are not allowed to take in or out more than 10,000 baht. Any goods exceeding this value also require a Certificate of Exportation.

The people, their languages, education and religion

Thailand has a population of 57.6 million of whom 40 per cent are under 15 years old and 83 per cent live in rural areas. Only around five million people of the total population are not ethnic Thais. Of these, eight per cent are Chinese, or 'Sino-Thais' and less than one per cent are ethnic Malays and hill tribe people. The country has also provided a refuge for large numbers of people from neighbouring countries who have been beset by wars for the last 15 years.

Thai is the national language but a great many of the people speak various Chinese dialects (Chiuchow is the most common) and in the south of the country a new Malay-Thai hybrid language has evolved. Several systems of romanisation are used.

Many of the Thai elite have long sent their sons and daughters to public schools in England (although the trend now is more towards sending them to the US) so there is no problem whatsoever with the English language throughout the course of normal business. A number of Thais also speak good French.

Over 90 per cent of the population are followers of Theravada Buddhism, but Mahayana Buddhism is practised by Sino-Thais and Vietnamese. Bangkok's Indian communities are predominantly Hindu and Sikh. In the south, there is a large concentration of Muslims, both Sunni and Shiite, who together make up the largest minority religious group. There are also Christians (Roman Catholics), Presbyterians, Baptists, and Seventh Day Adventists.

Education is compulsory from the age of seven till 15 and the literacy rate is well over 80 per cent. The system of higher education in Thailand has expanded rapidly and there are now 16 government universities and 23 private institutions offering degrees, diplomas and certificates of vocational education. There is also the Ratchamongkol Institute of Technology with 28 campuses, as well as 200 government vocation colleges and a further 363 private ones. The total number of graduates from vocational schools each year exceeds 150,000 of which about half specialise in technical fields, with the rest studying commerce. A particularly interesting feature is the Technological Promotion Association between Japan and Thailand which promotes industrial training and know-how and arranges language and specialist seminars.

Thailand has a number of international schools, with about 5,500 pupils shared between them all, including the International School of Bangkok, the Ruamrudee International School, the Bangkok Pattana School, the Thai-Japanese Association School, and the Chiang Mai International School.

Publications of note

The local English-language newspapers, *The Bangkok Post* and *The Nation* are of an excellent standard and there are three good business publications also available in English. The first of these is *Industry*, produced by the Association of Thai Industries every two months. There is also *The Investor*, put out by the Industrial Finance Corporation of Thailand and a very useful supplement that comes with *The Nation* newspaper, *The Business Review*. Some well-known Thai language newspapers are *Daily News*, *Siam Rath*, *Dao Siam* and *Thai Rath* which you might want to get a local Thai assistant to skim for you to find items of interest.

There are a number of television stations including an army television channel, the Bangkok Broadcasting Company, Thai Television, an education channel and the Bangkok Entertainment Company. Radio stations cater for all languages including English, Chinese, French, Japanese, Malay, Lao, Khmer, Vietnamese and Burmese.

Visa and health requirements

If you will be staying in Thailand for less than 14 nights/15 days, you will not need a visa providing you have a confirmed ticket out of the country at the end of your stay.

It is likely that you will need a 90-day non-immigrant visa to enter Thailand to do a feasibility study of any kind or to start a contract. Once in, it is necessary to apply for formal approval to stay beyond the initial period granted by the visa. Other types of visas are the non-quota and the immigrant visa, but it is important to get advice on these from either the BoI or the embassy.

Please note that foreigners can only own land in Thailand with special permission from the Ministry of the Interior, only up to certain levels and even then only if there is a reciprocal treaty with the country of your citizenship. The right to use land for business purposes is subject to the scrutiny of the Board of Industry. If a company buys land for commercial purposes and then ceases to operate in Thailand, it is obliged to sell the land within one year.

If you are arriving in Thailand from an area that is infected with either yellow fever or cholera, you must have proof of vaccination. Recommended inoculations are for cholera, typhoid and paratyphoid and malaria tablets are advisable. Animals in the countryside are fairly likely to be rabid.

Caution replaces heady optimism

Thailand's optimism is flagging. The country's three years of explosive growth are proving a mixed blessing. In 1990 82% of respondents to the *Asian Business* confidence survey were more optimistic about the country's overall economic prospects than they had been six months before. In 1991 53% were less optimistic.

While 71% of this year's respondents were more optimistic about their own company's prospects than they were previously, that's a drop of 14% from last year's figure. How quickly things change.

Corruption and infrastructure are the two big worries for these respondents. A staggering 90% say that corruption is a big problem for the economy as a whole. The country's infrastructure gets high marks from no one and 76% of respondents say the government isn't doing enough about it.

Foreign investment troubles Thai executives less now than it did before, when the majority felt that the country was too dependent on foreign money. Now 58% are either happy with the level of foreign investment or want more of it, and almost half are happy with the level of technology transfer that is coming to the country with the foreign money.

On the operations side, Thai executives were concerned with pretty much the same problems. Tight competition was cited by 22% as the main worry. Other prominent concerns were availability or cost of materials, high interest rates, industrial unrest, labour supply and political instability.

But overall, Thailand still looks pretty good to Thai executives when its economic prospects are compared with those of other countries. They rated it fourth – just behind Singapore, and ahead of Taiwan.

Thailand confidence index: 86

Asian Business provides readers with a Confidence Index for each country surveyed. To compare the results of confidence surveys conducted around the region, we process the data from each survey and (in conjunction with Frank Small & Associates) arrive at a numerical rating for each country. This Confidence Index measures the following six criteria used in the survey: local market, export market, turnover, profits, company prospects and economy.

ECONOMIC/POLITICAL

National economy: Are you more optimistic about the national economy than you were six months ago? Less? About the same?

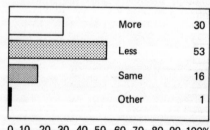

More	30
Less	53
Same	16
Other	1

0 10 20 30 40 50 60 70 80 90 100%

Local market: During the last six months, has your company been operating in an expanding, a static, or a contracting local market?

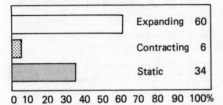

Expanding	60
Contracting	6
Static	34

0 10 20 30 40 50 60 70 80 90 100%

Export market: During the last six months, has your company been operating in an expanding, a static, or a contracting export market?

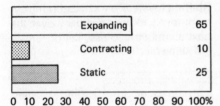

Expanding	65
Contracting	10
Static	25

0 10 20 30 40 50 60 70 80 90 100%

Corruption: How much damage is corruption doing to the economy?

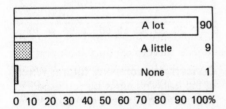

A lot	90
A little	9
None	1

0 10 20 30 40 50 60 70 80 90 100%

Infrastructure investment: Do you think the government has invested enough in developing the country's infrastructure?

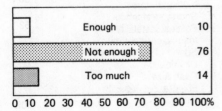

Enough	10
Not enough	76
Too much	14

0 10 20 30 40 50 60 70 80 90 100%

Foreign investment: Do you think Thailand is too dependent on foreign investment; has just about the right amount of foreign investment; or doesn't have enough foreign investment?

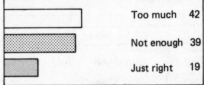

Too much	42
Not enough	39
Just right	19

0 10 20 30 40 50 60 70 80 90 100%

Technology transfer: Are you satisfied with the amount of technology transfer to domestic companies from foreign investors?

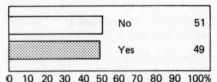

No	51
Yes	49

0 10 20 30 40 50 60 70 80 90 100%

Economic prospects: On a scale of one, for very poor, to 10, for very good, how would you rate the likely economic performance of the following economies in the next 12 months?

	Average Rating	Proportion who gave a rating
Japan	7.6	100%
South Korea	7.0	100%
Singapore	6.7	100%
Thailand	6.6	100%
Taiwan	6.5	100%
Malaysia	6.4	100%
Australia	6.2	100%
New Zealand	6.1	100%
US	6.0	100%
Indonesia	5.9	100%
China	5.6	100%
Hong Kong	5.5	100%
Vietnam	4.3	100%
Sri Lanka	4.1	100%
India	4.0	100%
Philippines	4.0	100%

CORPORATE

Company prospects: Would you say you are more optimistic, about the same, or less optimistic about your company's prospects than you were six months ago?

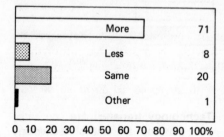

More	71
Less	8
Same	20
Other	1

0 10 20 30 40 50 60 70 80 90 100%

Company performance: Overall, would you say that your company is doing well, badly, or neither?

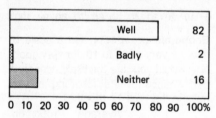

Well	82
Badly	2
Neither	16

0 10 20 30 40 50 60 70 80 90 100%

Gross profits: During the past six months, has the trend of your gross profits been up, down, or the same compared with the same period last year?

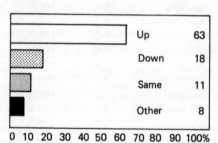

Up	63
Down	18
Same	11
Other	8

0 10 20 30 40 50 60 70 80 90 100%

Turnover: During the last six months, have your company's turnover/billings, compared with the same period last year, gone up, stayed the same or gone down (ie, in real terms excluding the effects of inflation)?

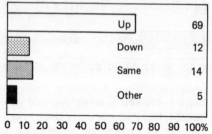

Up	69
Down	12
Same	14
Other	5

0 10 20 30 40 50 60 70 80 90 100%

Staffing levels: Do you expect employment levels in your company over the next six months to rise, fall or remain the same?:

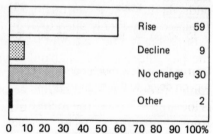

Rise	59
Decline	9
No change	30
Other	2

0 10 20 30 40 50 60 70 80 90 100%

Concern for company future: Which of the following areas do you expect to be your main business concerns during the next six months? (Multiple responses possible)

Tight competition	22
Availability or cost of materials	15
High interest rates	14
Industrial unrest	14
Shortage of labour	12
Political instability	12
Insufficient demand	3
Speed of service or deliveries	3
Devaluation	2
Cash flow	1
Fixed asset capacity	–
Other	2

The survey was compiled by Frank Small & Associates in Bangkok from telephone interviews with a quota sample of businessmen. Business directories were used to construct a sampling frame. Eligibility criteria were set for number of employees in the company and for respondent's seniority, and company quotas were set for different company types. Interviewing took place between January 15 and 31. A response rate of 92% among eligible companies was achieved.

Note: 'Other' category in charts includes those who answered 'Don't know' or declined to answer.

Investment risk: Thailand 62

Getting anything at all accomplished in Thailand is becoming increasingly difficult and expensive. Infrastructure is obstructive rather than helpful, and it's getting worse. Skilled labour is in short supply and unskilled labour is getting restless.

As the government totters from crisis to crisis, bureaucrats and vested interests are gaining more power and fattening their wallets.

Despite all this, Thai executives have expressed a great deal more confidence in their country than it would seem to warrant. They must know something; they live with the risk and, according to our survey, continue to make money.

Many Thais cite politics as one hopeful area. Even though the democratically-elected government is weak, it has persisted against all odds. If the next government has as much success in just surviving, Thailand may finally shed its reputation for political volatility.

But there can be no doubt that, after skyrocketing in the ratings over the past three years, Thailand is definitely heading downwards. It is interesting to note that while Indonesia – the subject of last month's confidence survey – scored five points lower than Thailand, that country is looking set to take the mantle of 'investors' flavour of the month' away from Thailand.

Thailand scored as follows:

1	Inflation	7
2	Interest rate	2
3	GDP growth	9
4	Infrastructure	4
5	Labour: Strife and shortages	5
6	Bureaucratic impediments	4
7	Government intervention	6
8	Threat of armed aggression (internal and external)	9
9	Political volatility	7
10	Business confidence level	9

Investment risk: 62
Last year's (1990) score: 69

Reproduced by courtesy of *Asian Business*

SOCIALIST REPUBLIC OF VIETNAM

Nominal GDP: (not measured; former COMECON's Net Material Product (NMP) used instead and unreliable. Somewhere in the range US$112-190.)
GDP real growth: (as above, but the ADB estimates five per cent in 1992)
Exports: US$2.4bn (+ 15 per cent)
Imports: US$3.2bn (+ 12 per cent)
Net foreign debt: US$14.6bn (ADB, 1990 figure)
Trade deficit: US$1.2bn (1986 estimate only)
Population: 64.4m (1989)
Work-force: 34m (1988)
Unemployment:
Inflation: 700 per cent (1988 – since sharply reduced)
Head of State: President Vo Chi Cong
Head of Government: Prime Minister Vo Van Kiet
Ruling party: Communist Party of Vietnam
Other political parties: None
Capital city: Hanoi (GMT+7 hours)

Note Statistics concerning Vietnam tend to be unreliable at best. The NMP – see above – is used to measure economic growth, and is largely unverifiable. These figures are therefore given as a rough guide only.

Membership of international organisations: Asian Development Bank, Colombo Plan, ESCAP, FAO, G-77, IAEA, IBRD, ICAO, IDA, IFAD, IFC, ILO, INTELSAT, IMF, IMO, IRC, ITU, International Bank for Economic Co-operation, International Investment Bank, NAM, UN, UNDP, UNESCO, UNICEF, UPU, WFTU, WHO, WIP, WMO, World Bank, WTO.

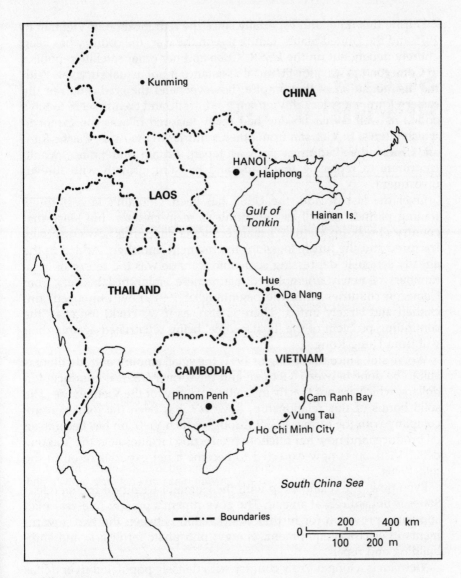

Vietnam

Brief history

The mere mention of the country Vietnam in the last 20 years has often caused emotional upsets and controversy, obviously in the United States of America with whom it was at war for so long, but also in Europe generally and other Western countries.

During this time, and especially since the reunification of Vietnam in 1975 and the United States' failure to win the war, the country has been entirely dependent on the USSR, Cuba and her other satellite republics in Comecon (as was) for financial assistance if not actual survival. With the disintegration of that empire, however, and the eradication of the eastern European bloc, all Vietnam's aid, trade and credits seem to have ended as well. What no one had really factored in was the extent to which interest in Vietnam from other countries in the Asian-Pacific Rim, and from other countries such as Japan, Britain and France would contribute to replacing this trade and boosting growth with foreign investment.

Over the last decade, the USSR has been Vietnam's largest single trading partner as well as the country's main creditor, but since that country's break-up Vietnam's main economic support is now essentially fractured and the future looks for the moment uncertain. Added to the already seriously depressing economic scenario was the return of large numbers of newly unemployed Vietnamese emigrant labourers from Comecon countries since the beginning of 1991, now unhoused, un-clothed and largely unfed. There is also, as if we could forget it, the continuing problem of the 'boat people' being repatriated against their will from Hong Kong.

Worse still, since the spring of 1991, the small amount of trade there is still to be done between Vietnam and the former USSR is conducted in dollars, which are not exactly in limitless supply for the Vietnamese. The solid bonus of this relationship, however, has been the joint venture company with the former USSR through which Vietnam has become an oil producer and now has offshore production facilities near the Mekong delta. Vietnam is now expected to become a net exporter of oil in the mid-1990s.

Even now, the relationship with the Commonwealth of Independent States is not entirely at an end. The government's present five-year plan stipulates provision for further co-operation between the two govern-ments in electrical equipment, energy, phosphate fertilisers, and ship-building and repair.

Vietnam is a long narrow country with densely populated river deltas at both ends. The geographical length of Vietnam is around 1,650 kilometres from north to south and, over this distance, it encompasses a string of archipelagos between two gulfs, Tonkin and Thailand. On the northern side is the People's Republic of China, in the west is the Lao People's Democratic Republic (Laos) and in the south-west is that much troubled country, Cambodia.

The capital city of Vietnam is the ten-centuries old city Hanoi with a population of about three million. It was founded in 1010 by Ly Thai To, the first ruler of the Ly dynasty. The largest city with 3.9 million people is Ho Chi Minh City. Smaller cities are Haiphong, Da Nang, Nha-Trang,

Qui-Nhon and Hue. Vietnam also lays claim to the two groups of islands in the South China Sea, the Spratlys and the Paracels. These are also being contested by China, the Philippines and Malaysia.

The first state of Vietnam was set up in around 2879BC as the Van Lang State, leaving traces of its culture to this day throughout the country. There followed a very long period of virtually a thousand years of sheer havoc with invasion and disaster. Then, in the last century, having been an integral part of China for hundreds of years, Vietnam became a French colony in 1867 which it continued to be until the end of the Second World War.

Vietnam was then to be occupied by both British and Chinese troops, the former being south of the 16th parallel, while the latter were north. At that very moment, however, the August Revolution took place when Ho Chi Minh declared Vietnam to be a democratic republic on 2nd September 1945, a state which was formally recognised by China and the USSR in 1945 providing the catalyst for the subsequent war.

There was, however, a brief re-introduction of French colonial rule from 1946 until 1954 when the French were defeated and routed and the country was split, *de facto*, north and south. Fighting magnified ultimately into the Vietnam war with the North Vietnamese, supported by the USSR and its allies, opposing the South who were in cahoots with the USA and her allies. In late 1961, the USA's involvement deepened with President John F Kennedy promising that he would 'bear any burden' to defend freedom.

As if to make him eat his words, the Communist 'Tet Offensive' in 1968 against the Americans was so very severe in terms of US casualties that public support for the war was irrevocably eroded, so much so that by 1970 US troops were being pulled out. By 1973, the conditions were such that a 'peace treaty' was eventually signed in Paris. It was not until April 1975, however, that the final US troops flew out of Saigon leaving us all with the heart-rending images that we remember so well of women and children clinging to troops and helicopters.

Vietnam was subsequently reunified and then, on 2nd July 1976, the whole country was proclaimed the Socialist Republic of Vietnam and became a member of the United Nations in 1977. Conflagrations in Indo-China raged on, however, till Vietnamese troops made an incursion into Cambodia in 1978 and a Vietnamese-backed puppet government was installed. The domestic problems in Vietnam were sorely exacerbated by her Cambodian incursions with dire results. In 1989, Vietnam announced it would make a withdrawal of its troops from Cambodia, and then, in 1991, the USA linked the normalisation of Vietnam-US relations to a four-stage UN-imposed plan for free elections in Cambodia.

This is how we now find Vietnam and her extremely unfortunate neighbour, Cambodia, though how long this situation will realistically hold remains anyone's guess. The motivation of economic growth for Vietnam, however, might just be the best conceivable provider of peace for her people, regardless of their political loyalties or dispositions, if real signs of prosperity and better conditions quickly materialise.

Politics and history apart, Vietnam has desperately been trying to achieve full-scale economic reform or renovation, 'doi moi' in their language, which was launched at the Sixth Party Congress during the nadir of 1986. Attempts have been made to try to turn the system around from a Soviet-style, centrally planned mechanism to one that is fully market-orientated. It would be miraculous, indeed, if just five short years later the real effects were truly palpable.

The devastation, both economic and physical from the Vietnam War, as well as from the then continuing internecine warfare, was almost total. There were no real foundations for the 'reformers' to start their work upon. As if the economic battle were not hard enough on its own, since 1989 they have also been trying to turn the clock back politically. Cynics say this has come about not so much because those at the top wanted real change or because they were fed up with their growing poverty, but rather because the government, watching with horror what was happening to eastern Europe, had absolutely no choice.

The economic reform began, it must be said, only after it became apparent that the communism imposed on the whole country since the fall of Saigon in 1975 had only brought Vietnam to a state of absolute destitution. Nowadays there are a number of ostensibly genuinely motivated economic reforms that allow private enterprise and foreign investment – the cornerstone of the industrialisation of the economy – but so far they have had only limited success.

The main restraint on the country's development is that Vietnam is still trying to function in the international community with both hands tied firmly behind its back in bonds that will not seem to loosen. The country remains diplomatically and economically isolated, with the key American trade and aid embargo still in place.

The present situation *vis-à-vis* trade has its origins in the United States Act, the Trading with the Enemy Act 1917, which prohibits both companies and individuals from the USA from either trading or investing in Vietnam either directly or indirectly. This even precludes Americans from providing any kind of service whatsoever to Vietnam.

While, as US Secretary of State James Baker obliquely suggested in 1991, this will probably be lifted at least partially within the next couple of years, the going is still extremely tough while the linkage remains to the four-stage plan for UN-administered elections in Cambodia. The Vietnamese are finding faith, however, in the huge number of Japanese businesses and corporations which, unrestricted by any legal or moral code, are all too eager to jump on the Vietnam bandwagon regardless of so-called political sensitivities. The Japanese clearly see it as an opportunity too good to miss and believe that, once the doors open, it will be too late to get the best seats.

The country's strengths

- Strategic positioning is such that there is enormous potential to develop its agricultural and other industries.
- Substantial undeveloped reserves of natural resources, including plentiful coal, oil, gas, hydroelectric potential, etc., for commercial development; masses of gold, copper, bauxite, iron ore, etc.
- The IMF reports that the country's progress on the economic front is exemplary and that the drive towards the market economy in Vietnam is now an accepted fact.
- A population of nearly 65 million (70 per cent under 35 years old) providing a cheap and capable labour force expanding at the rate of one million a year, all eager for consumer goods and with a literacy rate of 80 per cent, Vietnam has positive economic potential. (The literacy rate in the 14-45 age group is 90 per cent) The work ethic is undiminished, despite the war, as is clear in the south of the country and overseas.
- Having hit the pits, there is now nowhere for the Vietnamese economy to go but up.
- The ADB growth prediction of five per cent in 1992 is encouraging.
- Recent leadership chances in the country, together with significant progress in regional understanding (and the results of the July 1991 National Assembly election) all confirm that the government intends to continue on the path to reform that was started in 1987.
- The liberal foreign investment law introduced in December 1987 which expressly guarantees the right to repatriate profits, to make payments due for technology and services, to repay the loans and interest on loans and to repatriate capital in the original currency or any convertible currency of choice.
- 1991 saw significant advances on the political front including improvements in relations with the EEC, USA and the PRC.

The country's weaknesses

- Total absence of trade with the US until 'Trading with the Enemy Act' re Vietnam is lifted.
- As a result of the above, no aid from the US and now only limited aid from and trade with the USSR since the collapse of the Soviet empire.
- A history of flawed policies and international isolation.
- A per capita income on a par with Bangladesh or Malawi.
- Immense uncertainties on the road to reform, high political risk.

- A weak and vulnerable economy, after years of Stalinist policies, with a tendency to very high inflation.
- External debt represents a substantial proportion of Vietnam's earnings in currencies other than the dong and the country has defaulted on repayments in the 1980s. She continues to be in arrears and default on loans in both freely convertible and non-convertible currencies.
- As Asia's newest emerging market (and after the devastation of war) there is very little infrastructure to speak of.
- For the most part, Vietnam's industry, both light and heavy, is inefficient, unprofitable, technologically backward and concentrated in a narrow range of products.
- Unless new foreign investment is made available in the short term, the effect of the economic reforms will be diminished and slowed.

Goals

To press ahead with the radical reform programme, with liberal foreign investment incentives, so that market forces may be embraced. Prospects look good if the government can find it in itself to stick to this programme and if multilateral agencies are allowed to renew their vigorous assistance.

Politics

On 30th April 1991, it was the sixteenth anniversary of the fall of Saigon to the Communists but from the atmosphere in the streets you would hardly have believed it. The place was and still is positively buoyant and bristling, not with Communist fervour but with a vigorous, almost Thatcherite zeal for the commercial potential of the country's market place. Despite the hard line taken in the Seventh Plenum in August 1989, against 'bourgeois democracy', the pace of growth and liberalisation seems to be encouraging, almost in spite of itself, that very spirit. All the street markets are overflowing with produce (unlike in, say, Bangladesh or Malawi, which have the same per capita income but nowhere near the same availability of necessary basic consumer goods).

None of this means however that a multi-party system, or anything at all approximating democracy, is about to be ushered in to replace the Communist manifesto. The one brave soul in the Politburo who dared to mention the possibility of reform was summarily dismissed. The summer 1991 Seventh Communist Party congress saw what were, on the face of it, dramatic changes in leadership of the country but the new leaders were chosen, not in any kind of political departure, but specifically to gear the market place up for reform and to create a market place ripe for overseas investment.

There is no getting away from the fact, however, that underlying all this reform there lies the Vietnamese constitution which, practical Thatcherism apart, still rests upon the National Assembly of Vietnam ruled by the Communist Party. Elections to the Assembly are for a five-year term and sessions are held twice yearly in June and December. The State Council holds the fort between sessions.

It was the State Planning Commission which fixed the prices of goods and wages and organised the supply of input and the outlets of enterprises. It subsidised goods and wages massively and had open-ended pockets to finance all-comers in any form of enterprise. Goods were not produced and inflation ran riot.

It is the assembly, however, which rules the country on a practical and literal basis through the implementation of all legislation and all plans for development, economic, social or otherwise. The assembly also votes for the Chairman, the President of Vietnam's executive body, the Council of Ministers and the President of the State Council, as well as giving approval for all reforms and matters of national organisation. From the State Council is handed down decrees and policies which are in turn applied to the country at large through the ministries, state committees and government departments, and then on down through the provinces and cities and to the special zones and regional adminis-tration boards.

In other words, the country is still not a million miles away from the People's Republic of China in fact or feeling, even though reform is currently the buzz-word. It should remembered, the pessimists will argue, that the PRC too enjoyed a long period of reform under Deng Xiaoping but still managed to inflict the outright barbarianism of Tiananmen Square against its unsuspecting people. Calling a Confu-cian's bluff is always a bad idea.

As well as being a member of the UN for nearly 15 years, Vietnam is also a member of the non-aligned movement.

Domestic economy, current economic policy and forecasts.

The tiger awakens. Vietnam is a low-income, predominantly agrarian country which is strategically exceptionally well-placed in a region where high growth rates are the norm. Its society is a more cohesive, disciplined and industrially-minded unit than some others that have been identified in this book as future tigers and successors to the NICs of north-east Asia. Vietnam could, with solid infrastructural and consistent economic development, explore the markets of its neighbours to its own great advantage, as well as benefit from outsiders' interest in the country's abundance of investment opportunities.

In 1990, more than 3,000 delegations visited Vietnam from abroad to assess the investment potential. Of these some 40 per cent were Japanese. It is important for businessmen to remember that in the case of Vietnam, this book can only discuss the potential, not (as in the case of all other eight countries) the actual trade. Informed conjecture has to take the place of proof positive of the vastness of that potential.

However, with the prospect of the US embargo being lifted for trading with Vietnam in the not-too-distant future, the time is now ripe for exploring investment in the country and the populous Ho Chi Minh City particularly is attracting a lot of foreign money in the industrial sector. Soon the country will be establishing a number of export processing zones to attract further overseas investment, the first of which will, again, be near Ho Chi Minh City. Vietnam has already achieved over US $2.1 billion in foreign investment in just three years, invested in 280 authorised projects, and the future prospects look equally bright and will grow given bold government reforms designed to attract further interest.

Most foreign investment so far has been in the oil and gas exploration sector but the services sector, particularly hotel development, has also been a beneficiary. The Japanese have designs on turning Vietnam into a newer, fresher Thailand. Also attracting investment are the property and light industrial sectors. The Taiwanese, too, have a beady eye on Vietnam as a potential investment site for a number of their manufacturers as do nationals from other nearby countries. The higher level of education of the Vietnamese as compared to mainland Chinese, and the fact that a large ethnic Chinese population runs much of the business in Vietnam makes the country very attractive to the Taiwanese and others.

The picture is very different now from the late 1970s when industrial production was stagnating, agricultural production was failing to keep pace, there was an alarming increase in the population and all looked like death and disaster despite the fact that the Vietnam War was finally over.

Last year, two country funds were launched dedicated to Vietnam, perhaps just slightly too early for the money world's consciousness of the country and its potential. People now will remember that back in 1986 when the Korea, Thai or other emerging market funds were first launched, there was little interest in their potential either. The first of these was the Credit Lyonnais First Vietnam Fund which would, they hoped, play a big role in Vietnam's new privatisation programme with a target of $75m eventually being increased to US$100m. The fund was managed from Hong Kong by Jardine Fleming and shares were listed in Hong Kong and London. The other fund was the Vietnam Fund Management Co Ltd (c/o Smith New Court Far East Ltd; Martin M

Adams, executive director, 17th Fl, Wheelock House, 12 Pedder Street, Central, Hong Kong. tel 852-868 0330, fax 529 1704).

Whilst this investment will, of course, stimulate the country and its economy in just the right direction, the domestic problems are fairly dire. Inflation rose fairly drastically in the months after the Gulf conflict and can waiver up to heights that makes the Western mind boggle.

The country is nevertheless slowly emerging from years of economic neglect. There are two major factors which may help its progress and these are the recently discovered reserves of oil, which is being explored by such companies as BP and Broken Hill Proprietary Co Ltd and its pool of low-cost labour. As Vietnam's 'perestroika' policy, 'Doi Moi', progresses, the policy which is intended to stimulate economic growth and to help restore Vietnam's position in the international community, investment and to a lesser degree export opportunities are becoming more apparent. The UK has been the single largest investor in Vietnam, but this is mainly in the oil exploration sector and the Japanese are encroaching massively in this and other areas.

The economy is being manipulated through a series of five-year plans embracing the state, private and foreign-invested sectors. State-owned enterprises are still, in perception and in reality, the most important part of the economy although it is intended that this will change fairly rapidly, foreign investment willing. The United Nations Development Programme estimates that private investment in Vietnam is not less than 25 per cent of state investment, and investments by co-operatives and provincial authorities make up 20-25 per cent of state investment which has been declining over the last five to six years.

The recently updated Investment Law is widely regarded as the most liberal in the Asian-Pacific Rim. The only stipulation laid out is that foreign organisations and private individuals may invest capital in technology in Vietnam 'on the basis of respect for the independence and sovereignty of Vietnam, obvservance of Vietnam laws, equality and mutual benefit.' As far as anyone can tell to date (real practical and applied knowledge is still so rare) there are no hidden traps or pits for foreigners to fall into so far as interpretation of the law is concerned.

The IMF in April 1991 was very quick with its praise for the country's efforts in implementing a number of macro-economic measures to eliminate most price controls, to reduce inflation, to bring some measure of stability to the dong/US dollar exchange rate, to reduce the state sector borrowing requirement and to boost export competitiveness. The IMF went further however. It urged the international community to help Vietnam in the renovation and reform of its economy with inward investment and trade.

The government's target rate of economic growth over the next four to five years is nine per cent per annum. To this end, the government is setting about improving and reorganising the internal structure of the country so that it is best able to provide the optimum conditions for growth. The main targets for improvement are production of all kinds and management in general, as well as a general amelioration of the end-products and better use of raw materials. Labour productivity is also coming under scrutiny, as are the pricing structures for goods, and the re-equipment and modernisation of factories.

Vietnam has a young, efficient population of 65 million people with a passion for entrepreneurship and a drive to become wealthy in the run up to the privatisation which will take advantage of the new investment laws. Hampering all economic renovation efforts are the country's very low level of economic growth, an uncertain outlook on inflation, high unemployment, a potentially overwhelming debt burden and severe shortages of freely convertible currency.

Banking and finance, equity market outlook, stockmarkets

Financing from both domestic and foreign banks has been virtually unobtainable because of the primitive domestic financial system and the quality of credit risk demanded by international banks. It is an almost horrifying understatement to state quite simply, that banks everywhere are seriously under stress but in Vietnam there seems to be real hope that an excellent framework may now be in place to eliminate a great many pressing problems. Concerted and intelligent efforts are being made.

The biggest problems relate to foreign currency and financing, both of which will be substantially eased by the SCCI's very liberal foreign investment legislation. The ruling Vietnam Government has also recently passed a mandate to create a foreign exchange and a stockmarket in line with the accepted international market place, but it will naturally be some considerable time before these come into serious operation.

It is therefore unlikely, in the meantime, that significant sources of Dong or of foreign currency debt will be available from banks to finance companies or projects operating in Vietnam and most business is done on the basis of short-term credits of 180 days. So long as ECGD cover is not available for exports to Vietnam, British and other exporters will have to approach the market with great care. Some British and other Western companies have set up good connections and have allowed credit where business is ongoing. They can, for example, sell through traders in Singapore and other Asian-Pacific Rim countries with payment being made from credits granted by the third-party country.

Whereas other Asian-Pacific Rim countries discussed in this book are well along the road to making their financial infrastructure as user-friendly to foreigners as it can be, the Vietnamese are still in the earliest days of this process. The spirit is very willing, judging by the laws, but the system is inherently weak. That will, of course, change almost over night when relations are normalised with the US and money is once again allowed to flow into Vietnam throught the normal channels. For the moment, the central banking function has been streamlined into the State Bank of Vietnam as a result of the 1988 banking reforms and commercial banking operations have now been passed over to the state-owned commercial banks. One new foreign-invested bank has been established and several more have opened up representative offices.

In the meantime, foreign investors can make deposits in whatever currency they choose with banks in Vietnam to underwrite their own projects in that country. If you invest in Vietnam in dollars, it is dollars that will be returned to you at the end of the project. We have no reason to disbelieve the excellent intentions of this part of the law, but it remains to be seen how this would occur if large sums of money were to be repatriated in dollars all at once. Nevertheless, the point is there is no need to invest in a project with dong, and it could be said to be undesirable to do so.

There are also no restrictions whatsoever, in this era of apparent Vietnamese capitalist enlightenment, against opening bank accounts with domestic banks. Currency exchange is transacted through an authorised bank at a rate which must be within ten per cent of the official rate, so there is no room for severely unfair transaction levels. It should be borne in mind that it is very difficult to convert Vietnamese currency earned from an operation's profits back into a foreign currency, so these proceeds are probably best ploughed straight back into the operation (if it warrants it, of course) to obtain maximum tax-free benefits. This will improve as the country opens up and funds, hopefully, flow through.

French banks have been among the most active foreign banks in Vietnam. According to Clifford Chance, experts in the country, commercial transactions written in French with French law in mind and of relatively simple structure tend to work rather better than their equivalents in English or American. For further specific information and advice, contact Clifford Chance, Blackfriars House, 19 New Bridge Street, London EC4V 6BY; tel 071-353 0211, fax 071-489 0046 or one of their offices in New York, Paris, Saudi Arabia, Singapore, Tokyo and around Europe. Bear in mind that local lawyers are not used to dealing with financial transactions or to giving opinions of the type which foreign banks expect.

When repatriating capital, the usual form in Vietnam is for it to be remitted in three equal tranches after all taxes due have been deducted. If the amount of money being sent out is in fact larger than the original capital contribution, when all profits are included, the surplus money may only be sent or taken out of the country with permission of the

SCCI. If, however, you sell your commercial enterprise either to another Vietnamese or to another foreign party, all monies due for the purchase price may be repatriated immediately after taxes have been paid. There is no provision for reducing the capitalisation of an existing company or joint venture during the life of the operation. Joint ventures are allowed to operate in Vietnam for a term of up to 20 years.

Trade and industry

While, as has been pointed out in the summary of the country's weaknesses, Vietnam's industry is inefficient, unprofitable, technologically backward and concentrated in a narrow range of products, it is nevertheless true that the Government has managed, some would say almost miraculously, to attract significant companies from abroad to help them implement key heavy industrial projects in the fields of coal mines, oil exploration, power stations, pulp and paper production and engineering plants. Therefore radical improvement over time may be expected.

Vietnam's trading partners have been mostly dealing with the country in terms of long term credits. For example, Japan which is still the largest trading partner with a freely convertible currency, accounts for 24 per cent of Vietnam's exports and 40 per cent of imports, all financed through the credit of a major Japanese trading company. Singapore's share is 30 per cent of Vietnam's exports and only four per cent of the imports. Hong Kong was the third market for exports at 16 per cent but provided only eight per cent of its imports. Other countries trading with Vietnam in order of significance are South Korea, France, Belgium, Iraq, Australia, Germany and India.

For the moment, the most important sector of the economy continues to be agriculture, followed by industry and then trade. Quite a long way down in the scale of importance to the national economy are the construction sector, miscellaneous industries, transport and communications, and then forestry. This assessment, however, is based on the official Vietnames rating of national product, not the GNP as is commonly used by Asian-Pacific Rim countries, but the net material product (NMP) as commonly used by the former Comecon countries. This figure is fairly useless to us in judging the true worth of the country since it fails to include non-material services, depreciation and a number of other factors considered vital in obtaining an accurate picture.

As far as pioneers from the West are concerned, the electricity, oil and cement production fields have grown faster than most due to public investment and there is still room for further growth. Coal and steel, transport and communications, have been held back due to lack of public funding so would be ripe for joint ventures with appropriate external funding.

Machinery of all kinds, from the ground up, is in very heavy demand and the British industrial equipment that Vietnam has been sold in the past has enjoyed a very good reputation for being reliable. UK plant was recently purchased for a canning line for a Ho Chi Minh City brewery. The trouble is that the Vietnamese lack of experience with equipment other than that of Chinese or Soviet manufacture puts those trying to sell into this sector at a disadvantage. Quick orders are not the norm in Vietnam and a great deal of time needs to be spent on building a relationship. Towards the end of 1991, Vietnam curbed imports drastically to avert the ever-present threat of a currency crisis.

The government's policies have brought about a labour shake-out in the state sector. The State Commission for Co-operation and Investment (SCCI) is responsible for the concerns of the global business community with regard to investment in Vietnam. Domestic manufacturers and business enterprises have been given the right and responsibility to organise their own activities, including co-operation with foreign organisations and individuals.

A key part of this transformation is the development of the private sector. In June 1990, the Vietnamese law on foreign investment was amended to permit privately-owned business enterprises to engage in direct co-operation and and investment with foreign investors. Then, in December 1990, a comprehensive company law was passed which governs the establishment and activities of Vietnamese privately-owned enterprises.

Vietnam has an abundance of natural resources including coal, iron ore, tin, rubies, gold and marble and its very best resource possibly is its people. They are known to be industrious and skilful and able to learn advanced production techniques quickly in higher technology. Labour costs remain relatively low, probably more so than in any of the neighbouring Asian-Pacific Rim countries because of the condition of the economy and the generally low living standards.

The country's accounting, auditing and financial reporting standards are different from, and in no way equivalent to, those used generally in international practice. The legal system is relatively undeveloped still, even though a substantial legislative reform programme is being slowly worked through. At the moment though, there is no means of getting effective enforcement of commercial rights through legal or arbitration proceedings in the country.

Still today the main conduit to do business in Vietnam is through commercial activities specifically defined in the completely new and somewhat revolutionary (given the Communist dogma of previous laws) foreign investment legislation which was enacted in December 1987 by the Vietnamese National Assembly. Since then further laws and decrees have been passed for clarification purposes, but basically activities may be undertaken in one of three ways. The first is through a 'business co-operation' contract, the second through a joint venture company established in Vietnam and third, through a wholly foreign owned company established in Vietnam.

The business co-operation contract tends to be a production— or revenue-sharing relationship with the foreign investor providing the capital and the technology while the Vietnamese party contributes the manpower and the resources. These Vietnamese resources may include the right to use land, on a form of 'leasehold' for the duration of the contract up to a maximum of 20 years. While foreign investors are not allowed to own land in Vietnam, they are allowed to buy residential property for the length of their contract to do business in the country.

The National Institute for Urban and Rural Planning hopes to attract foreign funding for a US$600,000 project to survey the old parts of the city of Hanoi in an attempt to preserve what is left of the still largely intact but rotting blend of European and Asian-influenced property. The French construction firm, FEAL International, for example is working with Pullman International Hotels and will reopen a renovated version of the fabled Metropole Hotel this year.

The SCCI receives and vets all applications for all the various forms of business and is directly responsible to the Council of Ministers, the ultimate authority on all matters relating to foreign investment in the country. The SCCI is the sole government department with which those who wish to do business in Vietnam need to concern themselves. After a licence has been issued, the SCCI will monitor the business investment to make sure that everything is being carried out in agreement with the terms of the licence. This is not nearly as Big Brother-like as it may sound, but the process may involve ad hoc visits from departmental inspectors as well as progress reports which, in any case, have to be given to the government on a fairly regular basis.

These laws afford some measure of protection to foreign investment in the Vietnamese economy and allow investment in any sector whatsoever without restriction (quite unusual when compared with other countries in the Asian-Pacific Rim). There is no minimum percentage of Vietnamese participation required, but 30 per cent of a venture must be held by foreign investors. Specific guarantees are made in the law against expropriation or nationalisation.

One of the secrets to commercial success in Vietnam today lies with individuals and orgranisations from the USSR who were very active and experienced in Vietnam. Soviet organisations maintain comprehensive information about the Vietnamese economy and potential investment projects and are owners of substantial assets in the country. The All-Union Foreign Economic Association of the USSR, 'Technoexport', is one such organisation which was responsible for all of the main power projects in Vietnam and which reported to the Ministry for Foreign and Economic Affairs.

It is essential to tap into the network of Vietnamese officials, businessment, multinational and other non-Vietnamese companies who have substantial expertise in Vietnam. One British company already well into the country is Bovis which also provides project and construction management services elsewhere in the Asian-Pacific Rim, mainly in Hong Kong, Indonesia, Malaysia and Thailand.

Finally, the Vietnam Trading Corporation has set up a number of Vietnam Trade Service Centres in London (tel: 071-925 0144; Neil Shrimpton), and a number of other cities in Europe and the USA. These offices provide consultancy on doing business with Vietnam as well as helping with all travel arrangements. In Hanoi, the Vietnam Trade Service is establishing an International Business Centre to provide permanent and temporary office accommodation to the highest specification in downtown Hanoi. The refurbishment of the building for the offices is being undertaken by the UK chartered surveyors, Kennedy & Partners.

Sectors of note

Bach Ho oil field (and petrochemicals?)
Gold fields and mining
700 state enterprises in heavy industry
2,300 state enterprises in light industry (textiles, electronics assembly plants, packaging)
1,000 rice mills
200 state-owned food processing enterprises
Far East Shipping & Trading (FESTCO)

A thorough study of the history, as well as the annual reports (if available), of the entities of note will give you a good idea of the commercial 'inner game' psychology of Vietnam.

A new company law is leading to a rapid increase in private and foreign-owned sectors.

Agriculture

By far the majority of the population of Vietnam, between 70 and 75 per cent, are still and will continue to be for some time dependent on the agricultural sector for their livelihood. The sector is crucial to Vietnam in the development of its economy and should bring in good foreign earnings revenue.

Using the NMP again as the yardstick, the share of the market has in fact fallen between ten and 15 per cent to around 45 per cent of the total economy. With a better availability of fertilisers, improvement in the agricultural infrastructure and more investment and hard cash for the industry, the sector could grow from strength to strength. The Red River delta and the Mekong delta are so very fertile today that with the introduction of modern farming techniques, it is said that crop yields could be doubled to reach those of neighbouring countries.

The collectivisation of agriculture over the last 15 years has led to worse problems. It was supposed, according to the best dogma, to bring benefits and to increase production, so giving famers the kind of incentives they needed to maintain a steady growth in production and to keep working at very high levels of productivity. It failed miserably, completely demoralising the vast numbers of people in the country who look to the land for their sustenance and even managed to wreck what little good there had been before the socialists turned their fanatical minds to the paddy.

Three years ago, the Politburo issued a resolution called 'Renovation of Economic Management of Agriculture', which gave farmers new, realistic incentives to produce. The attempts at collectivisation in the southern part of the country have thankfully now been abandoned.

Around one fifth of the total land area in Vietnam is given over to agriculture. Rice production not surprisingly continues to be significant with around 19,000 tons produced in 1990, not only allowing the country to be self-sufficient in this crop but also to become the third largest exporter of rice in the world, after Thailand and the USA, for that year.

Arable land for cultivation makes up nearly seven million hectares but there is said to be nearly another three million hectares which could also be succeessfully cultivated. Key crops apart from rice are potatoes, cassava, pea-family food plants and other vegetables.

Tea, coffee and rubber have been designated at state level as key crops for increased production, especially for their potential to hook in lucrative foreign earnings in convertible currency for the country. Opportunities for foreign companies are limitless, it seems, as is witnessed by the involvement of one small British company, Vinatea of Southwark Bridge Road in London which is helping with the rehabilitation of the national tea industry and is involved with the marketing and distribution of other Vietnamese commodities. Other products the country produces are jute, sedge, cotton, mulberry and silkworm, sugar-cane and ground nuts. For animal foods, Vietnam produces mainly water buffalo, pigs, chicken and fish.

Vietnam's fishing grounds are rich and largely untapped and ripe for further streamlined development of the industry.

Tourism

The natural charms of Vietnam are abundant and the country's white sandy beaches certainly rival (some would say far exceed) those of Thailand as a tourist attraction. The country is centrally located to serve as a short-hop holiday destination for other more affluent south-east Asian countries and has substantial airport facilities to accommodate what will be explosive tourist growth. However, as in all other areas of her industry, Vietnam is desperately short of know-how, experience, capital, management and resources for skills' training. The greatest asset perhaps in this industry, though, is the charm of the people who are friendly and welcoming.

At the moment there is very little in the way of luxury accommodation, apart from the well-known Saigon Floating Hotel in Ho Chi Minh City, widely used by visiting businessmen, and the Rex Hotel. In Hanoi there is the Thang Loi Hotel and the Cuu Long Majestic and that is about it. The principal designated tourist centres, however, are at the Ha Long Tourist Compound at Ha Long Bay in Quang Ninh Province, the Tam Dao Resort in Vinh Phu Province, 30 kilometress from Hanoi, the Do Son Resort in Haiphong City, the Sa Pa Resort in Hoang Lien Province, famous for its fruit and vegetables and the Hanoi Tourist Centre with 600 international standard hotel rooms. There are many more all around the country.

Infrastructure

The very jolly and personable Commercial Attaché at Vietnam's London Embassy, Hoang Van Dung, jokes (what else can he do?) at the mention of his country's infrastructure. Simply put, there is none. Particularly in the north of the country, shipping, rail, road and telecommunications links are all lamentably deficient. There is massive opportunity for both foreign investment and joint ventures in this arena, providing what must surely be one of the world's hottest opportunities for those companies in this field. Those who are not investigating potential here, should ask themselves why not.

One of the most successful pioneers into this arena is FESTCO GB (Far East Shipping & Trading) which has formed a partnership between the UK company Chemex UK of South Ruislip, Middlesex, as a joint venture working together in the fields of general shipping, chartering, transportation, warehousing, insurance and general trading with particular reference to project work.

Infrastructure and industrial development have been crippled because of the US trade embargo which completely stopped the usual sources of funding, the IMF, the World Bank, and the US and Japanese governments, as well as the majority of the world's major corporations, from lending or investing in Vietnam. Taiwanese and Indonesian investors, amongst others, have already begun to put money into the property market which is ripe for investment and will, over a number of years, probably produce good returns.

Communications

It would be dishonest to overestimate the level of communications in Vietnam. It is extremely basic. However, things really are getting better all the time and the phone system especially seems to have got itself into better shape.

Telephoning Vietnam is now relatively uncomplicated with most calls getting through first time, and you are able to hear what is being said at the other end of the line. The Vietnamese still prefer to use telex rather than fax at the moment, although this is changing rapidly. Many post offices offer a fax service, especially in Ho Chi Minh City and in the Central Post Office in Hanoi.

The British Embassy does offer a service to help businessmen having difficulty contacting organisations in the country. Messages are passed on by the embassy courier in Hanoi and by internal mail to the rest of the country. Address such correspondence to British Embassy, Hanoi, BFPO 5, London, or British Embassy (Hanoi), FCO, King Charles Street, London SW1A 2AH.

Transportation

An increasing number of airlines now serve Vietnam including Thai International, Air France, Philippine Airlines and Garuda. Vietnamese air space provides the economical alternative to flights over mainland China for all commercial air routes from north-east Asia to the Middle East and then on to Europe. The domestic airline Vietnam Airlines is the subject of intense activity by the Japanese domestic carrier, JAL, who are closely co-operating with the Vietnamese Government in a programme to substantially upgrade standards both in the air, and on the ground, for both passenger and cargo traffic. At the moment, air freight facilities are very limited and subject to delay.

There are one or two flights daily between Hanoi and Ho Chi Minh City and these are supposed to increase in the not too distant future owing to the increasing volume of traffic. Details of the bookings and confirmation of such flights will normally be handled by the sponsor for your visit to Vietnam, although the system is becoming relatively more flexible as time goes on.

The principal shipping route from north-east to south-east Asia, the Middle East, Africa and western Europe passes within 200 miles of the Vietnamese coast. So, Vietnamese, ICS and eastern European ships call in at Haiphong and Ho Chi Minh City but there is not as yet a regular reliable cargo service. Most goods are transshipped at Hong Kong or Singapore, the latter being the most favoured. Most cargo is handled by the ship's own equipment and facilities for managing and unloading containers remain limited as yet. In southern Vietnam, the Mekong river provides a major water route into Cambodia for vessels up to about 3,000 tons, but the Cambodian market is not large and has its own port of entry at Kompong Som.

To date, roads and motorways have been developed faster than the rest of the transportation network and account for the largest volume of transport. The most recent figure is that the country is now covered by a network of some 90,000 kilometres, 10,000 of which is under asphalt. The main arteries are Highway One, (Vietnam border to Ho Chi Minh City, 2000km), Highway Five, (Hanoi to Haiphong, 105km), Highway Six (Hanoi to Lai Chau, 500km) Highway Four (Ho Chi Minh City to Nam Can), Highway Twenty (Bien Hoa to Dalat) and Highway Fifty-One (Bien Hoa to Vung Tau). There are 3,200 kilometres of railway, the most important line being the trans-Vietnam line from Lang So to Ho Chi Minh City.

In Hanoi and elsewhere throughout Vietnam, private cars and buses are still rare and taxis are almost non-existent, though given the natural entrepreneurial inclination of the people, versions of 'cabs' are springing up out of nowhere to earn their drivers extra bucks. Bicycles and pedicabs still provide the main form of transportation.

Conferences, conventions and trade fairs

The conferences on Vietnam to date have all been held outside the country, with a very popular location being Hong Kong and occasionally, when given by the government itself, Geneva. The government is said to be working on a number of conferences but it will be some time before the country has the facilities to manage exhibitions and delegations on a meaningful scale. In the meantime, the Chamber of Commerce and Industry of the Socialist Repubic of Vietnam will be most happy to keep you regularly informed of up-and-coming conferences in your sector if you advise them of your company's interest.

Taxation

Tax revenues as a percentage of national income have been comparatively low, running at around seven per cent of the NMP. The Government recognised the need to tackle this urgently in order to increase its revenue and introduced a new comprehensive income tax in 1991. Foreign entities trading in Vietnam are not liable to taxation on income derived outside the country. Profits from business co-operation contracts in Vietnam, however, are subject to tax and profits from dividends, interest or whatever, may also be subject to Vietnamese withholding taxes of between five and ten per cent. Joint venture companies and wholly foreign owned companies established in Vietnam also pay tax on their profits.

The rate of income tax depends on whether a business is a 'priority' or 'standard' category business. The former must pay tax of between 15 and 20 per cent, while the latter incurs a charge of between 21 and 25 per cent. Higher rates are payable to those companies working in the oil and gas exploration fields and in a few other areas working with scarce natural resources.

The new legislation allows exemptions from tax for joint venture companies in the 'priority' category for up to a maximum of two years from the time a joint venture company earns profits. Also allowed is a 50 per cent reduction of income tax for a further maximum of two years, ie the total tax holiday, at varying levels of reduction, is for a four-year period of investment. This only applies to joint ventures.

For the other two types of business, ie the business co-operation contracts or the wholly-owned foreign company, the usual tax rate is ten per cent but varies depending on the amount of legal capital, and can be as low as five per cent in those companies where foreign capital of more than US$10m is invested in a project. For some projects, funds that are reinvested back into Vietnam at a certain level for at least three years have a tax refund in the currency in which the tax was paid. Therefore, you will not always get dong back regardless of the currency you originally invested with in Vietnam.

A customs declaration must be filled out on arrival in Vietnam listing any valuable items which they might consider saleable for domestic currency. These include cameras, computers, etc. and all specified items must be taken out of the country when you leave. Foreign currency being brought in must also be declared.

Exchange rates and currency's posititioning relative to US$

The Dong, the Vietnamese unit of currency, is not freely convertible into other currencies, nor is it traded internationally. The dollar value of the dong has been deteriorating as of late (fluctuating from around 5,000 to 9,000 to the dollar) and confidence in the local currency remains low. There seems to be a very high incidence of counterfeiting, so people still keep what money they can scrabble together either in US dollars or in physical gold.

The people, their languages, education and religion

Even though Vietnam was essentially part of mainland China for aeons, it is wrong to think of her people as merely Chinese. They have a highly developed sense of national identity developed over decades of struggle and internecine warfare and are tough and determined.

The predominant language in Vietnam is Viet, the tongue spoken by those people, the Viet or Kinh, who in fact make up 85 per cent of the total population of nearly 65 million. The Vietnamese alphabet owes its use of the Roman script to the work of missionaries in Vietnam throughout the passage of time. It is the only Latinised script that the countries of the Asian-Pacific Rim have ever used, making culture shock substantially less of a problem for the visiting businessman. Other languages in common use in the country are of course, French (it was a former colony), English, Russian and Mandarin Chinese.

In total, Vietnam has 54 ethnic groups, each with its own language and culture. The most significant of these are the Viet (Kinh). Others, in decreasing order of size, are the Tay, the Thai, the Hoa, the Khmer, the Muong, the Nung and a number of others and these make up around 2.7 million ethnic people. The Viet tend to live in the deltas and the coastal areas while the ethnic groups prefer the moutainous regious, the midlands and the borders.

The Vietnamese are highly literate with over 90 per cent of the population being fluent readers. Some 11.18 million complete primary school, 3.118 million finish secondary education and around 1.3 million finish vocational training for a career. Nearly one million people have university or college degrees.

Sitting at the crossroads of the Asian-Pacific Rim, Vietnam has many of the features of other countries in the region in terms of cultural influence as well as those from other parts of the world. Other influences, from the earliest centuries, included Christianity, Buddhism and much from India. Confucian thought and the art and civilisation of China have been of paramount importance. Other points to remember when working in Vietnam are that the people attach a great deal of importance to personal relationships, as they do elsewhere in the Asian-Pacific Rim, and business will only really succeed when introductions are effected through respected intermediaries.

Visa and health requirements

When making arrangements to visit Vietnam on business, be sure to avoid the time around the Chinese new year, which is some time in January/February depending on the moon, because it coincides with the period of 'Tet'.

Travel to Vietnam is becoming significantly easier. You do still need visas, and that is unlikely to change for a very long time, but they are no longer the complete headache they have been in the past. Businessmen have been known recently to make impromptu visits after spur-of-the-moment decisions while visiting Bangkok, although such a lack of preparation is extremely ill-advised for those who want more than a look-see visit.

Officially, you must have a business visa 'sponsored' by a Vietnamese organisation that you intend to visit during your trip with a view to doing business. The sponsor can in fact be the Vietnamese Chamber of Commerce itself or any one of the trading organisations or companies authorised to do business in the country. Because of the high volume of visits made to Vietnam from Hong Kong, Bangkok and Tokyo, applications made from these cities are noticeably less troublesome.

The Chamber's own trade service company will network individuals with those who may be responsive to their business overtures, as will Investip (Bureau for the Promotion and Development of Industrial Property Activities) and Investconsult (Investment Consultancy & Technology Transfer Company). If in any doubt, the commercial attaché at the embassy can offer assistance.

Business visitors are still required to register at the local police station but this policy seems, with the increasing volume of traffic, to be rather lax. Travel permits are needed to travel from one city to another, but this is now just a routine feature of business travel and relatively trouble-free.

Hepatitis is a problem in Vietnam so inoculation is probably a sensible precaution, as are malaria tablets if there is any likelihood of you visiting an infected area, ie the countryside or indeed anywhere outside the larger cities. Vietnam is very, very short of medicine and facilities, although the doctors are excellent. If in doubt and feeling unwell, it is best to fly straight out to the next point on your itinerary.

7 The Asian-Pacific 'Little Black Book'

Who's really who in the Asian-Pacific Rim

In order to conduct successful business negotiations in the Asian-Pacific Rim, it is essential that you find a way into the very broad ethnic Chinese network of some 40 million people which largely controls most of the important transactions in the region. In the whole region, however, there are about half a dozen individuals in each market-place who rule the business roost.

Regardless of which country you choose for your business focus in the Asian-Pacific Rim, you will find that the Chinese are the dominant force in that arena and their operations tend to be tightly knit family affairs in every field of industry, finance and commerce. In this business culture, personal loyalty is of paramount importance and the person who brings you or your company into a deal is considered crucial. The act of introduction reflects both on you and on them, for good or for bad. As one Chinese businessman bluntly put it to me, 'No introduction, no business'. The value of these solid relationships is a trump card that no businessman, however powerful in the West, can afford to ignore.

Study this list of some of the key players in each of the Asian-Pacific countries and consider your possibilities for formal introductions, if not to them themselves, to someone in their operations. The embassies can be invaluable in playing their part in this important game. Ultimately, you will find that you cannot avoid crossing paths with these tycoons, however ephemerally, if you mean serious business.

Hong Kong

Sally **Aw-Sian**, a peripatetic businesswoman who is nevertheless frequently in Hong Kong, is the proprietor of the world-wide Sing-Tao group of Chinese-language newspapers and a member of Singapore's 'Tiger Balm' family.

The **Chen** family who own 50 per cent of the Hang Lung Development company, own major property interests in Australia, as well as Amoy Properties and Grand Hotel Holdings and interests in Amoy Industries, Denny's Restaurant, and the Matsuzakaya Department Store in Hong Kong.

Cheng Yu-Tung and his son Henry are members of the New World Development group family and are said to be in the league of the top ten of Hong Kong's richest men.

The **Fok** family, (Henry, Ying-Tung, 69, and his son, Tim), are said to have made their early fortunes through working with the Japanese during the Second World War. Today they virtually own Macau inasmuch as the Foks control nearly one quarter of the Sociedade de Turismo e Diversoes de Macau through their corporation, the Yau Wing Co Ltd, which owns the Portuguese colony's gambling licences, as well as substantial real estate. The Foks work in partnership with the legendary Stanley Ho and with Teddy Yip. Henry's son Tim, was a pioneer into the mainland in the very early 1980s with the White Swan Hotel in Guangzhou. The Foks are said to be worth some US$1.3bn.

The **Kadoorie**s, (Lord Kadoorie, 93, Horace, 90, Michael, 51), command a fortune between them of around US$1.5bn through substantial interests in China Light & Power (Daya Bay Nuclear Power Station, Guangdong Nuclear Power Joint Venture Company, etc), the Hong Kong and Shanghai Hotels, and Hong Kong Carpet. Originally of Parsee origin from Baghdad, the Kadoories are best known perhaps for their flagship Hong Kong hotel, the luxurious Peninsula, but 'young Michael' is now branching out into the newer territories of Vietnam and mainland China.

The **Keswick** family, whose Hong Kong operations are now headed by Simon, own about ten per cent of Jardine Matheson Holdings and are said to be the original model for the 'taipans' on which Robert Elegant based *Noble House*. Today the holdings company owns 50 per cent of the securities firm Jardine Fleming, as well as significant interests in Hongkong Land, Dairy Farm and the Mandarin Oriental Hotel group as well as various other insurance, shipping, consumer and property interests.

Robert **Kuok**, said to be worth around US$2.0bn, is generally considered to be the consummate Chinese networker and powerbroker in the Asian-Pacific Rim cutting real estate and other commercial deals everywhere he goes. His hotel group, Shangri-La International, has 14 supreme class hotels all around the Rim and in mainland China with many more currently on the drawing board. Apart from the hotels, Kuok also owns 34.5 per cent of Hong Kong's dominant television station and is developing shopping complexes in the Philippines as well as a causeway that will link Singapore to Malaysia. He is currently becoming more and more involved in a relationship with the almighty mainland-controlled corporation, China International Trust & Investment Corp (CITIC) and has formed a Hong Kong corporate takeover mechanism. CITIC presently owns around 20 per cent of Hong Kong Telecommunications, a chunk of Dragonair, 12.5 per cent of Cathay Pacific, part of the Eastern Cross Harbour Tunnel and substantial property interests. He is one of the few expected to be a big player once the mainland assumes control of the Colony after 1997.

The **Kwok**s (Walter, 42, Thomas, 41, Raymond 40), between them own nearly half of Sun Hung Kai Properties, the largest single landowning entity in the territory. They also own nearly 30 per cent of both the Kowloon Motor Bus Company and Hong Kong Cable Communications.

The **Lau** brothers own nearly half of Evergo International Holdings with its real estate interests and Paul Y International construction group which is heavily involved in Singapore and mainland China.

H.C. **Lee** and his family own nearly half of the Hysan Development Co with numerous commercial property interests in the territory as well as a very large number of shares in Cathay Pacific and Hong Kong Telecom.

Lee Shau-Kee, 54, is yet another Hong Kong billionaire (US$1.5bn) with his fortune firmly based in real estate. His interests lie in owning large chunks of Henderson Land Development, which in turn has interests in Town Gas and the Yaumati Ferry Company.

David **Li** is chief executive of the Bank of East Asia which has extensive contacts on the mainland. He is generally considered to be a putative Chinese governor of Hong Kong after the 1997 takeover.

Li Ka-Shing, 64, if the stuff of which Hong Kong dreams are made. Starting out as a youthful toy peddler on the streets of the colony, the Chiuchow-born billionaire now has substantial real estate interests. He also controls ownership of as much as one sixth of the Hong Kong stockmarket through shares in such companies as the Canadian Imperial Bank of Commerce, Cheung Kong Holdings, Hutchison Whampoa Cavendish and other securities.

The **Lo** family own Gold Peak Industries, making batteries, electrics and electronics and telecommunications and lighting equipment, as well as Great Eagle Holdings Co which has substantial real estate interests.

Y. S. **Lo**, of the Century City Group, the holdings company which owns over 70 per cent of Paliburg International Holdings, 49.9 per cent of Regal Hotels, 59.9 per cent of Cathay City, and 65 per cent of Richfield.

Simon **Murray** is the head of Hutchison Whampoa, one of Hong Kong's most blue-blooded companies which is largely owned by tycoon Li Ka Shing.

Dickson **Poon**, the Uppingham-educated entrepreneur is now just 36 and started his watch and jewellery business on a HK$5.0m loan from his father. Dubbed 'Hong Kong's Donald Trump' in the days when that could still be meant and taken as flattery, he now owns more than 50 per cent of Dickson Concepts Ltd with substantial overseas operations which recently acquired Knightsbridge's own Harvey Nichols. His companies own the rights to a number of prestigious luxury brands for Hong Kong including Charles Jourdan, Guy Laroche, Polo Ralph Lauren and S. T. Dupont which Poon recently bought outright. His Continental Holdings company exports and manufactures fine jewellery and his Innovisions Holdings company has at least ten outlets selling optical products.

Sir Run Run **Shaw**, media mogul, owns nearly 70 per cent of Shaw Brothers (HK) Ltd with interests in Hong Kong Cable Communications, TVB television, cinemas throughout Asia, and Shaw Towers in Singapore. Sir Run Run worked for the promotion of the Chinese film industry in Shanghai as long ago as the 1930s.

The **Swires**, (Sir John 65, and Sir Adrian, 60), both live in England but well over two-thirds of their US$1bn fortune is based on interests in Hong Kong. Swire Pacific has stakes in Cathay Pacific Airline, HAECO (Hong Kong Aircraft Engineering Co), South China Aero-Technology Ltd, the Kentucky Fried Chicken franchises and numerous real estate interests.

David **Tang** is the third generation heir to a fortune from his grandfather, Sir Shiu Kin Tang, director of the Kowloon Motor Bus company, amongst many other things. Young Tang is a proficient wheeler-dealer and merchant banker, as well as being Hong Kong representative for Algy Cluff and chief executive of his own company, DWC Tang Development Ltd. Tang has a well-established commercial and social presence in Britain, and will find no difficulty floating between the mainland and the UK whatever the political scenario in the years to come.

Peter **Woo** is the son-in-law of the late Sir Yue-Kong Pao who recently passed away leaving control of his ownership in World International and World-Wide Shipping to Woo and his other son-in-law the Austrian lawyer, Helmut Sohmen. The shipping and real estate fortune is said to be worth some US$1.3bn. Pao also had a number of daughters who survived him.

Princeton-educated Gordon **Ying Sheung Wu**, leading light of Hopewell Holdings Ltd, is the most pro-mainland of Hong Kong's movers and shakers and is playing his part in linking China with Hong Kong with the construction of the Guangzhou-Shenzhen-Zhuhai Superhighway, a 76-mile toll road, for which he is said to have arranged a US$800m loan. He and Hopewell are also involved in the construction of power plants in the Philippines and China, a US$1.0bn suspension bridge for Hong Kong and the proposed US$2.0bn overhead mass transit system for Bangkok.

Indonesia

Liem Sio Liong, 76, is patriarch of the US$8.0bn Salim Group and he and his family, of Fujian origin in Southern China, have interests in several hundred notable companies in Indonesia, including the Bank of Central Asia Group, the Bogasari Flour Mills, Indocement, Indomilk and Indo-steel. Today he is one of the prime movers in developing industry on Batam (see page 164, the new Golden Triangle – Johor, Batam, Singapore) and is working on a US$3.5bn tourist development on Bintan Island. He was also the founder in 1982 of the Hong Kong-based First Pacific Company which now has 75 companies in over 24 countries and is said to have assets worth more than US$1.0bn. His early fortune was said to be founded as a key supplier for troops led by Suharto fighting against the Dutch in the 1940s. Even today, the legacy of the Suharto connection continues to work for Liem and some of his enterprise is still conducted in partnership with one or other of the Suharto progeny. His two sons, who are fully involved in their father's operations, are Andrew **Salim** Liem and Anthony Salim **Liem** although the first concerns himself mostly with cars and industry, while the latter is more involved in cement and the Bogasari flour mills.

Oei Ek Tjong, or Eka Tjipa Widjaya, is the owner of the Sinar Mas group of companies and is said to be the third richest man in the country with a fortune of nearly one billion dollars.

William **Soeryadjaya**, 69, and his family founded his family's fortunes in the Astra Group on soft drinks but then diversified into a very valuable portfolio of interests which now include agribusiness, commodities, the sole distribution of Toyota cars, electronics, finance, forestry, and publishing. The family's fortune is said to be worth some one billion US dollars and includes over 80 per cent of Astra International.

South Korea

Chey Jong-Hyun, 62, and his family are said to be worth around US$1.3bn through ownership of interests in the giant Sungkyung Corporation (chemicals, oil refining and textiles) amongst others.

Chung Ju-Yung, 76, may never have got beyond secondary school in terms of his own scholastic education but as far as Hyundai (cars, construction and heavy industry) is concerned, he is a megastar. Today he and his family are said to be worth about $6.5bn and between them they personally own around 27.5 per cent of Hyundai.

Kim Seung-Yuon, 40, is a dynamite personality of a man owning as he does over 40 per cent of Korea Explosives Co Ltd. His interests are not solely confined to big bangs of the dangerous kind, however, and his interests also include construction, electronics, insurance and petrochemicals.

Ku Cha-Kyung of Lucky Goldstar, is another head of one of the five all-powerful Korean conglomerates and a billionaire said to be worth about US$1.8bn. Goldstar is a fast-rising star of the electronics world, more than meeting the world challenge earlier established by such Japanese giants as Sony.

Shin Kyuk-Ho, 70, and his family own a major stake in the influential Lotte Group (retail and department stores, hotels and real estate and confectionery) based on his early commercial successes with chewing gum. Today the family is said to be worth around US$3.5m and are thought to own about 41.4 per cent of the Lotte Group.

Malaysia

Loyheang **Heong**, 55, is an M&A whiz-kid and head of the MBF group of which he is said to own one third. He deals in acquisitions in all kinds of operations from printing to fast food companies.

Vincent **Tan**, 37, of Inter-Pacific Industrial is one of Malaysia's most pre-eminent real estate tycoons. He is a former part-owner of the national lottery Sports Toto, but these days concentrates on major take-overs of large corporations.

The man who was till recent crashes, Malaysia's wealthiest private landowner is former street hawker **Wong** Tee Tat, 65. He built his fortune from just one block of modest land and is today the boss of the giant Lian Seng group of companies. The portfolio includes hotels, as well as finance companies, insurance concerns and manufacturing operations. His daughter, Linda, is married to former 'taipan' David Davies who is a close friend of the Prime Minister's own daughter.

The Philippines

The **Araneta** family, father Amado, brother Jorge and daughter Maria Araneta-Fores own vast chunks of Manila including the Araneta Center, bought with the proceeds of a decades old import-export business specialising primarily in raw materials. Maria is said to be the second wealthiest woman in the Philippines after former first lady, Imelda Marcos.

Political aspirant, Eduardo 'Danding' **Cojuanco**, the ancient enemy of the slain Benigno Aquino is coconut king of the Philippines and head of the all-powerful Cocobank. Aquino's younger brother, Jose Cojuanco, is one of the wealthiest people in the congress and her sister-in-law, Teresa Aquino Ortega, also in congress, is said to be officially worth well over one million US dollars.

Alfredo **Ramos** or 'Pacman' as he is sometimes known, amongst many other property and business interests, co-owns the Shangri-La Properties company in Manila with Robert Kuok.

Industrialist Enrique **Sobel** is the head of the all-powerful Ayala Corporation.

The **Soriano** family, led today by Andres Soriano Jr own the San Miguel brewery empire.

Singapore

Tan Sri **Khoo** Teck Puat and his son, Khoo Ban Hock own the Goodwood Hotel in Singapore as the flagship of his real estate empire which has other hotels around the Pacific Rim including Sydney, Melbourne, Fiji, Tahiti, and New Zealand.

The **Kwek** sons of the late Kwek Hong Png [*sic*], Roland Kwek Leng Joo, the heir apparent, Kwek Leng Peng, together with nephew Kwek Leng Chan, have influence throughout the Malay Peninsula. Originally from Fukien province in China, their empire was founded on trade in general goods and then specialised in construction materials till they went on eventually to found Hong Leong Finance. After being denied permission to found a bank in Singapore, the group set up Dao Heng Bank in Hong Kong.

Lee Seng-Wee, 62, owns nearly one-third of the Overseas Chinese Banking Corporation as well as all of Lee Rubber. He is said to be worth around one billion dollars.

B. S. 'Benny' **Ong** made his initial fortune in hotels and real estate and is a former part owner of London's Inn on the Park. He recently opened the Halkin Hotel in London and works for many deals in close co-operation with Japan's C Itoh and Kowa Real Estate companies. He was the pioneer in Asia for the Hard Rock franchise outlets in Singapore and Bangkok.

Taiwan

Chang Yung-fa, 65, has recently branched out from the mainstay of his US$1.8bn fortune that is Evergreen Marine Corp to his new EVA Airways, which started service in July of 1991 flying from Taiwan to five major cities in the Asian-Pacific Rim. He also owns substantial chunks of the Uniglory Marine Corp and of the Evergreen Transport Corp. Chang's links with Marubeni of Japan are said to be very close.

Tsai Wan-Lin, 67, and his family come from a humble background of poor rice farmers yet today the family, including heir apparent, H. T. Tsai, 41, own nearly half of the powerful Cathay Life Insurance Co of which Tsai senior was chairman until quite recently. He is now said to be the wealthiest man in Taiwan and worth some $5.6bn. He owns 120 office buildings but is said to be unimpressed by his own wealth.

Y. T. **Wang**, 70, and his brother, Y. C. Wang, 75, who is based in the US, owe their fortune primarily to plastics through the ownership of major stakes in the Formosa Plastic Corp and the Nan Ya Plastics Corp. They also have substantial interests in the Formosa Taffeta Corp and the Formosa Chemicals & Fibre Corp.

Eugene T. C. **Wu**, 45, and his family (textiles, department stores and insurance) are said to be worth around US$1.9bn through ownership of major interests in Shin Kong Life Insurance, Shin Kong Spinning Corp, Shin Kong Synthetic Fibre Corp and the Taipei Gas Corp.

J. M. **Yang** is steel king of Taiwan and in his mid-fifties. He says the only education he ever received is that given to him by his father but that he had well-honed business instincts and was always very willing. He showed a very early inclination towards robotics.

Thailand

Pin **Chakkaphak**, 41, was born into one of Thailand's oldest trading dynasties, the owners of the company Yip in Tsoi, and is now the president of Finance Once, Bangkok's fastest growing finance house.

Sura **Chansrishawala**, real estate magnate, runs the Siam Vidhaya Group.

Dhanin **Chiaravanont** is a Thai agribusiness magnate through the Charoen Pokphand Group which is fast becoming the major player in the Asian-Pacific Rim for packaged foods, petrochemicals and prawn production and is already pre-eminent in animal feed and poultry production. His company is currently involved in a joint venture to develop a prawn farm in Hainan Island, and a joint venture in Shanghai manufacturing motor cycles.

The **Chirathivat** family runs the Central Department Stores chain, Thailand's leading retail group.

Akorn **Hoontrakul**, 46, is the Queen's University, Belfast-educated owner of a string of world-wide restaurants which include the eponymous Khun Akorn Thai on London's Brompton Road. Twenty or so more are planned in Europe, the US and Canada over the next three years. His family runs the Imperial Family Hotel chain which has seven hotels in Thailand.

The **Kanchanapas** family (Mongkol, 71, Anant, 50, Keree 42), own nearly 60 per cent of Bangkok Land Ltd, accrued from monies earned as distributor of Japanese watch company Seiko's products, and are said to be worth around US$1.3bn. They also have interests in cable television, cement, financial services, metals, shopping centres and sugar.

The **Phornpraphra** family has a controlling interest in Siam Motors which is Thailand's largest car manufacturer.

Thailand's so-called 'telecommunications mogul' is Thaksin **Shinawatra**, 41, chairman of the Shinawatra Computer Group. He owns the first non-government cable television station in Thailand and his company is now the market leader in mobile phones.

Chatri **Sophonpanich**, 58, or 'The Boss' and his family are based in Bangkok where they are said to own 35 per cent of Bangkok Bank, Thailand's largest financial institution, as well as major interests in over 200 other corporations, especially in textiles and shipping.

The **Tejapaibuls**, **Uthane** and **Athorn** are the heads of the family which controls the Metropolitan Bank.

Vietnam

It is early days for Vietnam in terms of visiting businessmen being able to hook into a Chinese network in order to be able to get deals done. For the moment, it would be best to concentrate on any introductions that may be effected through such people as former cabinet minister Peter Walker (who is involved with Smith New Court's Vietnam Fund) or through other experts such as Jim Walker, managing director of Credit Lyonnais Securities (Asia). Another name of note in the Vietnamese network connection is Vietnamese-born Taiwanese citizen, James **Hung**, who runs Asia Securities.

Ngo Van **Thuan**, on the government side in Hanoi, is a director of the Vietnam Trade Service Centre in conjunction with Neil V Shrimpton in London. The most accessible of bankers in the country is probably Nguyen Duy **Lo**, deputy general director of Vietcombank, the foreign trade bank. He is also chairman of the twice-weekly foreign exchange auction at the State Bank of Vietnam Ho Chi Minh City branch. Tran Duc **Luong** is a key government figure said to be closely involved with the reform programmes and is currently vice-chairman of the Council of Ministers of Vietnam.

Madame Nguyen Thi **Thi** has made her millions, it is said, through control of Vietnam's food distribution system and is in charge of 1,700 people in a company which has an annual turnover of around 400bn dong (about half a billion dollars). She is said to be one of the most influential of business people in the country today.

Finally, Madame Pham Chi **Lan** is deputy secretary of the General Chamber of Commerce & Industry in Hanoi.

8 Have you got what it takes?

A self-test questionnaire

Before entering into this complex but potentially highly lucrative business arena, it is essential that your current domestic operation is in very good order. These questions are designed to allow you an opportunity to begin the analysis and evaluation that will be required to build the foundations for a successful enterprise in or with countries in the Asian-Pacific Rim. They also serve as a very useful jumping-off point for exploratory management-level discussions on the subject.

Answer each question by allocating marks out of 10 (1 – the weakest, 10 – the strongest) and add up the numbers for a possible total of 100. During the answering process, make sure that you bring all the considerations into play, drawing up lists of strengths and weaknesses where appropriate, so that the outcome is not just a numerate summary of your status but has provided an opportunity for useful self-analysis and debate.

There are a number of expert business consultants who may help carry out the necessary and far more thorough investigation into your commercial readiness for the Asian-Pacific Rim and the Department of Trade & Industry is always ready to help explore all commercial possibilities for new business.

Questions

1. After studying the inherent strengths and weaknesses of your company's management team and organisational structure, are you currently in a position to cope with the administrative and financial demands of overseas expansion into the Asian-Pacific Rim?

2.   Have you achieved an internal consensus within top-level management in your company that will provide complete and unequivocal support for this area of new business?

3.   Are you able to identify a key senior management-level individual, or team of individuals, on whom the responsibility for the operation and expansion will devolve?

4.   Does that key person have the sensitivity to work with people of other cultures, as well as the integrity, flexibility and patience to cope on a personal level in these new markets in all situations?

5.   Are these people fully committed for at least a five-year period to developing new business in the Asian-Pacific arena?

6.   Are the back-office systems of your operation such that they can absorb the intricacies of this new area of business into their usual functions without major disruption to present commercial activities?

7.   Can you ensure that the new business into the Asian-Pacific Rim will be sufficiently funded, with or without outside financing for working or investment capital, to cover all eventualities?

8.   Are you prepared to undertake the necessary product or service evaluation, as well as investigations into likely demand, before launching into these markets to establish its suitability and likelihood of success?

9.   Do you have the in-built flexibility to adapt products and services where necessary in order to win new business in this arena?

10.   Are you prepared as a company to accept and adjust to the very different demands that the international marketing of your product and/or services will require?

Results

1–35: You have probably turned to the possibilities in the Asian-Pacific Rim out of desperation about the economic gloom on the home-front. The problems you seem to have in your domestic operation, displayed by a lack of confidence in your answers, can only be exacerbated once you expand into overseas markets. Furthermore, while these can be contained within the confines of a relatively simple domestically-based operation, they could be the cause of your commercial death and destruction if you dabble overseas too soon. The Asian-Pacific Rim is not a fad that you turn to because you are looking for commercial stimulation. If you are really serious about these new areas of business, you must first put your house in proper order to ensure a sound foundation upon which to build and then commit come hell or high water for at least a five-year period. Seek expert help immediately.

36–70: Like eastern Europe, the Asian-Pacific Rim could be said to be a bit of a management consultants' fad and you might well have been swayed by this. Some of the necessary ingredients seem to be in place within your existing operation but will need honing to a much greater degree of precision and reliability to ensure continued Asian-Pacific Rim success. Now go back to the above questions and pursue all the logical implications to their ultimate conclusions until you are satisfied you have a clear picture of what specifically needs to be worked upon. There is plenty of expert help available which you should not fail to make good use of.

71–100: All the superficial indications are that as a company you have the right commercial and management qualities for a foundation of business success in the Asian-Pacific Rim. While there are some areas open for improvement, you are aware of your weaknesses and prepared to tackle and eradicate them. If you can now apply the same formulae of thoroughness and application to business procedures in the Asian-Pacific Rim, your company may soon become one of the many emerging market success stories that we are increasingly hearing so much about. The opportunities are now just waiting for you. Jump at them.

Appendix 1

Essential contacts and addresses

Hong Kong

Official representation in the United Kingdom:

Hong Kong Government Office
6 Grafton Street, London W1X 3LB (tel 071-499 9821, telex 28404).

Hong Kong Trade Development Council
Swire House, 59 Buckingham Gate, London SW1E 6AJ (tel 071-828 1661, telex 916923).

Hong Kong Tourist Association
125 Pall Mall, London SW1Y 5EA (tel 071-930 4775).

American Chamber of Commerce in Hong Kong
Room 1027, 10th Fl, Swire House, Central (tel 526-0165, telex 83664).

Chinese General Chamber of Commerce
7th Fl, Chinese General Chamber of Commerce Building,
24-25 Connaught Road Central (tel 525-6385, telex 89854).

Banking, Securities, Insurance & Companies Division
24th Fl, Admiralty Centre, Tower 11, Central (tel 527-8337 fax 865-6146, telex 75776).

Business & Industrial Trade Fairs Ltd
28th Fl, Harbour Centre, 25 Harbour Road, Wanchai (tel 575-6333, fax 589-15347/583 41171, telex 64882).

Census and Statistics Department
Tower 1, 12 Harbour Road, Wanchai.

Chinese Manufacturers' Association of Hong Kong
3rd and 4th Fl, 64-66 Connaught Road, Central CMA Building, (tel 545-6166, telex 53526).

Exchange Fund Division
24th Fl, Admiralty Centre, Tower 11, Central (tel 529-0024, fax 865-6146, telex 75776).

Federation of Hong Kong Industries
4th Fl, Hankow Centre, 5–15 Hankow Road, Kowloon (tel 723-0818).

Finance Branch, Hong Kong Government Secretariat
Central Government Offices, Lower Albert Road, Central (tel 810-2540, fax 810-1530).

Hong Kong Convention & Incentive Travel Bureau (Trade fairs)
35th Fl, Jardine House, Central (tel 524-4191, fax 581-04877).

Hong Kong Export Credit Insurance Corp
2nd Fl, South Seas Centre, Tower 1, 75 Mody Road, Tsimshatsui East, Kowloon (tel 723-3883, telex 56200).

Hong Kong Exporters Association
Room 825, Star House, 3 Salisbury Road, Tsimshatsui, Kowloon (tel 730-9851).

Hong Kong General Chamber of Commerce
22nd Fl, United Centre, 95 Queensway, Central (tel 529-9229, fax 866 2035, telex 83535).

Hong Kong Industrial Estates Corp
107 Estate Centre Building, 19 Dai Cheong Street, Tai Po Industrial Estate, Tai Po, New Territories (tel 635-1183).

Hong Kong Productivity Council and Productivity Centre,
12th Fl, World Commerce Centre, Harbour City, 11 Canton Road, Tsimshatsui, Kowloon (tel 735-1656, telex 32842).

Hong Kong Standards and Testing Centre
10 Dai Wang Street, Tai Po Industrial Estate, Tai Po, New Territories (tel 653-0021).

Hong Kong Tourist Association
Connaught Place, Central (tel 801-7177).

Hong Kong Trade Development Council
36th-39th Fl, Office Tower, Convention Plaza, 1 Harbour Road, Wanchai (tel 833-4333, fax 824-0249, telex 73595).

Kowloon Chamber of Commerce
3rd Fl, KCC Building, 2 Liberty Avenue, Kowloon (tel 760 0393).

Securities and Futures Commission
32nd Fl, Alexandra House, 16–20 Chater Road, Central (tel 842-7666, fax 526-5304, telex 69429).

Academic/research institutes

Chinese University of Hong Kong
Shatin, New Territories (tel 635-2111). (Majority of teaching in Chinese)

University of Hong Kong
Knowles Building, Pokfulam Road (tel 585-9211, telex 71919).
(Centre of Urban Studies and Urban Planning – these are both set up to aid south-east Asia)

Other useful numbers

Emergencies: 999
Directory enquiries: 108
Problems: 109
International calls: 010
Calls to China: 012
International direct dialling code enquiries: 013
Reverse charge (collect) calls: 011
Tourist information: 801-7177

Indonesia

Official representation in the United Kingdom

Indonesian Embassy
38 Grosvenor Square, London W1X 9AD (tel 071-499 7661).
Commercial Attaché – Gusmardi Bustami
Trade Dept: 24 Upper Brook Street, London W1Y 1PD (tel 071-629 5924).

ASEAN Secretariat
Jalan Sisigamangaraja 70A, Jakarta (tel 716451, telex 47213).

Business Advisory Services
Kuningan Plaza Building, Jalan Rasuna Said Kav C-11-14, Jakarta (tel 5177295).

Central Bureau of Statistics
Jalan Dr Sutomo 18, Jakarta (tel 372808).

Co-ordinating Board for Capital Investment (Badan Ko-ordinasi Penanaman Modal)
Jalan Gatot Subroto 6, Jakarta (tel 51648/512008).

Department of Agriculture
Jalan Harsono RM2, Jakarta (tel 782131).

Department of Communications
Jalan Merdeka Barat 8, Jakarta (tel 366322).

Department of Finance
Jalan Lapangan Banteng Timur 2-4, Jakarta (tel 365364).

Department of Industry
Jalan Gatot Subroto Kav 52–53, Jakarta (tel 511738).

Department of Information
Jalan Medan Merdeka Barat 9, Jakarta (tel 374392).

Department of Tourism, Post & Telecommunications
Jalan Kebon Sirih 36, Jakarta (tel 366705).

Department of Trade
Jalan Ridwan Rais 5, Jakarta (tel 366318).

Directorate General of Tourism
Jalan Kramat Raya, PO Box 409, Jakarta (tel 359001, telex 45625).

Indonesia-British Association
Lippo Life Building, 2nd Fl, Jalan HR Rasuna Said Kav B-10, Jakarta.

Indonesian Exporters Association (GPEI)
Jalan Kramat Raya 4–6, Jakarta (tel 346892/350099).

Indonesian Importers Association (GINSI)
PO Box 2744/DDK,
Wisma Nusantara,
Jalan Maja Pahit 1, Jakarta (tel 360643/367269).

Investment Co-ordinating Board
Jalan Gatot Subroto 44, Jakarta (tel. 510023).

Ministry of Trade Foreign Corporation Division
Bureau of PR, Jalan Moh Ikhwan Ridwan Rais 5, Jakarta Pusat (tel 357412/347413, fax 375237, telex 45725).

National Development Information Office
12th Fl Wisma Antara, Jalan Kerdeka Selatan 17, Jakarta (tel 347412/347413, fax 347603, telex 44456).

National Development Planning Board
Jalan Suropati 2, Jakarta (tel 336206, fax 3105374, telex 51333/61623).

Pertamina (State oil and gas company)
Jalan Medan Merdeka Timur, Jakarta (tel 3031, telex 44302).

Chambers of Commerce

American Chamber of Commerce in Indonesia
8th Fl, Citibank Building, 55 Jalan HM Thamrin, Jakarta (tel 578 0800, telex 44368).

Indonesian Chamber of Commerce and Industry
Jalan Medan Merdeka Timur 11, Jakarta
(tel 377459/367906).

Jakarta Chamber of Commerce and Industry
Kadin Jaya Graha, Jalan I H Juanda 38, Jakarta (tel 365609/370943).

Other useful numbers

Police: 510110
Ambulance: 119
Fire: 113
Directory (local): 108
International information: 102
International operator: 101

Republic of Korea

Official representation in the United Kingdom:

Embassy of Republic of Korea
4 Palace Gate, London W8 5NF (tel 071-582 0247, fax 071-589 9134, telex 919620).
Commercial Attaché – Hyo Sung Kim
Consular Section tel 071-581 3330
Press & Cultural Information Office tel 071-584 3252

Korea Trade Centre
Vincent House, Vincent Square, London SW1P 2NB (tel 071-834 5082, fax 071-630 5233, telex 22375).
Managing Director – K. L. Chung

Korea Trade Advisory Group
OT2/2A, Room 336, Department of Trade & Industry, 1–19 Victoria Street, London SW1H 0ET (tel 071-215 4807, fax 071-222 2629, telex 881174).

For government departments and foreign organisations, correspondence can be addressed to the organisation name, followed by Seoul.

Association of Foreign Trading Agents of Korea (AFTAK)
45–20 Yoido-dong, Yungdungpo-ku, Seoul (tel 782-2206).

Federation of Korean Industries
28–1 Uoido-dong, Yungdungpo-ku, Seoul (tel 783-0821).

Foreign Investment Policy Division
Room 203, Complex No 3, 1 Chungang-dong, Kwachonshi, Kyongki-do, Seoul (tel 503-9276/7, fax 503-9324).

Korean Broadcasting Association
25, 1-st Taepong ro, Seoul (tel 735-7117).

Korean Broadcasting Committee
75, 1-ga Taepong-ro, Chung-ku, Seoul (tel 735-2640).

Korean Exhibition Centre
65 Samsung-dong, Gangnam-ku, Seoul.

Hunting with the Tigers

Korean Traders' Association (KTA)
World Trade Center, Korea Building, 10–1, 2-ka Hoehyun-dong, Chung-ku, Seoul (telex 24265).

Ministry of Finance
1st Chungang-dong, Kwachonshi, Kyongki-do, Seoul (tel 503-7171).

Ministry of Finance (Foreign Investment)
Promotion Division, Istchumgang-dong, Kwachomshi, Kyongki-do, Seoul (tel 503-9276).

Ministry of Justice
1 Chungang-dong, Kwachonshi, Kyongki-do, Seoul (tel 503-7011, fax 503-7507).

Ministry of Trade & Industry
77–6 Sejong-ro, Chongro-ku, Seoul.

Securities Exchange Committee
28–1 Yoido-dong, Yongdongpo-ku, Seoul (tel 785–7593, fax 785–3475).

Consultation Office for Overseas Companies (COOC)
Ministry of Trade and Industry, 1st Fl, KOEX Main Building, 159 Samsung-dong, Kangnam-ku, Seoul 135-731 (tel 551-6781, fax 551-6784).

American Chamber of Commerce in Korea
307 Chosun Hotel, 87-1 Sokong-dong, Chung-ku, Seoul (tel 752-3061, telex 242560).

The Korea Chamber of Commerce & Industry
CPO Box 25, Seoul (tel 757-0757, telex 25728).

The Korea Trade Promotion Corporation (KOTRA)
Korea World Trade Center, CPO Box 1621, Seoul (tel 753-4180/9, telex 23659, 27326, 28819, 28820).

Korea National Tourism Corporation
10 Ta-dong, Chung-ku, Seoul (tel 757-0757, fax 757-5997).

Korea Tourist Association
9th Fl, Kyongwun Building, 70 Kyongwun-dong, Chongro-ku, Seoul (tel 724-2702).

Other useful numbers

International calls: 1035/1037
Directory: 114
Police: 112
Fire/ambulance: 119

Malaysia

Official representation in the United Kingdom

Malaysian High Commission
45 Belgrave Square, London SW1X 8QT (tel 071-235 8033, fax 071-235 5161, telex 262550).

Senior Trade Commissioner:
Malaysian Trade Commission
17 Curzon Street, London W1Y 7FE (tel 071-499 7388).

Malaysian Tourist Development Corp
57 Trafalgar Square, London WC2N 5DU (tel 071-930 7932).

Investment Office
Basement, 17 Curzon Street, London W1Y 7FE (tel 071-493 0616/0411).

Associated Chinese Chamber of Commerce and Industry
Chinese Assembly Hall, 1 Jalan Maharajalela, 50150 Kuala Lumpur (tel 232-0473, telex 32995).

Associated Indian Chamber of Commerce
Wisma UOA, 36 Jalan Ampang, PO Box 12564, Kuala Lumpur (tel 238-7917, telex 31354).

Malay Chamber of Commerce
17A Fl, Plaza Pekeliling, Jalan Tun Razak, 50400 Kuala Lumpur (tel 292-8522).

Malaysian International Chamber of Commerce and Industry
10th Fl, Wisma Damansara, Jalan Semantan, PO Box 10192, 50706 Kuala Lumpur (tel 254-2677, fax 255-4946, telex 32120).

National Chamber of Commerce and Industry of Malaysia
Plaza Pekeliling, Jalan Tun Razak, Kuala Lumpur (tel 298987, telex 33642).

Sabah Chamber of Commerce
Bangunan Central, Jalan Sagunting, 88000 Kota Kinabulu (tel 088-54913).

United Chamber of Commerce of Sarawak
c/o Ernst & Whinney, Room 301, 3rd Fl, Wisma Bukit Mata, Jalan Tuanku Abdul Rahman, 93100 Kuching, Sarawak (telex 70920).

Advertising Standards Authority of Malaysia
c/o Coopers & Lybrand, Hong Kong Bank Building, Leboh Pasar, Kuala Lumpur.

Capital Issues Committee (Kementerian Kewangan)
11th Fl, Block 9 Khazanah Malaysia, Jalan Duta, Kuala Lumpur (tel 254-0011, fax 254-2636, telex 30242).

Federal Land Development Authority (FELDA)
Jalan Maktab, Kuala Lumpur (tel 293-5066, fax 292-0089, telex 30789).

Hunting with the Tigers

Federation of Malaysian Manufacturers
17th Fl, Wisma Sime Darby, PO Box 12194, 50770 Kuala Lumpur (tel 293-1244, telex 32437).

Foreign Investment Committee
Economic Planning Unit, Prime Minister's Dept, Jln Dato' Onn, Kuala Lumpur (tel 230-0133).

Kuala Lumpur Stock Exchange Bhd
3rd-4th Fl, Block A Komplek Bukit Naga, Damansara Heights, Kuala Lumpur (tel 254-6433, fax 255-7463, telex 30241).

Malaysian Export Trade Centre
Ministry of Trade & Industry, Wisma PKNS, Jalan Raja Laut, 50350 Kuala Lumpur (tel 292-8122, telex 33721).

Malaysian Industrial Development Authority
3rd–6th Fl, Wisma Damansara, Jalan Semantan, PO Box 10618, 50720 Kuala Lumpur (tel 254-3633, fax 255-7970, telex 30752).

Ministry of Finance
Block 9, Kompleks Pejabat-Pejabat Kerajaan, Jalan Duta, Kuala Lumpur (tel 254-6066, telex 30242).

Ministry of Information
Angkasapuri, Bukit Putra, 50601 Kuala Lumpur.

Ministry of Trade and Industry
International Trade Division, Block 10, Jalan Duta, 50622 Kuala Lumpur (tel 254-0033/254-8044).

Perbadanan Nasional Bhd (PERNAS)
16th Fl, Menara Tun Razak, Jalan Raja Laut, Kuala Lumpur (tel 242-5022).

Sarawak Economic Development Corporation
1st Fl, Bangunan Yayasa Sarawak, Jalan Masjid, PO Box 400, Kuching, Sarawak (telex 70063).

Tourist Development Corp (TDC)
24/27F, Menara Dato' Onn, Putra World Trade Centre, 45, Jalan Tun Ismail, Kuala Lumpur (tel 293-5188; fax 293-5884; telex 30093).

Automobile Association of Malaysia,
30 Jalan Datuk Sulaiman, Taman Tun Dr Ismail, Kuala Lumpur (tel 261-0042).

Kuala Lumpur Tourist Association (KLTA)
3 Jalan Sultan Hishamuddin, 50050 Kuala Lumpur (tel 238-1832).

Malaysian Tourist Information Complex (MATIC)
109 Jalan Ampang, 50450 Kuala Lumpur (tel 243-4929).

Malaysian Airline System
Information/reservations – Kuala Lumpur Airport (tel 746-3000/1014; DCA information tel 746-1235).

Academic/research institutes

National University of Malaysia
43600 Bangi, Selangor (tel 03-35001; telex 31496).

Northern University of Malaysia
Bandar Darulaman, 06000 Jitra, Kedan (tel Jitra(04)772066, telex 42052).

University of Agriculture
43400 UPM, Serdang, Selangor (tel 356101-10/355425-8).

University of Malaya
Pantai Valley, 59100 Kuala Lumpur (tel 560022, telex 31496).

University of Science (Universiti Sains Malaysia)
Minden, 11800 Penang (tel 883822, telex 40245).

Other useful numbers

Emergency: 999
Operator (trunk call) enquiries: 102
Directory: 103
International service: 108
Railway station, Kuala Lumpur: 274-7435
Telegrams: 104
Tourist police: 243 5522

Philippines

Official representation in the United Kingdom:

Embassy of the Philippines
9A Palace Green, London W8 4QE (tel 071-937 1600, fax 071-937 2925, telex 24411).

Office of the Commercial Counsellor
1A Cumberland House, Kensington Court Road, London W8 5NX (tel 071-937 1898).

Philippine Department of Tourism
199 Piccadilly, London W1V 0JJ (tel 071-439 3481/071-734 6358).

American Chamber of Commerce
2nd Fl, Corinthian Plaza, Paseo do Roxas, Legaspi Village, Makati, Metro Manila (tel 818-7911, telex 45181).

European Chamber of Commerce
3rd Fl, Electra House Building, 115–117 Esteban Street, Legaspi Village, Makati, Metro Manila.

Philippine Chamber of Commerce & Industries
CCP Building, Magellanes Drive, Intramuros, Manila 2801 (tel 403082).

Board of Investments Inc
Industry and Investments Building, 385 Sen Gil Puyat Avenue, Makati, Metro Manila.

Bureau of Export Trade Promotion
New Solid Building, 357 Sen Gil J Puyat Avenue, Makati, Metro Manila (tel 819-1809/818-8434, fax 819-1816).

Chamber of Agriculture and Natural Resource
3rd Fl, Rico House, 126 Amorsolo Street, Legaspi Village, Makati, Metro Manila.

Chamber of International Trade
Room 914, L&S Building No 2, 1515 Roxas Boulevard, Ermita, Metro Manila (tel 591372/3).

Department of Agriculture
Elliptical Road, Dilimann, Quezon City (tel 978586/998751, fax 978183).

Department of Trade & Industry
385 Sen Gil J Puyat Avenue Extension, Makati, Metro Manila (tel 875602/868485/818-1835/9, fax 851166).

Export Processing Zone Authority
Legaspi Towers, 300 Roxas Boulevard, Manila (tel 521-0419/0546, fax 521-8659.

International Economic Affairs & Development Division
Philippine International Convention Center, Roxas Boulevard, Manila (tel 831-8988, fax 832-3793).

Ministry of Finance
Finance Building, Agrifina Circle, Manila.

National Economic & Development Authority (NEDA)
NEDA Building, Amber Avenue, Pasig, Metro Manila (tel 673-6313, fax 631-3282).

Philippine Convention Bureau
4th Fl, Legaspi Towers, 300 Roxas Boulevard, Manila (tel 575031, telex 40604).

Philippine International Trading Corp
Tordesillas Street, PO Box 1056 MCC, Salcedo Village, Metro Manila (tel 818-9801, telex 63745).

Private Development Corp of the Philippines
PDCP Building, Ayala Avenue, Makati, Metro Manila (tel 850686).

Secretary of Finance
Finance Building, Agrifina Circle, Manila (tel 586719/596913, fax 521-9495).

Securities and Exchange Commission
SEC Building, E de los Santos Avenue, Greenhills, San Juan, Metro Manila (tel 780931/39, fax 722-0990).

Under-Secretary for Industry and Investments
377 Sen Gil J Puyat Avenue Extension, Makati, Metro Manila (tel 868485/818-1835/1839).

Department of Tourism
DOT Building, TM Kalaw Street, Rizal Park, PO Box 3451, Manila (tel 599031, fax 521-6165, telex 40183, 66412).

Philippine Air Lines Inc
Venida Building, Legaspi Street, Makati, Metro Manila (tel 818-0111).

Philippine Motor Association
683 Aurora Boulevard, Quezon City, Manila (tel 721-5761).

Tourism Council of the Philippines
Suite 326, PICC Building, CCP Complex, Roxas Boulevard, Manila (tel 831-2404/833-1462, telex 40771).

Singapore

Official representation in the United Kingdom

High Commission for the Republic of Singapore
9 Wilton Crescent, London SW1X 8SA (tel 071-235 8315, fax 071-245 6583, telex 262564).
Commercial section
5 Chesham Street, London SW1X 8ND (tel 071-245 9709, fax 071-235 9792, telex 921117).
Commercial Attaché – Hock Chee Tham

Singapore Economic Development Board
International House, World Trade Centre, London E1 9AA (tel 071-481 0745/4308).

Singapore Trade Development Bureau
5 Chesham Street, London SW1X 8ND (tel 071-245 9709, fax 071-235 9792, telex 921117).

Singapore & Malaysian British Association
1 Grangeway, London NW6 2BW (tel 071-328 3452).

Singapore Tourist Promotion Board
1 Carrington House, 126 Regent Street, London W1R 7HA (tel 071-437 0033, fax 071-734 2191)

Singapore Chinese Chamber of Commerce
09–00 Chinese Chamber Building, 47 Hill Street, Singapore 0617 (tel 337-8381, fax 339-0605, telex 33714).

Singapore Federation of Chambers of Commerce & Industry
03–01 Chinese Chamber of Commerce Building, 47 Hill Street, Singapore 0617 (tel 338-9761, telex 26228).

Singapore Indian Chamber of Commerce
23–01 Tong Eng Building, 101 Cecil Street, Singapore 0106 (tel 222-2855, telex 22336).

Singapore International Chamber of Commerce
03–02 Shell Tower, 50 Raffles Place, Singapore 0104 (tel 224-1255, fax 224-2785, telex 25235).

Singapore Malay Chamber of Commerce
20–01 International Plaza, 10 Anson Road, Singapore 0207 (tel 221-1066, telex 25521).

Monetary Authority of Singapore
MAS Building, 10 Shenton Way, Singapore 0207 (tel 225-5577, fax 229-09491, telex 28174).

American Business Council
10–12 Shaw House, 354 Orchard Road, Singapore 0923 (tel 235-0077, telex 50296).

British Businessmen's Association
3rd Fl, Inchcape House, 450–452 Alexandra Road, Singapore 0511 (tel 475-4192, telex 212400).

Civil Aviation Authority of Singapore
Singapore Airtropolis, Changi Airport, Singapore 1750 (tel 542-1122, fax 545-6222, telex 21231).

Controller of Immigration
Pidemco Centre, 95 South Bridge Road, Singapore 0105 (tel 532-2877, fax 530-1840).

Customs & Excise Department
1 Maritime Square, Unit 03–01 World Trade Centre, Singapore 0409 (tel 272-8222).

Economic Development Board
24–00 Raffles City Tower, 250 North Bridge Road, Singapore 0617 (tel 336-2288, fax 339-6077, telex 26233).

Export Credit Insurance Corporation of Singapore Ltd
17–03 MAS Building, 10 Shenton Way, Singapore 0207 (tel 220-8344, fax 224-2887, telex 21524).

Housing and Development Board
HDB Centre, 3451 Jalan Bukit Merah, Singapore 0315 (tel 273-9090, telex 22020).

Jurong Town Corporation
Jurong Town Hall, Jurong Town, Singapore 2260 (tel 560-0056, telex 35733).

Ministry of Communications & Information
36–00 PSA Building, 460 Alexandra Road, Singapore 0207 (tel 279-9793, fax 278-1526, telex 22428).

Ministry of Finance
Treasury Building, 8 Shenton Way, Singapore 0207 (tel 225-9911).

Ministry of National Development
21st Fl, National Development Building, Maxwell Road, Singapore 0106 (tel 222-1211, telex 34369).

Ministry of Trade & Industry
48–00 Treasury Building, 8 Shenton Way, Singapore 0207 (tel 225-9911, fax 320-9260, telex 24702).

National Productivity Board
2 Bukit Merah, Central NPB Building, Singapore 0315 (tel 734-5534, telex 36047).

Registrar of Companies and Businesses
Rooms 06–6, 6th Fl Colombo Court, Singapore 0617 (tel 278-6666, telex 36047).

Singapore International Monetary Exchange
09–39 World Trade Centre, 1 Maritime Square, Singapore 0409 (tel 278–6363, telex 38000).

Singapore Manufacturers' Association
SMA House, 20 Orchard Road, Singapore (tel 338-8787, fax 336-1251, telex 24993).

Singapore Telecom
28–00 Comcentre, 31 Exeter Road, Singapore (tel 730-3682, fax 733-1350).

Singapore Trade Development Board
10–40 World Trade Centre, 1 Maritime Square, Telok Blangan Road, Singapore 0409 (tel 271-9388, fax 274-0770/278-2518, telex 286171).

Vocational and Industry Training Board
Vocational Drive (Off Dover Road), Singapore 0513 (tel 775-7800, telex 50195).

Other useful numbers

Police: 999
Fire/ambulance: 995
Directory enquiries: 103
International calls: 104
International enquiries: 162
Trunk calls to Malaysia: 109
Flight information: 542-1234
Bus information: 287-2727
AA road service: 748–9911
Post Office information: 533-0234, 532-4536

Taiwan

Taiwan Trade Services
5th Fl, Bewlay House, 2 Swallow Place, London SW1R 7AA (tel 071-629 1516, fax 071-499 8730) *Managing Director* – James Chu.

General Chamber of Commerce of the Republic of China
6th Fl, 390 Fu Hsing South Road, Section 1, Taipei (tel 701-2671, telex 11396).

Taipei Chamber of Commerce
6th Fl, 72 Nanking East Road, Section 2, Taipei (tel 531-8217).

Board of Foreign Trade
1 Hukow Street, Taipei (tel 351-0271, fax 351-3603, telex 11434).

China External Trade Development Council
4–8th Fl, International Trade Building, 333 Keelung Road, Section 1, Taipei 10548 (tel 738-2345, fax 757-6653, telex 21676).

Chinese National Association of Industry & Commerce
13th Fl, 390 Fu Hsing South Road, Section 1, Taipei (tel 707-0111, fax 701-7601, telex 21676).

Chinese National Federation of Industries
12th Fl, 390 Fu Hsing South Road, Section 2, Taipei (tel 703-3500, telex 14565).

Council for Economic Planning and Development
9th Fl, 87 Nanking East Road, Section 2, Taipei (tel 551-3522, fax 581-8549, telex 11385).

Directorate-General of Budgets, Accounting & Statistics
1 Chung Hsiao East Road, Section 1, Taipei.

Industrial Development and Investment Center
10th Fl, 7 Roosevelt Road, Section 1, Taipei (tel 394-7213, fax 392-6835, telex 10634).

Industry of Free China
9th Fl, 87 Nanking East Road, Section 2, Taipei (tel 543-5988).

Ministry of Economic Affairs
Investment Commission, 8th Fl, 7 Roosevelt Road, Section 1, Taipei (tel 351-3151, fax 396-3970).

Ministry of Finance
Monetary Affairs Dept, 2 Aikwo W Road, Taipei (tel 321-3836, telex 11840).

Securities and Exchange Commission
12th Fl, Yangteh Building, 3 Nanhai Road, Taipei (tel 341-3191, fax 394-8249).

Taipei World Trade Center
5 Hsinyl Road, Section 5, Taipei (tel 725-1111, fax 351-3603, telex 28094).

Taiwan Stock Exchange Corporation
85 Yen Ping S Road, Taipei (tel 311-4020, fax 311-4004, telex 22914).

Taiwan Visitors' Association
5th Fl, 111 Minchuan East Road, Taipei (tel 594-3261, fax 594-3265).

Ministry of Communications Tourism Bureau
9th Fl, 280 Chung Hsiao East Road, Section 4, PO Box 1490, Taipei (tel 721-8541, telex 26408).

Tourist Service Centre
CKS International Airport (tel 383-4631/2).

Other useful numbers

Police: 110
Ambulance: 721-6315
Fire: 119
International calls: 100
Directory enquiries: 104 (Chinese language)
                                    311-6796 (English language)
Tourist information hot line: 717-3737

Thailand

Official representation in the United Kingdom:

Royal Thai Embassy
29–30 Queen's Gate, London SW7 5JB (tel 071-589 0173, fax 071-823 9695).
Commercial Counsellor's Office: 9 Stafford Street, London W1X 4RT (tel 071-493 5749).
Information Attaché's Office: 28 Prince's Gate, London SW7 1PT (tel 071-584 5421).
Commercial Counsellor – Nabthong Thongyai
Overseas Trade Division (OTD)

American Chamber of Commerce
7/F Kian-Nguan Building, 140 Thanon Withayn, Bangkok (tel 251-9266/1605, telex 82778).

British Chamber of Commerce
Room 206, Bangkok Insurance Building, 302 Thanon Silom, Bangkok (tel 234-1140/69).

Thai Chamber of Commerce
150 Thanon Rajabophit, Phra Nakhom, Bangkok 2 (tel 221-6532/4, telex 72093).

Association of Thai Industries
294/14 Thanon Samsen, Tamboi Dusit, Bangkok 3 (telex 72202).

Board of Investment
555 Viphavadee Rangsit Road, Bangkhen, Bangkok (tel 270-1400, fax 271-0777, telex 72435).

Board of Trade of Thailand
150 Thanon Rajabophit, Bangkok 2 (tel 221-9350, telex 84309).

Department of Export Promotion
22/77 Thanon Rachadaphisek, Chatuchak, Bangkok 10900 (tel 511-5066 ext 347, fax 512-1079, telex 82354).

Economic and Social Commission for Asia and the Pacific (ESCAP)
United Nations Building, Rajadammernnok Avenue, Bangkok 2 (tel 282 9608, telex 82392).

Ministry of Commerce
Export Service Center, Department of Commercial Relations, 22–77 Thanon Rachadaphisek, Bangkok 10900 (tel 513-1905).

General Post Office
1160 Thanon Jaroenkrung, Bangkok 10501 (tel 233-1050).

Industrial Estate Authority of Thailand
618 Nikhom Makkasan Road, Phayathai, Bangkok (tel 253-0561).

Ministry of Finance
Rama VI Road, Bangkok (tel 271-4672, fax 271-3378, telex 82823).

Port Authority of Thailand
Thanon Sunthomkosa, Bangkok (tel 249-0362).

Securities Exchange of Thailand
2nd Fl, Sinthorn Building, 132 Wireless Road, Bangkok (tel 254-0960/9, fax 254-3040, telex 20126).

Royal Automobile Association of Thailand
151 Soi Aphaisongkram, Phaholyothin, Bangkok 10900 (tel 511-2230/1).

Tourism Authority of Thailand
4 Thanon Ratchadamnoen, Bangkok (tel 282-1143/7, telex 72059).

Thai Airways International Ltd
6, Thanon Larn Luang, Bangkok (tel 280-0090); Internal travel reservations (tel 280-0700); 89, Vibhavadi Rangsit, Bangkok (tel 513-0121; reservations (tel 233-3810, telex 82359).

Other useful numbers

Metropolitan mobile police: 123,191,246-1338/42
Tourist assistance centre: 195,281-5051
Capital security police: 123
Ambulance: 252-2171/75
Fire: 199,246-0199
Directory (Bangkok): 13
International calls: 100

Vietnam

Official representation in the United Kingdom

Embassy of the Socialist Republic of Vietnam
12–14 Victoria Road, London W8 5RD (tel 071-937 1912/8564, fax 071-937 6108, telex 887361) *Commercial Counsellor* – Dung Hoang Van.

Bureau of the Promotion and Development of Industrialist Property Activities
39, Trang Hung Dao Street, Hanoi (tel 52731 ext 32–35, telex 287).

Chamber of Commerce and Industry of the Socialist Republic of Vietnam
33, Ba Trieu Street, Hanoi (tel 529862); branch office – 69, Dong Khoi Street, Ho Chi Minh City (tel 20101/2, telex 8215).

Investment Consultancy & Technology Transfer Company
91, Ly Nam De Street, PO Box 615, Hanoi; Bo Ho, Hanoi 10000 (tel 64554, telex 411502).

Trade Services Company
33, Ba Trieu Street, Hanoi.

Saigon Shipping Company (Saigonship)
9 Nguyen Cong Tru Street, District 1, Ho Chi Minh City (tel 96316,25067,963902, fax 84825067, telex 811260).

Vietnam National Foreign Trade Corp (TRANSAF)
46 Ngo Quyen, Hanoi.

FOREIGN & COMMONWEALTH OFFICE – Diplomatic Service Directory for Pacific Rim Countries

Local embassies and High Commissions have a wide network of local contacts and absolute access to key decision makers. They also have fully comprehensive and valuable knowledge of local market conditions as well as of local culture, customs and business practises. One of their key roles, as they see it, is to give practical assistance to UK businesses so they are delighted to help you and their advice is there for the asking. Whether you are a new exporter selling your product into that market for the first time or an established multinational seeking major projects, make sure you take advantage of what must undoubtedly be some of the best market intelligence available. As with the DTI, not all services offered are entirely free. Where costs are incurred, reasonable charges are made.

Hong Kong

British Trade Commission
9th Fl, Bank of America Tower, 12 Harcourt Road, Hong Kong (tel 523-0176, fax 852-8455/2870, telex 1234).
Senior Trade Commissioner – P. W. Heap; Deputy Senior Trade Commissioner – C. C. Hayward; Trade Commissioner (China Trade) – Ms P. M. Barnsley; Assistant Trade Commissioner (Hong Kong Trade) – D. J. Smith

Hunting with the Tigers

Indonesia

British Embassy
Jalan M. H. Thamrin 75, Jakarta 10310
(tel 330904, fax 321824, telex 61166).
Ambassador – R. Carrick; Counsellor (Commercial) – M. H. Hope; First
Secretary (Commercial) – M. B. G. Plumb; Second Secretary (Commercial) – R. F.
Terry; Second Secretary (Commercial) – R. N. G. Sinclair.

Korea

British Embassy
4, Chung-Dong, Chung-ku, Seoul 100 (tel 735-7341, 737-7689, fax 733-8368).
Ambassador – D. J. Wright; Counsellor (Commercial) – R. M. Jackson; First
Secretary (Commercial) – D. M. Grey; Second Secretary (Commercial) – I. A.
Worthington; Second Secretary (Commercial) – S. Buckley; Second Secretary
(Commercial) – S. J. Bridges.

Malaysia

British High Commission
185 Jalan Semantan Ampang, PO Box 11030, 50732 Kuala Lumpur (tel 248-2122)
Consular section: tel 248-7122, 7348, 7430, fax 248-0880, telex 35225).
High Commissioner – Sir Nicholas Spreckley; Deputy High Commissioner and
Counsellor (Commercial/Economic) – A. C. Thorpe; First Secretary (Commer-
cial) – Mr A. C. Gallie; Second Secretary (Commercial) – Mr R. R. Avery.

Philippines

British Embassy
15–17th Fl, LV Locsin Building, 6752 Ayala Avenue, (cnr Makati Avenue),
Makati, Metro Manila (tel 816-7116, fax 817-2421, telex 63282).
Ambassador – K. G. MacInnes; Deputy Head of Mission – P. J. Priestley; Second
Secretary (Commercial) – E. J. McEvoy.

Singapore

British High Commission
Tanglin Road, Singapore 1024; Commercial Department: Tanglin PO Box 19,
Singapore 1024 (tel 4739333, fax 475-9700, 2320, telex 21218).
High Commissioner – Gordon Duggan
Counsellor (Economic/Commercial) – Mr T. D. Curran
First Secretary (Commercial) – Mr D. R. Shaw
Second Secretary (Commercial) – Mr R. Mackenzie

Taiwan

No representation

Thailand

British Embassy
Wireless Road, Bangkok 10330
(tel 253-0191, fax 255-8619, telex 82263).
Ambassador – M. R. Melhuish
Counsellor – D. W. Fall; First Secretary – D. Bleakley; First Secretary (Commercial/Development) – M. J. E. Mayhew; Third Secretary (Commercial) – D. M. Hartley

Vietnam

British Embassy
16, Pho Ly Thuong Kiet, Hanoi.
(Mailing address: c/o British Embassy, Wireless Road, Bangkok 10330, Thailand)
(tel 425-2510 telex 411405).
Ambassador – P. K. Williams; Second Secretary – Miss R. L. Foxwell.

Department of Trade & Industry Country Desk

Department of Trade & Industry, 1 Victoria Street, London SW1H 0ET
(tel 071-215 5253/5849, fax 071-222 2629, telex 8811074/5).

For specific business and export advice, as well as the latest information on export opportunities in individual countries, contact the 'Country Desks' at the DTI's Overseas Trade Divisions in London. The staff manning them and their departments are responsible for export promotion and the protection of UK commercial interests overseas. They are extremely helpful and will give general background information, (free of charge), country profiles, economic and trade intelligence, as well as specific industry and sector information.

To contact a country desk, dial the London number 071-215 and add the relevant final four digits from: Hong Kong 4828/4829; Indonesia (4738/4741); Korea (4747/4809); Malaysia (5143/5465); Philippines (5253/5489); Singapore (5143/5465); Taiwan (4821/4824); Thailand (5253/5489); Vietnam (4736/4737).

For consumer goods and general enquiries, including regulations and tariffs 071-215 5179. Capital goods market information only 071-215 5179.

Department of Trade & Industry Regional Offices

DTI North East
Stanegate House, 2 Groat Market, Newcastle-upon-Tyne NE1 1YN (tel 091-232 4722, fax 091-232 6742/222-1496).

DTI North West
Sunley Tower, Piccadilly Plaza, Manchester M1 48A (tel 061-838 5000, fax 061-228 3740/838 5326).

DTI North West (area office Liverpool)
Graeme House, Derby Square, Liverpool L2 7UP (tel 051-224 6300, fax 051-236 1140).

DTI Yorkshire and Humberside
25 Queen Street, Leeds LS1 2TW (tel 0532-443171, fax 0532-338301).

DTI East Midlands
Severns House, 20 Middle Pavement, Nottingham NG1 7DW (tel 0602-506181, fax 0602-587074).

DTI West Midlands
77 Paradise Circus, Queensway, Birmingham B1 2DT (tel 021-212 5000, fax 021-212 1010).

DTI South West
The Pithay, Bristol BS1 2PB (tel 0272-272666, fax 0272-299494).

DTI South East
Bridge Place, 88–89 Eccleston Square, London SW1V 1PT (tel 071-215 5000, fax 071-828 1105).

DTI South East (area office Reading)
40 Caversham Road, Reading, Berkshire RG1 7EB (tel 0734-395600, fax 0734-502818).

DTI South East (area office Reigate)
Douglas House, London Road, Reigate, Surrey RH2 9QP (tel 0737-226900, fax 0737-223491).

DTI East
Building A, Westbrook Research Centre, Milton Road, Cambridge CB4 1YG (tel 0223-461939, fax 0223-461941).

For Scotland
Scottish Office, Industry Department Exports Division, Alhambra House, 45 Waterloo Street, Glasgow G2 6AT (tel 041-242 5495, fax 041-242 5405).

For Wales
Welsh Office Industry Department, New Crown Building, Cathays Park, Cardiff CF1 3NQ (tel 0222-825097/823258, fax 0222-823088).

For Northern Ireland
Industrial Development Board for Northern Ireland, Export Development Branch, Marketing Development Division, IDB House, Belfast BT1 4JX (tel 0232-233233, fax 0232-231328).

Export Market Information Centre (EMIC), 1–19 Victoria Street, London, SW1H 0ET (tel 071-2315 5444 fax 071-215 4231, telex 8811074).

You can do your own research here in its Library and the staff are extremely helpful. If you prefer, they will give you a list of independent research consultants who will work for a fee. Information available includes:

Essential contacts and addresses

- DTI's own database of export information
- Production and trade statistics
- Selected commercial databases
- Mail order catalogues
- Foreign telephone and telex directories
- Overseas company directories
- Development plans for the Third World

Overseas Trade (Magazine)

Available free of charge to UK exporters is *Overseas Trade* magazine which provides current and usable export news and stories of opportunities in foreign markets. For inclusion on the mailing list of DTI's Overseas Trade magazine, contact *Overseas Trade*, Room 711, Bridge Place, 88–89 Eccleston Square, London, SW1V 1PT

World Aid Section (WAS)

This provides information about projects funded by multilateral development agencies who help finance projects in developing countries (including a number in the Asian-Pacific Rim, esp. Vietnam) and loan $30bn annually. Their database is available for visitors by appointment. Contact: Department of Trade & Industry, World Aid Section, Room 290, Ashdown House, London SW1E 6RB (tel 071-215 6512).

DTI Export Data Branch

This is a very useful guide to help the uninitiated in the selection of an overseas agent or if you want to confirm the reliability of a candidate. There are over 50,000 status reports an overseas businesses, giving local standing and suitability for acting on behalf of a UK business.

Export Opportunities Ltd (EOL), Export House, Wembley Hill Road, Wembley, Middlesex HA9 8BU (tel 081-900 1313, fax 081-900 1268).

This provides information of selling opportunities and market information received daily from Diplomatic Service Posts, including loan information, calls for tender concerning aid-funded projects and specific market pointers.

Export Network

Trade Network International Ltd, Regency House, 1–4 Warwick Street, London W1R 5WA (tel 071-494 4030; fax 071-494 1245).

DTI export publications

DTI have a list of excellent country and sector reports updated each year as well as *Hints to Exporters* and other useful publications.

Technical Help for Exporters (THE)

British Standards Institution, Linford Wood, Milton Keynes, MK14 6LE (tel 0908-22022, fax 0908-320856, telex 825777).

287

Hunting with the Tigers

The British Standards Institution runs Technical Help for Exporters (THE). THE aims to help UK exporters in overseas markets, providing information regarding technical requirements and interpreting approval procedures, foreign standards and regulations. THE also helps with translations, codes of practice and legislation and produces various publications and an updating service for some product fields. Information service is charged pro rata.

Export Credits Guarantee Department (ECGD)

No 2 Exchange Tower, Harbour Exchange Square, London E14 9GS tel 071-512-7000, fax 071-512-7649, telex 290350.

The Export Credits Guarantee Department offers insurance to UK suppliers against the major financial risks of exporting goods and services to far-flung markets. It also provides a conduit to low-cost export finance. Also available are buyer credit facilities for capital goods contracts for 1 million or more, which enables buyers to obtain finance direct from a UK bank with ECGD's guarantee. This allows the UK supplier to receive payment on shipment. ECGD also covers third country trade by UK companies or their overseas subsidiaries.

Other organisations

BBC World Service

PO BOX 76, Bush House, Strand, London, WC2B 4PH (tel 071-240 3456).

It seems almost too obvious to remind readers of this but the World Service broadcasts in 36 languages throughout the world and is very keen to report British industry successes in contracts, trade fairs and new developments. It also has excellent (and very necessary to do business successfully in the Asian-Pacific Rim) coverage of world affairs. The best available in background information for Asian-Pacific pioneers.

INSEAD – Euro-Asia Centre

Boulevard de Constance, 77309 Fontainebleu, France (tel 33 (1) 60 72 40 40, fax 33 (1) 60 72 40 49, telex 690389).

The Euro-Asia Centre is part of INSEAD, the renowned international post-graduate business school. Its objective is to promote understanding among all communities doing business in the Asian-Pacific and to develop management skills for application in the region. It is a centre for information, communication, management skills and research (social, economical and political). They offer various specified programmes and seminars in Fontainebleu as well as in the Asia-Pacific Rim cities themselves. Membership fees are FF20,000 for each academic year.

Incomterms

For crystal-clear interpretations of those international rules most commonly used in foreign trade, ie 'cif', 'fob' etc and fully compatible with developments in electronic data interchange (EDI). Exporters will undoubtedly find Incomterms useful for identifying specific obligations for the safe delivery of goods under the terms of international contracts.

International Chamber of Commerce (ICC United Kingdom)

Centre Point, 103 New Oxford Street, London, WC1A 1QB (tel 071-240 5558, telex 21332).

Publicity

Central Office of Information, Hercules Road, London SE1 7DU (tel 071-928 2345, fax 071-240 8776, telex 915444)
Government information service provides publicity for British exporters. Ring the head office for more information.

Useful addresses

Arthur Anderson & Co,
1 Surrey Street, London WC2R 2PS (tel 071-836 1200)

Association of International Courier and Express Services
PO Box 10, Leatherhead, Surrey KT22 OHT (tel 037-284 2953).

British Chambers of Commerce
Sovereign House, 212a Shaftesbury Avenue, London WC2H 8EW (tel 071-240 5831)

British Exporters Association
16 Dartmouth Street, London SW1H 9BL (tel 071-222 5419).

British Overseas Trade Board
Kingsgate House, 66–74 Victoria Street, London SW1E 6SW

Business Statistics Office
Government Buildings, Cardiff Road, Newport, Gwent NP9 1XG (tel 0633-815696).

Central Office of Information (COI)
Hercules Road, London SE1 7DU (tel 071-928 2345).

Centre for Information on Language Teaching and Research
Regent's College, Inner Circle, Regent's Park, London NW1 4NS (tel 071-486 8221).

Confederation of British Industry
Centre Point, 103 New Oxford Street, London WC1A 1DU (tel 071-379 7400).

Coopers & Lybrand
Plumtree Court, London EC4A 4HT (tel 071-583 5000).

Defence Export Services Organisation
Room 707, Stuart House, 23–25 Soho Square, London W1V 5JF (tel 071-632 4826).

The Design Council
28 Haymarket, London SW1Y 4SU (tel 071-839 8000).

Deloitte Haskins & Sells
PO Box 207, 128 Queen Victoria Street, London EC4P 4JX (tel 071-248 3913).

Dun & Bradstreet Ltd
Holmers Farm Way, High Wycombe, Bucks, HP12 4UL (tel 0494-422000).

Ernst & Young
Becket House, Lambeth Palace Road, London SE1 7EU (tel 071-928 2000).

The Export Buying Offices Association
c/o Portman Ltd, 360 Oxford Street, London W1A 4BY (tel 071-493 8141).

Export Licences
The Enquiry Unit, Export Control Organisation, Room 540, Kingsgate House, 66–74 Victoria Street, London SW1E 6SW (tel 071-215 8070).

Fairs & Promotions (DTI)
Dean Bradley House, Horseferry Road, London SW1P 2AG (tel 071-276 2414).

Finance Houses Association
18 Upper Grosvenor Street, London W1X 9PB (tel 071-491 2783).

Freight Forwarders
British International Freight Association, Redfern House, Browells Lane, Feltham, Middlesex TW13 7EP (tel 081-844 2266).

HM Customs & Excise
Dorset House, Stamford Street, London SE1 9PS (tel 071-620 1313).

Hongkong & Shanghai Banking Corporation
99 Bishopsgate, London, EC2P 2LA (tel 071-638 2300).

Institute of Export
Export House, 64 Clifton Street, London EC2A 4HB (tel 071-247 9812).

International Chamber of Commerce
ICC United Kingdom, Centre Point, 103 New Oxford Street, London WC1A 1QB (tel 071-240 5558).

Language Export Centres
Co-Ordinating Unit, Regent's College, Inner Circle, Regents Park, London NW1 4NS (tel 071-486 0141).

London Chamber of Commerce (International Division)
69 Cannon Street, London EC4N 5AB (tel 071-248 4444, fax 071-489 0391).

London Enterprise Agency
4 Snow Hill, London EC1A 2BS (tel 071-236 3000).

London World Trade Centre Association
International House, 1 St Katherine's Way, London E1 9UN (tel 071-488 2400).

Market Research Society
15 Northburgh Street, London EC1V 0AH (tel 071-490 4911).

Profile Information (Financial Times)
Sunbury House, 79 Staines Road West, Sunbury-on-Thames, TW16 7AH (tel 0932-761444, fax 0932-781425).

Resource
1–3 Birdcage Walk, London SW1H 9JH (tel 071-222 5373).

The Simpler Trade Procedures Board (SITPRO)
Venture House, 29 Glasshouse Street, London W1R 5RG (tel 071-287 5751).

Small Firms Service
Dial 100 and ask for 'Freefone Enterprise'

Statistics and Market Intelligence Library
1 Victoria Street, London, SW1H 0ET.

Appendix 2

Useful publications

Entering an Export Market – Midland Bank International.
A guide to developing a particular export market, including research, marketing and setting up an overseas operation. Very useful contacts included.

Tradebrief – Midland Bank.
Outlines economic and fiscal development opportunities overseas. A follow-up service of telephone and telex is offered for interested readers.

Britain's Aid Programme: Business Opportunities – Overseas Development Administration.
This leaflet covers how the UK's aid programme provides opportunities for British business and gives a useful list of contacts.

Executive Guide to the Countries of ASEAN – Citibank.
Provides background information of Indonesia, Malaysia, Philippines, Singapore and Thailand together with foreign investment opportunities and regulations, forms of business enterprise, taxation, labour and doing business.

Business Advisory Service series – Peat, Marwick, McLintock.
Finance for exports is among the series of four-page leaflets on current management and business topics.

Support for World Trade: a series including such titles as *An Introduction to Exporting and Importing Documentary Letters of Credit, Foreign Exchange for Export/Import, An Introduction to Importing* – Barclays Bank International, Barclays House, 1 Wimborne Road, Poole, Dorset BH15 BB.

The Business Travellers Handbook – How to get along with people in 100 countries – Foseco Minsep Ltd.
A handbook for the business traveller giving advice on etiquette and codes of behaviour.

Croner's Reference Book for Exporters – Croner Publications Ltd, Croner House, London Road, Kingston upon Thames, Surrey KT2 6SR (tel 081-547 3333). A regular update on all exporting procedures. It costs £60.50 but is available on a ten day free approval. (Also *Croner's Reference Book for Importers*).

Directory of Export Buyers in the United Kingdom – by Tookey; Published by Trade Research Publications, 6 Beech Hill Court, Berkhamsted, Herts HP4 2PR (also *Directory of British Importers*).

Doing Business – Ernst & Young, Becket House, 1 Lambeth Palace Road, London SE1 7EU (tel 071-928 2000). A series of free publications setting out the economic and commercial climate in most of the developed countries.

Export Handbook – A guide from the British Overseas Trade Board giving invaluable advice on UK import and export regulations, finance, credit insurance, international transport etc.

Export Step by Step to Success by Brian Ogley – Harper & Row. Written on behalf of the Small Business Research Trust, this book guides you from assessing the market through to financing the sale.

Importing for the Small Business by Max Morris – Kogan Page Ltd, 120 Pentonville Road, London N1 9JN (tel 071-278 0433).

Handbook of International Business – John Wiley, Baffins Lane, Chichester, West Sussex, PO19 1UD (tel 0243-784531). It details virtually every area of international business.

Appendix 3

Bibliography

General background reading on the Asian-Pacific Rim

Southeast Asia in the World Economy, by Chris Dixon (Cambridge: Cambridge UP, 1991).

Political Change in Southeast Asia, edited by Donald Altschiller (New York: HW Wilson, 1989)

ASEAN in the 1990s – Growing Together, by Sarwar Hobohm (London: Economist Intelligence Unit, 1989).

Foreign Trade and Investment: Economic Growth in the Newly Industrializing Asian Countries, edited by Walter Galenson (University of Wisconsin Press, 1985).

God's Dust: A Modern Asian Journey, by Ian Buruma (Vintage, 1991).

Pacific Destiny: The Rise of the East, by Robert Elegant (Headline, 1991).

Behind the Myth – Business, Money and Power in Southeast Asia, by James Clad (London: Unwin Hyman, 1989).

International Marketing Research, by Susan P Douglas, and Samuel Craig (Englewood Cliffs, NJ: Prentice-Hall, 1983).

International Marketing, by Vern Terpstra (4th ed, Hinsdale, IL: Dryden Press, 1987).

Asia's Top 7500 Companies (published by Dun & Bradstreet).

294

Specific titles of particular interest by country

City on the Rocks: Hong Kong's uncertain future, by Kevin Rafferty (New York: Viking, 1990).

Perfidious albion: the abandonment of Hong Kong, 1997, by William McGurn, foreword by William F Buckley Jr (Washington, DC: Ethics & Public Policy Center, 1991).

Indonesia to 1993 – Breakthrough in the Balance, by Sarwar Hobohm (London: Economist Intelligence Unit, 1989).

The Endogenous Dynamics of Social Transformation in Traditional Korea, by Jae-Hyeon Choe (Bielefeld: University of Bielefeld, Faculty of Sociology, Sociology of Development Research, 1985).

The Malaysian Economy – Spatial Perspectives, by George Cho (London: Routledge, 1990).

A Changeless Land – Continuity and Change in Philippine Politics, by David G Timberman (Armonk, NY: ME Sharpe, 1991).

The Philippine state and the Marcos regime – the politics of export, (Ithaca, London: Cornell University Press, 1987).

Key prospects and market conditions in Singapore and the newly industrialised countries, by Richard Baker (Cardiff: CSP Economic, 1987).

Policy Options for the Singapore Economy, by Lim Chong Yah (London: McGraw-Hill, 1988).

Thai insurgency – contemporary developments, by R Sean Randolph and W Scott Thompson, foreword by Fay S Cline (London: Centre for Strategic & International Studies, 1981).

National Unification and Economic Development in Vietnam, by Melanie Beresford (London: Macmillan, 1989)

All the *Country Reports* from the Economist Intelligence Unit.

Commercial cultural literacy

The Asian Mind Game: Unlocking the Hidden Agenda of the Asian Business culture: A Westerner's Survival Manual, by Chin-Ning Chu. (New York: Maxwell Macmillan International, 1990).

Venturing Abroad in Asia – the Complete Business Guide to Cultural Differences in eleven Asian Countries, by Robert T Moran (Maidenhead: McGraw-Hill, 1988).

The Cultural Environment of International Business, by Vern Terpstra and Kenneth David (2nd ed, Cincinnati, US: Southwestern, 1985).

Do's and Taboos around the World – a guide to international behaviour, by Roger E Axtell (New York: John Wiley & Sons, 1986).

Asia Guide to Business Travel, by Robert K McCabe (London: Black, 1987).

The Global Edge, by Sondra Snowden (New York: Simon & Schuster)

Dealing with the Chinese: A Practical Guide to Business Etiquette, by Scott D Seligman Scott (Mercury Business Books, 1990).

Korean Etiquette and Ethics in Business, by Boye de Mente (Merehurst Press, 1988).

Simple Etiquette in Thailand by Derek Tonkin, illustrated by Irene Sanderson (Folkestone: Norbury 1990).

Essential periodical publications

Asia Computer Weekly, (Asian Business Press, Singapore). Fortnightly, English.
Asia Magazine, (Hong Kong) fortnightly free insert in major regional English-language Sunday papers.
Asia Technology
Asia Travel Trade
Asian Advertising & Marketing
Asian Business
Asian Wall Street Journal Weekly (Dow Jones) – recapped version of stories of interest from the Asian version of the Wall Street Journal
Asiaweek, Hong Kong
Business Asia (Business International)
Business Traveller Asia-Pacific
Computerworld Asia
Far Eastern Economic Review, Hong Kong
The Economist (Asian edition)
Global Executive (North American Publishing Co., Philadelphia)
International Trade Forum (Intl. Trade Centre, Geneva)
PATA Travel News Asia/Pacific
Shipping & Transport News (Singapore)
South Magazine (Hong Kong)
Travelnews Asia

Appendix 4

Databases

Business Opportunities
(Available through Data-Star)
Worldwide trade opportunities and business contacts may be searched for in this German database with over 25,000 references in English, French and German. Sources for the information on the database include directories, exhibition catalogues, trade journals and trade promotion literature from the relevant countries concerned. New opportunities are added monthly.

Compuserve, etc
Many of the widely used electronic mail information systems, but particularly Compuserve with well over 800,000 participants online worldwide, may provide invaluable insight and contacts into the market of your choice through small business networking. Many of the more than 175 professional Special Interest Groups (ie public relations, law, IT and computing) offer a forum in which you can ask specific questions on precise business problems in the Asian-Pacific Rim and get answers from personal experience. This system also provides access to more than 900 additional databases including DIALOG, BRS, NewsNet, Pergamon Infoline, Questel, Orbit and VU/TEXT. For further information about joining the system, call 0800-289458, 9am-9pm daily.

Dow Jones Text-Search Services
(Available through Dow Jones News/Retrieval or MCI Mail)
Search for articles electronically in The Business Library on the Asian-Pacific Rim in Forbes, Fortune, McGraw-Hill Library, Financial World and many others. An excellent source of useful and applicable information.

Dun & Bradstreet – International Dun's Market Identifiers
(Available through Dialog)
More than 200,000 companies in 90 countries including from around the Pacific Rim with name and address, type of business, CEO, etc. and updated quarterly.

Financial Times Company Abstracts
Summaries of all FT articles (both editions) back to 1981 and searchable by industry, location, personnel or product. Daily updates.

Investext
Available through CompuServe, Data-Star, Dialog, Dow Jones News/Retrieval, Mead, NewsNet, Thomson Financial Networks & Market Barometer Reports available through Investext/Plus.

Information on both international and domestic markets, indexes and industries useful for determining future outlook.

Jordan's Business Information Service
Jordan House, 21 St Thomas Street, Bristol, BS1 6JS (tel 0272-230600).
This gives details of an international network of information sources and agents throughout the world. The network will provide specific destination country information in far greater detail than standard directories. Excellent information brokerage for searching out companies which are very small or newly formed.

Moody's Corporate News – International
(Available through Dialog)
Business news and financial information on thousands of companies in over 100 countries, covering financial institutions, investment trusts, manufacturers, public utilities and shipping companies, back to January 1983.

NewsNet
NewsNet offers 13 worldwide wire services as well as a whole host of indepth newsletters covering 35 specific professions and industries. Of particular interest is Asian Intelligence. For more information, call Thompson Henry Ltd, Ascot, UK (tel 0344-291072).

World Trade Centre Network
To access this invaluable up-to-the-minute data, it is necessary to first join the World Trade Centers Association.

Appendix 5

Glossary

ADB – The Asian Development Bank exists primarily to redirect lending to fight poverty and to encourage private sector business in new economies.

ANRPC – Association of Natural Rubber Producing Countries.

APEC – Asia Pacific Economic Co-operation. A twelve-nation inter-governmental regional initiative launched in Canberra in November 1989 to establish some form of economic mutuality.

ASEAN – Association of South East Asian Nations: Singapore, Indonesia, Malaysia, the Philippines, Thailand and Brunei

ESCAP – Economic & Social Commission for Asia & the Pacific (UN).

FAO – Food and Agriculture Organization (of UN).

G-7 – Group of seven: the finance ministers and central bankers of the United States, Canada, Japan, West Germany, Britain, France and Italy who co-ordinate monetary policies in order to achieve a stable international economic environment.

GATT – General Agreement on Tariffs and Trade.

IAEA – International Atomic Energy Agency.

IBRD – International Bank for Reconstruction and Development (UN).

ICAO – International Civil Aviation Organization (UN).

ICO – International Commodity Organization.

IDA – International Development Association (UN).

IFAD – International Fund for Agricultural Development (UN).

IFC – International Finance Corporation (UN).

IHO – International Hydrographic Organization.

ILO – International Labour Organization (UN).

IMO – International Maritime Organization.

IMO – International Maritime Organisation.

INRO – International Natural Rubber Organization.

INTELSAT – International Telecommunications Satellite Organization.

Interpol – International Criminal Police Organization.

IPU – Inter-Parliamentary Union.

IRC – International Red Cross.

ITC – International Trade Commission.

ITU – International Telecommunications Union (UN).

NICs – Newly industrialised countries, these are the tigers (sometimes called dragons) that are Hong Kong, Taiwan, South Korea and Singapore.

NIE – Newly industrialised economy.

UN – United Nations.

UNDP – United Nations Development Programme.

UNESCO – United Nations Educational, Scientific and Cultural Organization.

UNICEF – United Nations (International) Children's (Emergency) Fund.

UNIDO – United Nations Industrial Development Organization.

UPU – Universal Postal Union.

WFTU – World Federation of Trade Unions.

WHO – World Health Organization.

WIPO – World Intellectual Property Organization.

WMO – World Meteorological Organization.

WTO – World Tourism Organization.

World Bank – Each year the World Bank grants loans of billions of dollars to finance a variety of development and other projects.

WEC – World Energy Conference.

Index

Index

Index

Index

Index